Books are to be returned on
the last date below.

ROOM USE

The Irish in Britain
1815–1914

GRAHAM DAVIS

GILL AND MACMILLAN

Published in Ireland by
Gill and Macmillan Ltd
Goldenbridge
Dublin 8
with associated companies in
Auckland, Delhi, Gaborone, Hamburg, Harare,
Hong Kong, Johannesburg, Kuala Lumpur, Lagos, London,
Manzini, Melbourne, Mexico City, Nairobi,
New York, Singapore, Tokyo
© Graham Davis 1991
Index compiled by
Helen Litton
Print origination by Seton Graphics, Bantry, Co. Cork
Printed by Colour Books Ltd, Dublin

British Library Cataloguing in Publication Data
Davis, Graham
The Irish in Britain 1815–1914.
I. Title
941.08
ISBN 0–7171–1656–5
ISBN 0–7171–1907–6 pbk

*To Brian Stevens,
my old History teacher,
at Monmouth School*

Contents

Acknowledgments

To Patrick O'Sullivan of Bradford University and to David Brooke of Bath University, I am indebted for their attention to detail in scrutinising my first draft of chapter 2, Little Irelands. I am very grateful to Roger Swift and to Sheridan Gilley, the editors of the *The Irish in Britain, 1815–1939*, (Pinter Press) 1989, for including the same material in the form of an article. To colleagues at Bath College of Higher Education, Paul Hyland and Neil Sammells, I am thankful for their editorial work on part of chapter 1 which takes the form of an article on 'John Mitchel and the Great Famine', in their collective volume of essays, *Irish Writing: Exile and Subversion*, to be published by Macmillan. Other colleagues at Bath, Jon Press and Terence Rodgers, have also been helpful in discussing particular points of contention in the book. Course Secretary, Jill Palmer, was of great clerical assistance to me in completing the final drafts. I am especially indebted to Penny Bonsall who provided unfailing support as my Research Assistant on this project, whilst studying for her own doctorate at Warwick University.

My greatest debt is to my wife, Beth, and to my four sons, Matthew, Adam, Ben and Sam, who have been wonderfully patient, albeit mildly amused, at my 'Irish obsession' over the last few years.

Preface

'The difficulty indeed the impossibility of writing about Ireland in such a way as to win the approval of Irishmen may arise from the ambiguity of their own feelings towards her. If she is criticised they are publicly furious and privately amused; if praised they are outwardly pleased while inwardly condemning the writer as a fool.' Honor Tracy's warning suggests that writing about the Irish in Britain may be foolhardy twice over. It not only means running the gauntlet of Irish opinion but may easily fall foul of the repeated misunderstanding that marks the relation between the Irish and the British. However, the time is long overdue for a greater tolerance and respect on both sides, and, happily there are a few omens pointing in this direction for the future. The release of the 'Birmingham six' could mark a new chapter in Anglo-Irish relations for the benefit of both peoples.

One of the joys of historical research is turning up the unexpected. While engaged on the study of a 'notorious' street at the heart of a slum district of Victorian Bath I was surprised to discover a colony of Irish migrants who had settled there from County Cork. Further analysis revealed a community that was not subjected to the kind of racial and religious hostility which appeared to be the 'standard' experience of Irish migrants in British cities. Nor did the condition of the Irish differ significantly from their English working-class neighbours in a poor district. Moreover, the disdain of outside commentators, in describing the people of Victorian slums which included Irish migrants, appeared to be driven by class prejudice and contemporary ideology. Yet important differences separated middle-class perceptions from working-class reality. Within the framework of Victorian moral earnestness and the awesome foreboding of an urban crisis, the Irish who settled in British cities in the middle decades of the nineteenth century became caught up and stigmatised.

This realisation was to prove the starting point for my study of the Irish in Britain, a study that has taken me to Dublin, Cork and Mayo and to touring a country of breath-taking beauty, beguiling mystery and maddening frustration. It has involved a journey of exploration into the Irish experience in Britain, interviewing Irish migrants, meeting Irish and British scholars, and engaging with a bewildering array of opinions drawn from specialist research. For someone 'trained' as a British local historian, used to grubbing among primary sources, this study presents a very different scale of operation and style of activity. Instead of searching for the proverbial needle in a haystack for evidence relating to a single street, there was superabundance of secondary material written by scholars and relating to the whole of Britain and Ireland. Yet old habits die hard. Whilst sifting through the detailed research of key authorities on the subject, I needed to consult some contemporary sources to catch the mood and opinions of the time. So, some of my own research supplements that of a host of individuals, who have made certain subjects and certain places their own.

If I have done a disservice to any author in the selection of material and interpretations from their work, I willingly apologise in advance. In the transplanting from a specialist journal or thesis to meet the needs of a broader overview, some loss of depth and vitality may result but, perhaps, there is compensation in being part of a hybrid species formed in a process of cross-pollination with other authors. In the last resort I must take responsibility for the balance of selection and emphasis that emerges from a synthesis which also suggests new themes for productive debate.

Introduction

Since the pioneering work of J.E. Handley and J.A. Jackson there has been no substantial, single-author history that has addressed the subject of the Irish in nineteenth-century Britain.[1] Over the last thirty years, a great deal of work has been done that extends our knowledge and understanding of the Irish experience, especially in the critical middle decades of the last century. Much of it is written in the form of learned articles, published in specialist journals, or in local history series that may be inaccessible to a general reader. The Irish in Britain also feature, albeit marginally, in books that ostensibly deal with other subjects, such as Chartism or railway navvies.[2] Very few books take the Irish as a central focus, either in a particular place, such as the work by Lynn Lees, Frank Neal and Frances Finnegan on London, Liverpool and York, respectively, or collectively as in the contributions of specialist scholars—for example, in the two important volumes edited by Roger Swift and Sheridan Gilley.[3]

The Irish in Britain 1815–1914 is heavily dependent on previously published work in providing a historical overview and synthesis of current scholarship. Inevitably, the process involves the making of a personal choice of emphasis and interpretation. It also allows new themes to be presented which determine the historical approach and focus of discussion in the book.

It is written for the general reader, who may or may not be of Irish descent, and for those of any nationality engaged in Irish Studies who may compare the Irish experience in the United States, Canada, Australia, and elsewhere, with the Irish in Britain.[4] The impact on and the response of the host community is a theme of the growing body of literature on migration and the study of ethnic minorities in Britain, which means that, inevitably, such a focus is revealing about the nature of British society.[5] The very close integration of history and culture between the peoples of Ireland and Britain, the Irish being the oldest and largest ethnic minority in Britain, adds force to the general argument.

The central themes of published work on the Irish in Britain, migration, settlement, and relations with the host community, are common to all migrant studies. Much of the work has an inevitable focus on the identifiable problems of racial intolerance, religious sectarianism, the Irish association with slum housing, crime and disorder, and with political violence. The surge of immigration, especially in the 1830s and 1840s, brought a hysterical response among certain sections of the British press and from local officials and commentators. Fears were aroused, by 'Irish fever', of cheap Irish labour, and of an alien religion, and doubts were expressed about Irish loyalty to the crown. Indeed, Swift and Gilley adopt a theme of outcastness to describe the Irish experience in Victorian cities.[6] Due recognition is given to these central concerns, in surveying the range of available sources, but other themes have also suggested themselves which have the effect of qualifying the traditional emphasis on the migrant Irish, merely depicted as a problem.

Firstly, there is the theme of *diversity*, which allows an exploration of the wider Irish experience, beyond that of a few major centres of Irish settlement. This extends the work of individual town histories, not only broadening our understanding fully to recognise the differences between Glasgow, Liverpool and Manchester, but also the variety of conditions that affected an Irish presence in other towns like Dundee, Edinburgh, Newcastle, Hull and Bristol. The overall effect is to take the emphasis away from a continued sense of crisis and oppression to a more mixed pattern of Irish experience. In turn, this raises further questions on why the reception of Irish migrants varied considerably from place to place. It reveals something about the Irish who settled and something about the places they settled in.

Secondly, a theme emerges from examining *popular images and historical myths*. This allows a discussion, within the broader context of substantive chapters on specific areas of interest, of the historical meaning of the Irish Famine, the Irish in the ghetto, the comic 'Paddy' stereotype, the archetypal, fighting Irish navvy, the religious images of the Catholic faithful and of sectarian violence, the Irish as revolutionaries, and the myths surrounding Irish nationalism. The historical context in which such images were created, and have persisted, applies a corrective to their enduring appeal.

Thirdly, an attempt is made to recognise what may be described as the *Irish and British dimensions*, in assessing the Irish in Britain. This not only involves paying attention to nineteenth-century Ireland, as a background to Irish emigration to Britain, but recognises that emigrants brought Irish culture with them, or, indeed, wished to escape from it. The class interests particular to each society were also influential in promoting emigration and in determining the reception of Irish migrants. The British response to an Irish presence was also informed by the dominant ideologies of the day, and alarm was generated by the Irish association with issues of contemporary concern. The integration of British and Irish dimensions stemmed from the influence, for good or ill, that flowed from British rule after the Act of Union, and from the ever-present Irish question in British politics, throughout the nineteenth century.

In trying to establish what the Irish brought with them from Ireland, it became clear that the Irish could not be described as a homogeneous group. Such was the diversity of experience in Ireland, in the extent of the 'modernisation' of the economy and society, as revealed in varied patterns in economic condition, demographic trends, and in religious practice, that uniform generalisations become unsustainable.[7] So, too, with the identified patterns of Irish migration and settlement in Britain. The Irish experience varied enormously. If most of the attention focused on the Irish living in slums in the great Victorian cities, detailed research reveals that the Irish settled in every district of mid-Victorian London and Bristol.[8] Moreover, the Irish were more widely dispersed throughout the country than has been recognised, settling in thirty-one towns, including places such as Bath and Colchester, which in 1851 and 1861 had over a thousand Irish-born populations.[9] The Irish experience was determined by what skills they brought with them, their age, sex, and religious allegiance, when and where they settled, and whether they wished to retain an Irish identity or to merge into the crowd. Assimilation, as suggested by inter-marriage, appeared to have increased by the late century, and was greater in Birmingham, Cardiff and London than in northern industrial cities.[10]

Nor was there a uniform British response to the presence of Irish migrants. It is no accident that the most heated reaction to Irish immigrants was found in the key reception points of Glasgow, Liverpool and Cardiff. The impression of being 'swamped' was real enough in Liverpool, the main point of entry, not only for the Irish settling in Britain, but also for the thousands of Irish who were on short-stay migration before embarking on the Atlantic voyage to North America. For a period in 1847, Liverpool was engaged in distributing famine relief to many thousands of starving immigrants. Its institutions, already struggling to cope with its own resident population, were quite incapable of coping with the scale of an unprecedented emergency situation.

This crisis, already apparent before the famine influx, was exploited by local religious and political leaders, among whom Protestant Irishmen were prominent, whipping up anti-Catholic feeling as a means of gaining political control of the city council. This proved spectacularly successful, and as a consequence, religious hatred and sectarian violence found its most extreme and prolonged form in Liverpool.[11] Religious riots blighted the Irish experience in other cities, Glasgow, Stockport, and Cardiff.[12] The annual rituals of St Patrick's Day and Orange Day processions were rallying points for Catholics and Protestants which could spark off rioting and violence between the two communities. The establishment of the Catholic hierarchy in England in 1850 or the virulently anti-Catholic lectures of William Murphy and other Protestant zealots in the 1860s, provoked rioting from indignant Protestants and Catholics. Yet, even in cities affected by the 'Murphy Riots', accompanying the anti-Catholic rhetoric aimed at the Irish, there was a pronounced revulsion among the majority of moderate Protestants, fearful that vulgar Catholic baiting only led to the destruction of property. [13]

Less headline-grabbing but more widespread, was the liberal response to the Irish presence in Dundee, Edinburgh, Newcastle-upon-Tyne, Hull and Bristol. Enlightened individuals holding key positions in the Church, as local officials, or as editors of local newspapers, including several Irishmen, could exercise an important leadership over local opinion. The Irish presence was not held responsible for epidemics of typhoid and cholera in Newcastle or in Bristol, as it was in Cardiff and Manchester.[14] Social and religious harmony was created through intelligent church leadership in Edinburgh.[15] The repatriation of Irish paupers was stopped in Hull by the campaign of the Irish editor of the *Hull Advertiser*.[16] In Bristol, magistrates were very concerned at the way poor immigrants were cheated by 'sharpers' of their few belongings, or were exploited by local employers. They even took an extraordinarily sympathetic view of Irishmen regularly committed on charges of drunkenness.[17]

A key factor in the Irish experience was the context of the place of settlement. Irish workers were often appreciated by English and Scottish employers, were an essential part of the seasonal labour force in agriculture, and, as bricklayers in Birmingham or as dockers in London and Liverpool, they achieved a near-monopoly position.[18] Conflicts were more likely to occur when the local labour force, rightly or wrongly, felt threatened by the prospect of 'cheap' Irish labour, sometimes used by unscrupulous employers as 'blacklegs' or employed to foment sectarian division within the labour force. Surveying the range of work available adds to the conviction that the Irish experience went beyond the inflated images of poor, tramping harvesters, distressed hand-loom weavers, or drunken, riotous railway navvies. The exceptional mobility of Irish workers, able to migrate on a seasonal basis, eager to move from town to town in search of better prospects, ensured that the life experience of an individual Irishman or woman included a range of employment that suited each stage of the life cycle and the needs of the whole family.[19] The Irish were attracted to industrial cities where employment was available for husband and wife, with school provision and employment prospects for the children, and the family standard of living was immeasurably improved. Irish communities also provided employment through a network of personal contacts from Irish priests, publicans, shopkeepers, and lodging-house keepers. Upward social mobility, although slow by comparison with the Irish experience in the more dynamic society of the United States, varied according to the economic and social structure of each area of Irish settlement. Despite the background of sectarian hatred, the Irish in Liverpool rose to civic and commercial prominence, including being represented by the first Irish Nationalist MP, T.P. O'Connor.[20]

Perceptions of the Irish in Britain were shaped by contemporary ideologies, and the Irish involvement in specific crises aroused understandable fears among the native British. The hysteria of the adverse comment directed at the Irish in the 1830s and 1840s has to be seen in the context of the urban crisis that afflicted burgeoning cities lacking the administrative means to cope with rapid expansion. The Irish were a very useful scapegoat for a society struggling to adjust to the severe growing pains that accompanied the onset of an urban, industrial economy. Epidemic disease, squalid overcrowding, rising crime, and the ever-present threat of disorder, sparking off a mass rising from the labouring poor, were central concerns embodied in the dominant 'condition of England' question. The Irish did not create these problems, even if their presence was to lend them a higher profile.

However, for some local officials and commentators, unwilling to suggest additional burdens on the rates, the Irish offered a welcome diversion of public attention away from their own responsibilities, and a means of harnessing popular support against an alien threat. A strain of militant Protestantism, bent on the destruction of Catholic 'heresy' provided the emotive rhetoric. The doctrines of laissez-faire and self-help provided the intellectual justification for despising the poor English and Scots, as well as the Irish who lived among them. Contemporary racial theories, which curiously elevated the English as a mongrel race, naturally possessing the best qualities of Saxons, Normans and Celts, raised fears of contamination from an allegedly 'inferior' race of Irish immigrants [21] To complacent mid-Victorian Englishmen, events confirmed a natural sense of superiority. The defeat of Napoleon, Britain as the 'workshop of the world', Europe in revolutionary turmoil in 1848—all lent substance to the agreeable certainty of English genius.

With such an ideological background, it is not surprising that one interpretation of the Irish Famine also confirmed notions of English moral superiority.[22] The Malthusian explanation of a disaster caused by overpopulation was compounded by English condescension about the backward state of Irish agriculture and the wholesale dependency of the labouring poor on a subsistence economy dominated by the potato crop. This is the view that has formed an essential part of the nationalist version of events, condemning British rule in Ireland for a failure to feed the Irish people. It is an argument that can be turned round to one of dependency justifying the retention of the Union, or one of moral justice demanding its repeal.

Yet, perceptions about the tragic unfolding of events in the famine years varied on both sides of the Irish Sea. Whilst Malthusianism exerted a dominant influence in British government circles and was articulated in the editorials of *The Times* newspapers, ordinary British citizens responded in a humanitarian spirit of charitable famine relief. Within Ireland there were mixed feelings amidst the severe psychological shock that attended the disaster. Among the poor in the south and western counties, those most affected by starvation, disease and death, the famine was seen as a punishment by God for past wastefulness of the Lord's bounty.[23] A few landlords heroically looked after their poor tenants at great personal cost. Others planned wholesale evictions and organised emigration schemes to rid their estates of a poor peasantry seen as an impediment to the modernisation of agriculture. 'Strong' farmers and corn merchants were able to seize opportunities to enlarge their holdings and to inflate their prices in response to the emergency. Poor law officials and the Catholic Church organised emigration schemes as a way of ridding the propertied classes of the burden of pauperism and of spreading the faith abroad. Irish newspapers were ambivalent in lamenting large-scale emigration as the loss of the brightest and best among the Irish people, and emigration was also encouraged as the only salvation for Ireland's economic misery.

The idea of the 'Famine' was to be deployed with devastating effect by the journalist-historian, John Mitchel, as a propaganda weapon in the cause of Irish nationalism. He accused the British government of deliberately using the Famine to reduce the population of Ireland by resurrecting Jonathan Swift's old charge of genocide. The Mitchel thesis has long been influential among historians and remains the accepted version amongst the public, but more scholarship has incorporated a greater plurality of views. If the 'Famine' remains a potent political symbol, its significance as a crucial watershed in the history of nineteenth-century Ireland has been challenged, not least by demographers and economic historians, who have argued that the Famine accelerated trends already present in pre-famine Ireland.

A number of important historical questions are also raised in what may be called the Irish dimension of British popular politics. A debate has been continuing on the Irish contribution to English Chartism.[24] What is evident from the literature on the subject is that more is at stake then whether the Irish in Britain were involved or not. Irish involvement, it is argued, included both positive and negative influences on Chartism. These can be identified in the leadership and philosophies of the movement, and amongst the rank and file membership. Except in 1848, when Irish Repealers joined forces with English Chartists, the positive contribution was less than some historians have wanted to believe. The negative influences were not merely those of Catholic priests or the use of Irish bully-boys, deployed by the Anti-Corn Law League to break up Chartist meetings. The most important negative influence was the fear of an uprising in Ireland, occurring simultaneously with one in England, that prompted a heavy crackdown by the police and the army, even deploying Irish troops in the northern industrial districts most affected by Chartism. Unwittingly, the Irish reputation for political violence contributed to the defeat of English Chartism, just as it contributed to the establishment of police forces in England.

It is also worth reconsidering the importance of the Irish question in British politics in the nineteenth century. It tends to be treated as a marginal part of the drama of high politics, making an occasional entrance at particular points in the national story, Catholic Emancipation in 1829, the Repeal of the Corn Laws in 1846, the disestablishment of the Irish Church in 1869, the Irish Home Rule crisis in 1885, repeated in 1912. Yet, throughout the nineteenth century, although many Englishmen may have wanted to ignore the Irish question, it never went away. Indeed, the Irish question represented a key part of the radical agenda in the concept of 'justice for Ireland'. It is possible to construct a continuous radical tradition drawing on the inheritance of late eighteenth-century thinkers such as William Cobbett, Bronterre O'Brien, and even including the legislative reforms of William Gladstone. 'Justice for Ireland' embraced a philosophy of citizen rights in a reform programme that was applicable throughout Britain.

The fear of Irish political violence, spilling over into mainland Britain, was also an important influence in the response to the Fenian movement in the 1860s, to American-Irish bombers in the 1880s, and to the pressure for Home Rule over a period of thirty years.[25] It is argued that the insensitive and inept blunders on the part of the British authorities more than compensated for the comical incompetence associated with Fenian 'outrages'. The cause of Irish nationalism was sustained only fitfully by the ability of Fenian leaders to turn military defeat into theatrical 'victory' by a series of brilliant publicity strokes. What has been reconstructed, with hindsight, as a heroic struggle for national freedom, tends to exaggerate the extent of Irish popular support for a separatist state, at least until the execution of Irish Republican leaders after the Easter Rising in 1916. Throughout the nineteenth century, British government policy towards Ireland veered from coercion to reform. The redress of Irish grievances, which included more radical land reforms than were enacted in England, invariably came too late, and too often were accompanied by mindless repression. Even today, relations between the Irish Republic and the United Kingdom are bedevilled by the spectre of political violence, sustained by the myths of the past.

1

Emigration

This cannot last, Heaven disowns it. Earth is against it;
Ireland will be burnt into a black unpeopled field of ashes that
this should last . . . The time has come when the Irish
population must be improved a little or exterminated.
(Thomas Carlyle. 1839)

The population history of nineteenth-century Ireland draws powerfully on two haunting images—the shadow of the Great Famine and the spectre of emigrants fleeing overseas. Traditionally, the chronology of the two events has persuaded historians to connect the one with the other.[1] The population of Ireland doubled in the period 1785 to 1841 from an estimated 4 million to 8.2 million. Then between the censuses of 1841 and 1851 the population fell dramatically by some 20 per cent and during the seven long years of potato blight, 1845 to 1852, about a million and a half people emigrated.[2] Yet this unprecedented loss was not a once and for all adjustment to a Malthusian 'over-population'. It is now clearly established that Ireland's population increase disguised extensive emigration in the pre-famine era. Then, following the appalling loss of population through death and emigration during the famine years, further waves of emigration continued through to the end of the century and beyond into our own time. A pattern of continuous emigration from Ireland had become established. By 1901, Ireland's population at 4.5 million was approximately half the level it had been on the eve of the Great Famine.[3]

Even these figures may well underestimate the true loss of population through emigration. As Cormac O'Grada has demonstrated, the official figures were compiled from a number of sources of varying dependability.[4] It is likely that collectively they under-recorded the real extent of the human traffic leaving Ireland in the nineteenth century. The official estimate by the

Registrar-General of total emigration from Ireland between 1852 and 1910 is 4.0 million people. Significantly, the numbers recorded as emigrating to Britain do not match the numbers of Irish-born people enumerated in the 1911 census. O'Grada reaches two important conclusions. Firstly, the total figure for Irish emigration was probably nearer to 5 million than 4 million, and secondly, the proportion of Irish emigrants who settled permanently in Britain was rather more important than has been recognised to date. 'I would give the movement across the Irish Sea', he writes, 'far greater importance than the original estimates implied: instead of the emigration to Britain accounting for about one-eighth, a revised estimate suggests a share of between one-fifth and one quarter.'[5]

Not merely the scale of mass emigration but the complex nature of its economic and social context is under review. With hindsight, the tragedy of the Great Famine was widely interpreted as the inevitable consequence of too great a population, fatally dependent on a subsistence agriculture. This view can be traced to the influential writings of the Rev. Thomas Malthus. The Malthusian doctrine offered a seductively simple explanation of the poverty of Ireland. Population growth was ultimately limited by the availability of resources. When population began to outstrip resources a number of 'Malthusian checks' to further population growth would come into play—war, famine, disease—to restore the natural equilibrium. Malthus's theory of population growth implied that natural law would not tolerate 'overpopulation' indefinitely and, where it occurred, a proper corrective to the relationship with resources was inevitable.

Joel Mokyr quotes Malthus writing to Ricardo in 1817: 'the land in Ireland is infinitely more peopled than in England: and to give full effect to the natural resources of the country a great part of the population should be swept from the soil'.[6] His analysis contained a moral imperative and although Malthus had his critics, his 'overpopulation' thesis fitted well with the dominant orthodoxy of the day. Moreover, the awesome prediction of imminent disaster, based on the notion of the Malthusian checks of famine and disease, took on a powerful credibility with the scale of death and emigration of the famine period in Ireland. Significantly, the Malthusian view became not only the conventional wisdom in Victorian England but has remained a dominant influence for most of the twentieth century. The importance of Mokyr's work is that he subjects the 'overpopulation' thesis to a series of statistical tests and finds that the results are at best inconclusive. Firstly, he argues that the behaviour of the Irish economy, after the Famine, lends little support to the Malthusian approach. The standard of living of those who survived increased as a result of a rise in agricultural prices and due to structural changes in the economy, not because of the loss of population. Secondly, on the basis of international comparisons, it is by no means clear that Ireland was more densely populated than England and Wales; and Belgium, for instance, had a higher density of population than Ireland. If there had been no famine and economic circumstances had been more favourable, Mokyr concurs with Blacker's prediction in 1834 that Ireland could have sustained a population of around 17 million people by the end of the century. He concludes that there appears to be no statistically significant relation between poverty and population pressure variables in pre-Famine Ireland. Moreover, he questions whether emigration acted as a Malthusian check. Since pre-famine emigration emanated from the more advanced counties of Ireland it was unlikely that there was any reduction of pressure on the poorest province of Connaught.

Mokyr offers a further insight into the nature of rural Irish poverty which explains both the reluctance of smallholders to leave their plots and the often critical reception they got, as emigrants, when they arrived in Britain. Even before the famine years, descriptions of travellers were unanimous in deploring the appalling level of domestic squalor of smoke-filled cabins in which pigs and humans cohabited. Yet the outsider perspective was based on the consumption patterns and values of a separately ordered society. Where Englishmen saw only the outward signs of what they took to be a primitive and poor existence, we might have recognised that many Irishmen enjoyed certain benefits from a subsistence way of life.

The Irish diet, although monotonous, was clearly superior to that of agricultural labourers in southern England and was probably richer than in all but the most advanced regions of Europe. Despite a heavy dependence on the potato crop, particularly marked in the south and western counties, potatoes were supplemented by dairy products, oatmeal, fish and eggs. The pre-famine diet was certainly sufficient in vitamins, proteins and minerals, and although much is made of the dependency on the potato, the

than hints that potato harvests were less important than the changing economic developments within the British Isles in promoting Irish emigration in the pre-famine era.

Interestingly, Collins also demonstrates how Irish weavers clung to their familial work patterns and migrated to the textile areas of Scotland and the north of England. In the 1820s and 1830s, Irish weavers continued their craft in Lancashire, Yorkshire and in the Scottish cities of Aberdeen and Dundee, both centres of coarse linen production. When the potato harvests failed in successive years in the 1840s, a stream of emigrants from north-central Ireland found their way, via Drogheda, to Dundee. The 1851 census records that 60 per cent of the Irishmen in Dundee were employed in the handloom weaving trade while Irish women and girls made up over half the mill spinners in the town. The dependence on Irish labour in Dundee was so great that the familial patterns and population structure of north-central Ireland were transported intact to the east coast of Scotland.

The importance of textiles in early nineteenth-century Ireland is echoed by Eoin O'Malley in a study of the decline of Irish industry.[13] He estimates that one-third of Irish counties in 1821 had a greater number employed in manufacture, trade or handicraft than in agriculture and that as late as 1841 one-fifth of the labour force were occupied in textile manufacture. Ulster was the most heavily industrialised of the Irish provinces and significantly was least affected by the general experience of industrial decline in Ireland throughout the century. Indeed, the region centred on Belfast continued to flourish on the same pattern as the large industrial centres in Britain. Belfast, itself, became 'the largest centre of linen manufacture in the world and by the 1900s her shipyards were building up to a quarter of the total United Kingdom tonnage'.[14]

O'Malley echoes Collins in arguing that the phenomenon of general industrial decline and a concentration of industry in Ulster can be explained by the advantages of the early development of large-scale, centralised production and proximity to markets.[15] The decline of the Irish woollen industry in the 1820s and 1830s was comparable, as Cullen points out, to the decline of the smaller British centres, such as East Anglia and the south-west, in the face of the growing strength of the Yorkshire woollen industry.[16] In Ireland, as in England, it was the peripheral areas that suffered a dramatic reduction in both production and employment.

The consequences of the decline in the woollen industry and the concentration of linen spinning in Belfast were most acutely felt by the rural poor. For landless labourers, cottiers and small farmers, spinning had contributed a vital additional income, particularly in Ulster and in Connaught. With agriculture also becoming less labour intensive, with the expansion of beef relative to other agricultural products, there were fewer opportunities for employment on the land.[17] So the emigration already evident in the 1820s and 1830s was a response to the shortage of industrial and agricultural employment in Ireland.

The relationship between poverty and emigration in Ireland, referred to earlier and highlighted by the devastating loss of population during the Great Famine, retains some surprising features. Kerby Miller has shown that emigration was less evident among the poor than among farmers and tradesmen in the period 1815 to 1845, and this pattern persisted to an extent in the second half of the century.[18] As S. H. Cousens has demonstrated, the poorest districts of Ireland lost most population during the famine crisis, but this was the result of extensive mortality rather than through excessive emigration.[19] Moreover, despite the holocaust of the 1840s, the demographic pattern of the pre-famine era survived from the 1850s to the 1880s.[20] Whereas the population of Ireland as a whole continued to fall, population continued increasing in the poorest and least fertile parts of the west of Ireland. With the exception of urban areas, the marked disparity in population growth between the east and west of Ireland persisted until 1881. Further crop failures in the late seventies and early eighties prompted exceptionally heavy emigration from the western counties.

So what is required is an explanation that holds equally good for the persistence of the pre-famine pattern of population increase until late in the century and a sudden exodus from the western counties in the 1880s. The different rates of rural population growth between the east and the west of Ireland were bound up with the availability of land. The population density of the western coast in 1871 was three times as high as in the southeast of Ireland.[21] High population densities inevitably meant smallholdings and the continuation of a subsistence agriculture largely dependent on the potato crop. Contemporary opinion had it that a holding of 10–15 acres was insufficient to support a family on poor western soils, yet half the holdings in nineteen western unions in 1861 were in this category. What appeared to be a reduction in the size of holdings, already insufficient to support an increasing population, spelt imminent trouble should there be further failures in the potato crop. Whereas improvements were taking place in the condition of Ireland as a whole, the west of Ireland remained dangerously dependent on subsistence agriculture.

Sustaining the east/west division in population growth was the regional variation in marriage rates in Ireland, and despite the intervention of the Great Famine, these actually widened between 1841 and 1871. The relatively high propensity to marry, and at an early age, was closely related to the opportunities for occupying land in the western counties. There, the presence of wasteland enabled people to throw up a cabin and to cultivate potatoes, on tiny plots near the coast, manured with the application of seaweed. Also, the common holding of land under the rundale system, as in County Mayo in the west, allowed an increase in the number of dependent households through the subdivision of plots. In the more fertile east of Ireland, the comparative absence of wasteland and the difficulty of subdividing tenancies under leaseholding agreements, meant that occupation of the land had to wait on natural inheritance.

The impact of the Great Famine on the availability of land served to accentuate the differences between the east and west of Ireland. In the east, the drive to amalgamate smallholdings into substantial farms led to the systematic removal of the smaller tenants but a continual cultivation of the land. In the west, the peasantry, who were unable to pay their rent, were evicted and landlords threw down their cabins, leaving large areas of wasteland available for letting as smallholdings. The increase in the number of holdings below thirty acres was a western phenomenon of the 1850s which continued into the 1870s. Once it became difficult to obtain holdings in the western counties, the demographic patterns of the pre-famine era came to an end. Conditions in the west began to approximate to those of the east and the trend was towards a more uniform age of marriage throughout the country. By 1881, far fewer women were married in their early twenties than a decade before, with the decline most marked in the western counties. In 1871, over a third of the age group 21–24 were married in Kerry in the south-west compared with less than a sixth of the same age group in Wexford in the south-east. Ten years later, the gap had narrowed to a fifth of the age group in Kerry and an eighth in Wexford.[22] The age of brides was a critical factor in determining the rate of population growth in Ireland as in England.

Cousens concludes that the poverty of western Ireland had the effect not of promoting but of restricting emigration between 1861 and 1881. The persistence of high marriage rates and population growth in the west was associated with the availability of land. These pre-famine characteristics were only brought to an end with the further crop failures of the 1870s and 1880s, which in turn were accompanied by major emigration from the western counties, predominantly to North America.

How those poor smallholders were able to cling to their plots, for a generation after the Great Famine, is more fully explored by Cormac O'Grada, who attaches considerable importance to seasonal migration in the subsistence economy of the western counties.[23] O'Grada argues that the extent of seasonal migration to Great Britain was greater than has been recognised and increased in scale between the 1840s and 1860s, facilitated by the provision of special trains by the Midland Great Western Railway, transporting harvesters from the west to the east coast ports. In the 1860s, some 60,000 seasonal passengers were carried by the railway en route to the harvest fields of Scotland and the north of England, and O'Grada estimates the annual total of seasonal migration was of the order of 100,000 for the whole of Ireland.

Seasonal migration on this scale, most prominently from those western counties furthest away from mainland Britain, requires explanation. O'Grada argues that there was a close association between the continued poverty experienced in the subsistence agriculture of the west, specifically the need to find the annual rent to maintain the family plot, and the pattern of seasonal migration to Britain. Seasonal work could add about £10 to the family budget, amounting to a third of its income—sufficient indeed to pay the annual rent. He cites the evidence of the Registrar-General, Grimshaw, who if anything underestimated the extent of seasonal migration:

> The County of Mayo represents the extreme of the peculiar-
> ities depending upon this curious example of social economy.
> In this county we find that at least 41.7 per thousand of the
> population habitually migrate, nearly all to Great Britain, in

order to obtain an essential portion of their livelihood, that these migratory labourers constitute 17.3 per cent of the adult male population, that 44.3 per cent are landholders, and of these only 8.9 per cent are occupiers of the smallest class of holdings, and that although Mayo is the most remote of Irish counties that furnish migratory labourers in large numbers, yet the proportion of these who proceed to Great Britain, especially England, is greater than any other county in Ireland.[24]

Dependence upon seasonal migration leads O'Grada to suggest that the drying up of demand for harvest labour in Britain contributed, along with the near-famine conditions of 1879–83, to permanent emigration from the west of Ireland. The crisis in British agriculture from the late 1870s, when a series of disastrous harvests coincided with the importation of cheap American wheat, reduced the demand for seasonal labour from Ireland. The mechanisation of agriculture gradually took hold, accompanied by a reduction in cereal growing, as a structural change in British agriculture took place in the closing decades of the century. The American inventions of mechanical reapers, in the 1850s and 1860s, contributed ultimately to a lower demand for Irish seasonal workers as the use of machines increased in British harvest fields from the 1870s. This, in turn, led to a substantial emigration from the western counties to the United States in the 1880s.[25] The number of seasonal migrants from Ireland to Britain subsequently halved between the 1880s and the 1910s, with a demand remaining largely for picking potatoes and turnips,which were difficult to mechanise.

The diversity of the regional economy of nineteenth-century Ireland has been associated not only with differing population structures, as highlighted by Collins and Cousens, but also with a variety of destinations for Irish emigrants. These may be identified fairly accurately, as David Fitzpatrick has shown, from 1876, when the detail of the Irish county of origin was no longer subject to the arbitrary competence of the local constables.[26] In examining the emigration figures from 1876 to 1895, Fitzpatrick identifies four main destinations, each possessing a distinctive regional association. Moreover, he speculates that the patterns identified for the late nineteenth century may well have applied to earlier decades, including the period of the Great Famine, when the figures prove less reliable indicators of regional patterns of emigration. From his analysis for the period 1876 to 1895, he concludes that about three-fifths of Irish emigrants found their way to the United States and these tended to come from the more 'backward' counties along the Atlantic seaboard. The western counties 'had many Irish speakers, few Protestants, large agricultural populations and low farm value per capita'.[27]

Fitzpatrick poses the problem of why 'backward' emigrants should have chosen the more expensive destination of America rather than Britain. He speculates that many more emigrants fled from the western counties in the generation after the Great Famine than have been recorded, supported by generous remittances received from America, which largely financed a chain migration. The accident that the Great Famine in Ireland coincided with industrial recession in Britain also encouraged dispossessed Westerners to struggle across the Atlantic, often taking advantage of cut-price passages from British ports and risking their lives in the process.

The Irish who settled in Britain formed about one quarter of emigrants in 1870 and were naturally subject to under-recording as hard-pressed officials found the passengers on cross-channel ferries too numerous to count. Certainly, on the basis of the sample who were counted, the post-Depression emigrants to Britain came predominantly from north-east Ulster and from parts of the southern and eastern seaboards. In England, Irish settlement concentrated in the industrial midlands and the north, in Cheshire, Lancashire, Yorkshire and Northumberland, with minor clusters in London, the West Country and south Wales. In Scotland, the Irish concentrated in the Glasgow region in the west, and on the east coast were found in other industrial cities— Aberdeen, Dundee and Edinburgh.

Five main conclusions emerge from recent work on Irish demography and migration. Firstly, the primacy of the Great Famine period in the population history of nineteenth-century Ireland has become less certain with the recognition of mass emigration in the pre-famine era and the continuous outflow of Irish migrants in the second half of the century. Secondly, the lack of homogeneity in the structure of population, the variety in the patterns of agricultural development and in the incidence of both domestic and manufacturing industry in Ireland are fundamental to an understanding of the economic pressures behind

Irish emigration. Thirdly, the association between poverty and emigration is founded on a false premise. Not only did the poorest section of Irish society figure less prominently among the emigrant population than is commonly supposed but, more significantly, the subsistence way of life with its communal culture and values, predominant in the western counties was ignorantly condemned as a state of primitive poverty. This air of superiority, despite evidence to the contrary on the well-being of the Irish peasantry, was naturally incorporated into ideologically convenient explanations of famine and emigration in Ireland. Fourthly, migration flows from different provinces in Ireland at different periods in the century can be identified with a variety of destinations overseas, including Britain. And lastly, the Irish migrated to Britain, not only in greater numbers than recognised formerly, but in three distinctive forms of migration that collectively had the effect of increasing alarm about the Irish presence in mainland Britain.

Before 1870, the great majority of Irish emigrants bound for the United States, Canada and Australia, first came to Britain as short-stay migrants. Secondly, there was an annual migration of seasonal workers to Britain, mostly harvesters but also navvies on contract work constructing railways, canals and docks. Thirdly, there were those who may originally have come as short-stay migrants or as seasonal workers but settled more or less permanently in Britain.[28]

Where does this analysis leave the status of the Great Famine in the story of nineteenth-century Ireland? If it is diminished by recent interpretations of demographic trends, the Great Famine remains an epic monument for Irish people all over the world. To a people conditioned to look backwards, its potency as a political symbol has, if anything, been reinforced by a process of repetition. In spite of the careful qualifications made by a generation of historians since the 1950s, the events of the late 1840s—the woeful catalogue of starvation, death and emigration—still exercise a pervasive influence on Irish understanding of the past.

The idea of the Great Famine did not emerge spontaneously from the famine years. As Patrick O'Farrell has argued, it was largely the creation of one man, the journalist historian, John Mitchel (1815–1875).[29] As editor of *The United Irishman* he made his own colourful contribution to the nationalist politics of the period, as a result of which he was tried, convicted of treason and exiled to Australia in 1848. Having spent five years in British prisons, he escaped to America where he took the Confederate side in the Civil War,[30] and returned to Ireland in the 1870s to become MP for Tipperary. As a convicted felon he was denied the seat. Mitchel has been described as the 'quintessential Irish rebel', a man who never bowed the knee to British rule in Ireland.[31] His talent for elegant and forceful prose in advocating a peasant uprising and the establishment of an Irish Republic made him a leading figure on the left of the nationalist movement of his day. Yet his enduring influence may be traced to two works; *Jail Journal or Five Years in British Prisons* (New York: 1854) and *The Last Conquest of Ireland (Perhaps)* (New York: 1860).

In the Introduction to the *Jail Journal*, Mitchel produced a version of Irish history in which everything was subordinated to a diatribe against the tyranny of England. In a powerful polemic, by turns scathing and sarcastic, Mitchel constructed the history of Ireland from the time of Oliver Cromwell to the failure of the repeal movement in 1848, as a catalogue of the oppression of the Irish people by the British Government. Mitchel's withering prose stands comparison with the vitriolic pen of that English radical journalist of an earlier generation, William Cobbett. It was Mitchel's purpose to create an image of 'The Famine' as starvation in the midst of plenty. He succeeded in this by presenting the bitter prospect of thousands of Irish people starving to death while Ireland sent its surplus produce to feed the industrial population of England. Thus Mitchel's account of the Famine was transformed into a terrible indictment of English colonial rule and, by a masterly propaganda stroke, the tragedy became harnessed to the bandwagon of Irish nationalism. It is easy to admire the rhetorical skills Mitchel employed in creating his version of events:

> At the end of six years, I can set down these things calmly; but to see them might have driven a wise man mad. There is no need to recount how the Assistant Barristers and Sheriffs, aided by the Police, tore down the roof-trees and ploughed up the hearths of village after village—how the Quarter Acre clause laid waste the parishes, how the farmers and their wives and little ones in wild dismay, trooped along the highways;—how in some hamlets by the seaside, most of the inhabitants being already dead, an adventurous

traveller would come upon some family eating a famished ass;—how maniac mothers stowed away their dead children to be devoured at midnight; . . . how husband and wife fought like wolves for the last morsel of food in the house; how families, when all was eaten and no hope left, took their last look at the Sun, built up their cottage-doors, that none might see them die nor hear their groans, and were found weeks afterwards, skeletons on their own hearth; how the 'law' was vindicated all this while; how the Arms-bills were diligently put in force, and many examples were made; how starving wretches were transported for stealing vegetables at night; how overworked coroners declared they would hold no more inquests; how Americans sent corn, and the very Turks, yea, negro slaves, sent money for arms: which the British government was not ashamed to administer to the 'sister-country'; and how in every one of those years, '46, '47, and '48, Ireland was exporting to England, food to the value of fifteen million pounds sterling, and had on her own soil at each harvest, good and ample provision for double her own population, notwithstanding the potato blight.[32]

Mitchel claimed that the events of 'The Famine' were no accident. The sinister intention of the British government was evident in the establishment of the Devon Commission in 1843. Lord Devon and a few landlords were appointed to

Go through Ireland, collect evidence, and report on the best means (not of destroying the Irish enemy—official documents do not now use so harsh language, but) of ameliorating the relations of landlord and tenant in Ireland. On this commission, O'Connell observed that it was 'a jury of butchers trying a sheep for his life,' and said many other good things both merry and bitter, as was his wont; but the Devon Commission travelled and reported; and its Report has been the Gospel of Irish landlords and British Statesmen ever since.[33]

Mitchel focused on 'the most remarkable sentence' in Lord Devon's 'Digest of Evidence' which stated:

We find that there are at present 326,084 occupiers of land (more than one-third of the total number in Ireland), whose holdings vary from seven acres to less than one acre; and are therefore, inadequate to support the families residing upon them. In the same table, No 95, page 564, the calculation is put forward showing that the consolidation of these small holdings up to eight acres, would require the *removal* of about 192,368 *families*. [34]

Mitchel seized on the point:

That is, the killing of a million persons. Little did the Commissioners hope then that in four years, British policy, with the famine to aid, would succeed in killing fully two millions, and forcing another million to flee the country.[35]

Here we have Mitchel's method exposed. The Commission's straightforward analysis of the size of holdings with the need to make them economically viable (albeit in the interests of the landlords and 'strong' farmers), is interpreted as a plot to murder the cottiers and the labouring poor of Ireland. The recommendation of the Devon Commission (one of the more liberal reports on Irish agriculture, which was to advocate tenant-right in Ireland beyond the province of Ulster), was very much the standard one that agrarian reformers applied to agriculture in England at the time.[36]

Mitchel developed his theme beyond the charge of coercion, in the central thesis of *The Last Great Conquest of Ireland (Perhaps)*. Here, he accepted the religious context of the times but neatly turned it into a deadly political weapon: 'The Almighty, indeed, sent the potato blight, but the English created the Famine.'[37] Mitchel converted the seemingly unintelligible sequence of events in the famine years into the form of a sinister conspiracy to exterminate the Irish people. After explaining how the idea of 'surplus' population in Ireland had become axiomatic in English political circles prior to the famine period—regardless of the great potential in improvable wasteland in Ireland and the importance of Irish food exports to England—the charge of genocide was laid like a slowly ticking bomb at the door of the Imperial Government:

But the potato blight and consequent famine, placed in the hands of the British government an engine of state by which they were eventually enabled to clear off not a million, but two millions and a half of the 'surplus population'—to 'preserve law and order' in Ireland (what they call law and order) and to maintain the integrity of the Empire for this time.[38]

O'Farrell makes a convincing case that Mitchel's charge of genocide lifted the tragedy of the potato blight to the status of high drama, with 'villains in the highest political places' constructing a monstrous inhuman plot, 'designed to achieve racial extermination, emigration and land clearances in the interest of economic principles and power'.[39] Historically, the importance of the Mitchel thesis lay not only in its early acceptance among Irish emigrants, especially in North America, but also in the influence it was to exercise over later historians and in popular fiction.[40] The popular success of Woodham-Smith's *The Great Hunger*, published in 1962, derived from its portrayal of the shortcomings in the administration of famine relief by the Treasury official, Sir Charles Trevelyan. Although the tone was politer than the emotive rhetoric employed by Mitchel, Woodham-Smith's narrative of the unfolding drama was equally forthright in condemnation of the ideological blindness demonstrated by the British government.

Despite an interval of a hundred years the Mitchel thesis was largely accepted and indeed developed in *The Great Hunger*, a book that ran to six impressions between 1962 and 1980. What had been common currency among poor Irish emigrants in the New World was now the established view among a popular readership in Britain. An even wider audience was gained for the Mitchel/Woodham-Smith view in Robert Kee's treatment of the Great Famine as set out in *The Green Flag*, published in 1972 and popularised in his book, *Ireland, a Television History*, based on the BBC series broadcast in 1981.[41] Once more, Trevelyan was made the villain of the piece and the British government charged with failing in the fundamental responsibility of protecting its own citizens. Kee included an editorial from the *Cork Examiner* in 1846, as an ironic endorsement of the Mitchel view:

Talk of the power of England, her navy, her gold, her resources—oh yes, and her enlightened statesmen, while the broad fact is manifested that she cannot keep the children of her bosom from perishing by hunger . . . when the Queen at her coronation swore to protect and defend her subjects, it is not recollected that in the words of the solemn covenant there was any exception made with regard to Ireland. [42]

That Mitchel's influence remains as persuasive as ever is evident from the work of an Irish-American writer, Thomas Gallagher. His book, *Paddy's Lament: Ireland 1846–47: Prelude to Hatred*, was first published in 1982 and produced in paperback in 1985. It aims to speak for the victims of the Great Famine and to explain how centuries of hostility was turned into undying hatred on the part of their descendants by the events of 1847–8. The book turns out to be an unashamed and unqualified endorsement of the Mitchel thesis. Committed to the unifying theme of starvation amidst plenty, Gallagher contrasts the distress in Ireland with a satisfyingly superior tone of complacency found in England. In readdressing targets identified by Mitchel, Gallagher amplifies the nationalist case with stomach-churning descriptions, designed to make an emotive appeal to a popular readership.

Common to the work of Mitchel, and those who have followed his lead, is the prominence given to the plight of the district of Skibbereen in County Cork during the famine period. Skibbereen was perhaps the most reported of all famine locations and became, in the form of poems and popular songs, a powerful symbol of nationalist propaganda.[43] Gallagher, employing Mitchel's technique of creating vivid contrasts, sets two newspaper reports alongside each other, one from the *Cork Examiner* and the other from *The Times* to point up the unfeeling and inhumane character of the British response to starvation in Skibbereen. Thus the *Cork Examiner*:

> A terrible apathy hangs over the poor of Skibbereen; starvation has destroyed every generous sympathy; despair has made them hardened and insensible, and they sullenly await their doom with indifference and without fear. Death is in every hovel; disease and famine, its dread precursors, have fastened on the young and old, the strong and the feeble, the mother and the infant, whole families lie together on the damp floor, devoured by fever, without a human being to wet their burning lips or raise their languid heads; the husband dies by the side of the wife, and she knows not that he is beyond the reach of earthly suffering; the same rag covers the festering remains of mortality and the skeleton forms of the living, who are unconscious of the horrible

continguity; rats devour the corpse, and there is no energy among the living to scare them from their horrid banquet; fathers bury their children without a sigh, and cover them in shallow graves, round which no weeping mother, no sympathising friends are grouped; one scanty funeral is followed by another and another. Without food or fuel, bed or bedding whole families are shut up in naked hovels, dropping one by one into the arms of death. [44]

This was not mere reportage on 'the skeleton forms of the living', but a carefully constructed cry for help, designed to appeal to sympathy and respect for family values in the world at large. Along with the vivid pictures of the Famine featured in *The Illustrated London News* and other publications, such descriptions as those of the *Cork Examiner* were intended to prompt a generous response from the British people. In fact, the response in Britain was ambivalent. On the one hand, large sums of money were raised by charities in aid of famine victims in Ireland, rather in the same spirit as occurred with the famine in Ethiopia in 1984. The British Association collected over £470,000 and many local organisations and private individuals added immeasurably to that sum. [45] On the other hand, the spectre of misery and starvation depicted by the *Cork Examiner* struck no such sympathetic chord in the editorials of *The Times*. This can be explained, if not forgiven, by the ideological framework in which many propertied and educated Englishmen interpreted the events in Ireland. Words such as 'apathy', 'indifference', 'hardened and insensible', confirmed the Malthusian rationale for the starvation so colourfully depicted. Here was a picture of appalling squalor, of a people aparently removed from civilised conditions and sensibilities. To the editors of *The Times*, this was no natural disaster but the result of idleness and dependence on public money. In a damning analogy with disease, using language more normally associated with the potato blight, the moral corruption of the Irish peasantry was proclaimed:

> The season has come when not only the herb of the field should shoot forth, and the tree should blossom, but the hopes of men also bring forth their fruits. But in Ireland, alas! the voice of nature strikes upon listless ears and sluggish hearts. In vain has spring returned to men of idle hands and nerveless purpose. In vain has the iron tongue of

experience spoken its warning to men who hug their indolent misery as a treasure, far more precious than the wages of unaided industry. They have tasted of public money, and they find it pleasanter to live on alms than on labour. The alternative raises no feeling of shame or self-abasement. *Deep, indeed, has the canker eaten. Not into the core of a precarious and suspected root—but into the very hearts of the people, corrupting them with a fatal lethargy, and debasing them with a fatuous dependence!* . . . Thus the plow rusts, the spade lies idle, and the fields fallow.[46]

Contrast is central to Woodham-Smith's detailed narrative of the famine in Skibbereen, which chronicles the reports sent to Trevelyan by local magistrates, clergy and government officials, directly involved in famine relief. Those accounts contained the most heart-rending scenes—a woman and 4 naked children described as wretches huddling together on filthy straw and moaning in a fevered state beside a male corpse; frozen corpses lying upon a mud floor half-devoured by rats; witnesses besieged by 200 frightful spectres with demonic yells, and nearly having their clothes torn off them as they escaped from a throng of pestilence all round.[47] Trevelyan's response is depicted as unfeeling and cruel in the extreme: 'The great evil with which we have to contend, is not the physical evil of the famine, but the moral evil of the selfish, perverse and turbulent character of the people.'[48] In refusing to send more food, he argued that there were 'principles to be kept in view'. Private enterprise had to be protected: 'We attach the highest public importance to the strict observance of our pledge not to send orders abroad, which would come into competition with our merchants and upset all their calculations.'[49]

Woodham-Smith explained Trevelyan's position in terms of the prevailing ideology of the time. From London, there seemed no need to send food to Skibbereen when it was known there was ample food in the district. Trevelyan insisted on the resources of the country being 'drawn out' and the responsibility firmly placed on local landlords who, between them, drew an annual income of some £50,000. Relief was to be given to the inhabitants of Skibbereen through the agency of the local Relief Committee, and the Government would donate money to support the funds raised by local subscriptions. Local landowners were urged to contribute to the relief of their own people, on the principle that Irish property should provide for Irish poverty.[50] As mere exhortation proved insufficient to meet the needs of the crisis, the Government stood accused of abdicating its ultimate responsibility.

Alongide the charge of incompetence and neglect on the part of the British government, is an explanation that recognises the contribution of the economy and social structure in the scale of the devastation in Skibbereeen. It suffered from an especially primitive economy. The Skibbereen Union was a district of very high population density: 400 people per square mile, double that of many surrounding areas. With over half the occupiers of land holding between five and twenty acres, the valuation of land and buildings was less than one pound per head of population and the dependence on the potato was more complete than that of any other union in the county. On all counts, Skibbereen was extremely poor and desperately vulnerable. When the potato blight hit the district, there were few tradesmen or resident landlords to relieve the situation. In the decade 1841 to 1851, Skibbereen lost 36 per cent of its population, a greater loss than for any other union in County Cork.[51]

Running parallel with the enduring nationalist view of the Great Famine, a generation of historians has extended the scope of inquiry beyond the political and administrative spheres to explain the famine period in a broader social and economic context. The surviving evidence from folk memory, compiled by Roger McHugh, points to a predominantly religious explanation of the potato blight.[52] It was believed that the very abundance of the crops in good years had made people careless of their good fortune and wasteful of the Lord's bounty. People scarcely knew what to do with their surplus potatoes and wasted them. Potatoes were stacked in heaps and left to rot, burnt or buried, or even used to fill up gaps in fences. Such waste created a foreboding of retribution, and as famine spread over the land, it was assumed to be a scourge from God, a punishment for the abuse of plenty. Reinforcing this belief was what McHugh described in biblical terms as 'an ominous season of mist, of storms, of rain and wind alternating with periods of vast and terrible stillness; of the names of fields where the blight first appeared and of men who first noticed the heavy smell of decay or saw the brown spots spreading on the leaves, the blackened stalks slowly leaning over the potato-pits ominously sagging.'[53] How else could one explain how some crops and even some communities, escaped the swathe of decay that spread rapidly from field to field?

Folk memory also records how people survived the Famine through the miraculous appearance of food. The most popular of such stories featured the 'charitable woman' who embodied the traditional Irish virtue of sharing what little she had with poor neighbours, only to find that food given away was miraculously replaced. Such stories are found in a variety of forms in Mayo, Galway, Cork and Wexford. Others emphasise the virtues of hospitality in the shape of the stranger who is welcomed by poor people and, in turn, rewards them by causing food to appear. Others still have the miraculous appearance of food in response to prayer. The enduring belief in these tales, long after the famine years, is a tribute to the power of religious and communal values among surviving Irish-speaking people, especially in the south and west of Ireland.

Those disposed to leave the country were more open to fresh influences. The successive failures of the potato crop had by early 1847 induced a condition of hysteria in particular communities. Oliver McDonagh cites the newspaper stories about people suddenly making feverish arrangements to leave, about fights for contract tickets at the ports, and deliberate felonies being committed in the hope of transportation—an emigration driven by panic and the contagious example of neighbours. Whereas the exodus was only slight in some places, it was alarmingly high in others, even in adjoining parishes. McDonagh cites the example of the diocese of Elphin where emigration was as low as 1 per cent in some parishes and as high as 17 per cent in others. He suggests this marked the beginning of a profound social disintegration, prompting a fatal loss of morale among respectable farmers and tradesmen, whose flight left the peasantry scrambling in imitation to get out of the country. Further disastrous crop failures, and the fiasco of the 1848 Rising, brought on 'a deep mood of staleness and defeat', that was to last through the next three seasons.[54]

This emphasis on the successive moods of panic and depression, discernible in the evidence of commentators, contemporary witnesses and newpaper reports, marks an important distinction between how the scale of emigration was viewed at the time and how it was to be reconstructed subsequently. All that people could have known during the famine period was based on local incidents and drawn from anecdotal evidence. The mood was shaped by often despairing first-hand descriptions of the loss of family and friends through death or emigration. Almost certainly, these tended to exaggerate the actual level of loss sustained in any district, without reference to the broader context of events throughout Ireland. It was only later, and largely through Mitchel's agency, that the idea of the Great Famine was created and only then was a particular interpretation fixed upon it to support the nationalist cause.

In examining some of the structural changes that occurred during the Famine, an alternative interpretation to that of Mitchel's oppression model becomes apparent. Social changes were not confined to demographic trends that only gradually responded to the shock of the famine years. A more sudden and enduring transformation took place in the structure of Irish rural society. One estimate records a 40 per cent decline in the number of labourers and cottiers and a 20 per cent decline in the number of farmers in the period 1845 to 1851.[55] This trend continued over the next sixty years with the number of labourers and cottiers falling by a further 40 per cent while the number of farmers declined by only about 5 per cent. Broadly, there was a strengthening of the position of the more substantial farmers who were able to consolidate their holdings at the expense of those with less than fifteen acres. Between 1845 and 1910, the number of labourers and cottiers in Ireland fell by two thirds, small farmers on five to fifteen acres were halved in number and those who occupied holdings above fifteen acres increased by 10 per cent. Effectively, the large underclass at the base of Irish rural society was severely reduced and the power of 'strong' farmers greatly increased. The sudden and violent process of change made rural Ireland more sharply divided on class lines during the famine years.

The Great Famine accentuated a process that was already under way through the modernisation and commercialisation of Irish agriculture.[56] The failure of the potato crop in 1846 undermined what was left of the traditional relationship that existed between farmers and their bond labourers. Both parties could no longer meet their obligations. Labourers repudiated agreements to work for farmers in return for a cabin and a patch of ground, demanding the money wages needed to escape starvation. For their part, farmers demanded at least a portion of rent in advance for conacre land to unbound labourers and largely refused the payment of money wages. Abandoning their plots, labourers were compelled to seek relief through public works or in the workhouses.

At every level of society, the devastating impact of the successive failure of the potato crops in 1846, 1847 and 1848 brought not only starvation and eviction for labourers and cottiers, but spelled economic ruin for many farmers and landlords in the worst affected districts. Inevitably, there was a decline in farm rents collected, yet landlords faced greatly increased burdens from poor rates, and were being pressed to relieve the distress amongst the labouring population by providing employment on a much greater scale.

Bitterness and conflict grew as each sectional interest sought to protect itself in the face of the economic blizzard of the famine years. Landlords complained of farmers who dismissed their labourers and threw responsibility on to them, despite the good prices that farmers had received for corn in 1846 and 1847. The failure to pay farm rents prompted the distraint of goods in lieu as at Dungarvan on the Duke of Devonshire's estate in April 1847. Distraint was practised widely on estates in east and west Cork and landlord seizures led to tenants adopting counter-measures. Some farmers resorted to gathering friends to remove a whole crop on the Sabbath to a safe place to avoid seizure of goods which was unlawful on a Sunday. The law, however, was disregarded by both sides. Other tenants attempted to obstruct seizure or even to rescue cattle or crops already seized. In the face of large hostile crowds, landlords called out a strong force of constabulary to enforce a distress notice, and occasionally violence and death ensued. In Connaught many tenants, faced with landlords intent on securing their rents at all costs, sold their crops and stock and disappeared.[57]

Similar attempts to evade the law arose from the implementation of the notorious quarter-acre clause.[58] A provision of the Poor Law Amendment Act of June 1847, it attracted widespread hostility in promoting enforced starvation and the clearance of paupers from estates. Pauper tenants were evicted and their cabins levelled. Evasive action was taken by tenants, transferring their holdings to friends or relatives, on the understanding that they would reclaim the land once out of the workhouse. Such collusion was common to districts with a high proportion of smallholders. Clinging to tiny plots and trying to send wives and children into the workhouse to avoid starvation, smallholders often found themselves faced with refusal of their applications by vigilant Poor Law Guardians, who wanted to preserve the regulation workhouse test.

As towns were the centres for administering poor relief and public works, the famine-stricken rural poor flocked to them, so creating tensions between the towns and country districts. 'On an average', *The Cork Constitution* reported in April 1847, 'about 300 of these miserable creatures come into the city daily, who are walking masses of filth, vermin and sickness.'[59] The authorities feared being swamped by a horde of refugees. After some 20,000 paupers had invaded the city and an estimated 500 were dying each week, special constables were armed to guard the city entrances and turn the famine victims away.

A more sympathetic response was evoked from the young Marquis of Sligo when thousands of rural poor descended on the town of Westport in County Mayo in the spring of 1847. As chairman of the Westport Guardians and of the Westport Relief Committee, he was sensitive to the extent of distress in the area and along with some of the local clergy (Catholic and Protestant), he was able to offer some relief to the starving population. He chartered a ship, the *Martha Washington*, to sail from New Orleans to Westport with a 1,000 tons of flour on board. The ship arrived in June 1847, and its cargo was sold at half price, with Lord Sligo bearing most of the loss incurred, amounting to £3,012. His personal contribution to support relief meant that he had to borrow to pay the rates, close up the family home and move into town.[60]

If landlord reactions varied, so too did the operation of the Poor Law. Christine Kinealy's study of the Poor Law in County Mayo makes a case for local diversity.[61] Even as early as 1842, some unions in Mayo were unable to collect poor rates as the small occupiers lacked the means to pay them. By 1843, in the Ballina, Swinford and Castlebar Unions, the Guardians received no rates and were without funds. Opposition to rate collectors was widespread. Three were assaulted and beaten in the Ballina Union and the Guardians requested the presence of a Stipendiary Magistrate and the military, to secure the collection of rates and to keep the workhouse open. Following further resistance to the collection of rates, the authorities relented, making all occupiers of dwellings below £4 per annum exempt from payment. The result was to transfer the rate burden on to the landlords, who not only faced the prospect of bankruptcy as the Famine progressed, but became the scapegoats for non-payment of rates. When the Commissioners allowed the presence of a magistrate and the military, the collection of rates in Mayo was improved.

With the onset of the Famine in 1845, the limitations of the Poor Law were exposed. It was totally incapable of providing relief on the scale required. In Mayo, the workhouses had a total capacity of 4,400 inmates and when funds were exhausted, the Guardians were compelled to turn paupers away. Yet on one day in 1847, 2,000 paupers applied for relief at Ballina, when the workhouse was full, and the Guardians could only provide them with a meal. During the same year, the weekly expenses of the Poor Law Unions were met by private donations by the Earl of Lucan at Castlebar and the Marquis of Sligo at Westport. Despite the Commissioners' insistence on local distress being met by local taxation, the severe financial difficulties experienced by all the Mayo unions forced the Government to provide additional relief.

The prolonged distress in the western counties diverted the Government from its ideological stance over the Poor Law in Ireland. Whilst the situation was improving in Ulster and other parts of Ireland, the distress in Mayo, Galway, Clare and parts of Kerry was at its greatest in 1849. So in those areas, external financial assistance continued to supplement what could be collected from the poor rates. The Government introduced Rate-in-Aid as a national rate designed to compel the wealthier unions to subsidise the poorer ones.

Accompanying the inadequacy of poor relief and a desperate migration to the towns, food riots and the stealing of food assumed unprecedented proportions. In February 1847, an armed mob of labourers broke through the outer gate of Cork city and attacked the bread shops, and only after a long struggle were they dispersed by police, charging with fixed bayonets. Over the succeeding months such scenes were to be repeated in towns throughout the south of Ireland. Soup depots, corn mills, provision stores and even cars laden with Indian meal, under police escort, were targets for attack by mobs of starving people in the summer of 1847. Donnelly concludes that only the forbearance of the police and military authorities prevented bloodshed among potentially violent crowds.[62]

In rural districts, the forbearance of magistrates, in dismissing cases against labourers charged with stealing turnips, brought local objections from the farmers, some of whom took the law into their own hands by protecting their crops with shotguns. Not surprisingly, intimidation through warning shots directed against potential theft occasionally led to loss of life in defence of property interests. Even more serious was the astonishing increase in the stealing of cattle, sheep and poultry, as widely reported in the *Cork Examiner* from late 1846 to early 1849.[63] Farmers, in addition to being subjected to raids on their stock by the starving population of rural districts, also faced serious losses from gangs of thieves roaming the county.

Sheep and cattle stealing were regarded as serious offences and convicted labourers, even when driven by starvation, were sentenced to transportation to Australia for between seven and fifteen years. Transportation from Ireland rose from 600 to 2,000 a year during the famine years. Whilst this represented a draconian policy by magistrates to protect the property of farmers, it also probably included many labourers who saw transportation to Australia as preferable to destitution in Ireland. Self-interest and survival became the rule. In Counties Cork and Leitrim, the most distressed in Ireland, the Great Famine created an opportunity for landlords to clear their estates of bankrupt middlemen, for the larger farmers to increase the size of their holdings, and for tenants to fly the country without paying their rents. As a result, class antagonisms were sharpened and confiicts arose between farmers and magistrates, landowners and poor law officials, and between merchants, shopkeepers and the labouring poor.

The severity of the Famine varied in different parts of Ireland and continued longer in the poorer south and western counties than in other parts of the country. Landlord reaction also varied, ranging from the selfless and humane to the cynically opportunist. While some landlords impoverished their estates in relieving the distress of poor tenants, others exploited the situation by clearing their estates of poor cottiers and increasing the size of holdings. In the desperate scramble for survival, strong farmers, merchants and tradesmen looked to defend their economic interest, either at the expense of their neighours or by fleeing the country to avoid having to shoulder the burden of widespread distress.

Interestingly, county levels of mortality were commonly at variance with county levels of emigration. Five Irish counties, Cork, Kerry, Clare, Galway and Mayo—all on the Atlantic coast—had an average excess mortality of above an eighth of the total population in the period 1846 to 1850. At the same time, the rate of emigration from the southern counties was relatively moderate in relation to other parts of Ireland. For instance, County Cork is estimated to have lost 10–12 per cent through emigration between 1841 and 1851, a rather lower proportion than the estimated 20 per cent who left Mayo, Roscommon, Sligo, Monaghan, Cavan, Longford and Leix in the same decade. Of these, the midland counties had the highest rates of emigration where the small farmer, on holdings of 5–15 acres, possessed the means to emigrate and had the least incentive to stay.[64] S. H. Cousens explains the lower level of emigration from southern counties in relation to the heavy concentration of labourers within the region.[65] Put simply, the high level of poverty found in many of the southern districts meant that many people simply lacked the means to leave. Where there was a higher incidence of assisted emigration, as in Clare, Limerick and Kerry, more landless labourers did manage to emigrate. The most distressed areas of the south and west, which experienced high levels of mortality, attracted most public attention, but the midland counties from which there was the greatest exodus of population, were relatively ignored.

Certainly there were glaring shortcomings in the provision and administration of relief. A failure to control the grain trade, and the inadequate wages available on the public works in the autumn of 1846, made all the more likely the widespread starvation and disease in early 1847. Yet, inspired by the success of private relief schemes, the Government reversed policy, providing food relief from January 1847—free to the destitute, and directly to all distressed applicants outside the workhouses. Stirabout (a thick soup made from Indian meal and rice) was sold cheaply or distributed free. Through the auspices of the Poor Law unions, relief committees set up soup kitchens throughout the country, and by the summer of 1847, at the height of the operation, government kitchens distributed soup rations to over three million people throughout Ireland.

Distribution of food on this massive scale kept thousands alive and prevented a fearful mortality rate from rising still further. It was made possible only by huge imports of foreign grain, some 2.85 million tons during the first six months of 1847, resulting in a dramatic reduction in the price of Indian corn, from £19 a ton in February to £7.10s by the end of of August.[66] Plentiful supplies at low prices enabled the relief committees to operate their   soup kitchens effectively. Although intended as a temporary form of relief until changes in the Poor Law could be introduced, it represented a triumph of pragmatism over dogma. Trevelyan's rhetoric and the fulminations of *The Times*, designed to appease propertied interests in England concerned about the cost of relief to Ireland, were at variance with some of the practical steps taken by the British Government during the famine crisis.

The theme of starvation amidst plenty, a key part of Mitchel's nationalist propaganda, may also be seen as an oversimplification. Donnelly has shown that food exports from Ireland were affected severely during the famine years. Drastic reductions occurred in the level of grain exports as grain was diverted to home consumption, partly to provide food for livestock to compensate for the deficiencies in the potato crop.[67] Before the Famine, about a third of the annual potato crop was consumed by livestock, and over half of that went to feed pigs. The potato blight severely reduced pig-breeding but the raising of cattle expanded as farmers turned to using oats for cattle feed. Dairy farming also prospered and butter exports went on increasing through the late 1840s. The reduction in domestic consumption through poverty, death, and emigration, had the effect of diverting butter on to the export market. Irish agriculture, like Irish industry, was part of the wider British economy, and in the free play of market forces, the bigger cattle and dairy farmers not only weathered the storm but even prospered during the famine years, while the smaller farmers, dependent on cereals, pigs and sheep, faced adverse conditions.

Emigration from Ireland during the famine and post-famine period was not simply the result of a conspiracy by the British Government. Kerby Miller, in a major study of Irish emigration to North America, has argued that it was driven primarily by 'push' factors in Ireland—changing economic conditions, social structures and cultural patterns.[68] Miller pinpoints three dominant social forces in nineteenth-century Catholic Ireland that emerged from the break-up of a traditional Gaelic culture to spearhead the process of modernisation. He associates all three with the growing *embourgeoisement* of Catholic society—the strong-farmer type of rural Irish family, greatly strengthened by the clearances of the 1840s and 1850s; the Catholic Church, which imposed, through a 'devotional revolution', a coherent moral order on its followers; and Irish nationalism which found most of its support for constitutional change among strong farmers, the urban middle classes and village tradesmen. Commercialisation created the right conditions for such groups to emerge the more powerful from the devastation of the famine years.

Paradoxically Miller argues that all three of these agents of modernisation were also 'exponents of certain traditional attitudes' which ensured cultural continuity'.[69] In strong-farmer families, the concentration of capital through impartible inheritance, although it violated the older communal values, nevertheless preserved the traditional authoritarian family. Increasingly, this involved a prolonged adolescence and postponed marriage, tied to less opportunity for inheritance. On smaller farms, where the resources could not be found to provide non-inheriting children with dowries or with an education to establish themselves independently, emigration for both sexes was commonly the only alternative.

The Catholic Church in Ireland not only achieved a successful 'modernisation', replacing old forms of worship with those prescribed by Rome, but established a remarkable degree of clerical power over its parishioners. With the support of the Catholic middle class for church and school building programmes and the domination of the national school system, parochial attitudes were eroded. Also the reverence for celibacy and strict clerical injunction against sexual licence served to protect the planned marriages and inheritance in strong-farmer families. Increasingly, in the post-famine period, visitors to Ireland commented on the sinister influence of the priest, an influence not confined to the spiritual domain but extending to political and domestic issues. The Catholic clergy took over the allegiance that tenants had formerly given to their landlords. In troubled times, the clergy offered explanations in traditional terms, chiding their congregations for lapses in communal values and advocating charity, humility and acceptance of spiritual authority. Miller explains the impressive control exercised by the clergy, in terms of their providing 'psychic solace to the poor', and through their obscuring 'class and intergenerational conflicts within the Catholic community'.[70]

Modern and traditional elements were also present in Irish nationalism. Supported primarily by commercial farmers, businessmen and tradesmen, who viewed it as a necessary supplement to their increasingly powerful position, nationalist ideology also reinforced old habits of dependence and a lack of responsibility. In addition to a tradition-bound rhetoric, all Ireland's woes were put down to external causes. In having the English to blame for Ireland's problems, the Irish absolved themselves of all responsibility. Miller offers a compelling explanation of this phenomenon in what he terms the 'culture of exile'. In reality, he argues, Irish emigration was surrounded by conflicting pressures and emigrants themselves had highly ambivalent attitudes. Many farmers and tradesmen believed that the process of modernisation, a process synonymous with increasing bourgeois dominance, was only made possible by a clearing out of the poor cottiers and landless labourers. Emigration reduced the fear of potential agrarian violence in resistance to the consolidation of holdings among the larger farmers. For parents on smallholdings, it eased the way for the painful disinheritance of children without the prospect of unbearable family conflict.

For the Catholic Church, emigration provided the opportunity for the faith to be spread abroad. Not only might Catholic freedom thus be established in the United States but new settlements were consciously planned to rival those of earlier Protestant colonies in Australia and Canada.[71] Moreover, Irish emigrants abroad were seen as providing, through generous remittances, vital financial support for the building of Catholic churches and schools in Ireland. Emigrant money also paid for farm rents and financed improvements for tradesmen at home. Likewise, Irish emigrants in Britain and America gave aid in the form of capital and arms, and exercised diplomatic pressure in favour of the nationalist cause. More obviously, however, emigration aroused considerable fears that the country was losing its bone and sinew, its brightest and best. This loss could leave the people so pacified that the country would succumb to the English dream of a Protestant Ireland. The Church feared, too, that those who left for individual gain would violate the old values of family and faith. Parents would be abandoned to their fate as young people fled to a new life abroad.

To reconcile these conflicting tensions and anxieties, Miller suggests a unifying theme of emigration as exile took hold in the popular imagery, manifest in speeches, the press, and most especially in emigrant songs of the period. By explaining the phenomenon of emigration as enforced banishment, the result of continuing oppression and appalling neglect, England became the universally acknowledged scapegoat. This was politically convenient in harnesing support for the nationalist cause, and it also supplied an emotional need in coping with the sense of loss and defeat that emigration represented. More precisely, it diverted attention from the conflicting pressures within families and communities and in the hearts and minds of emigrants themselves. The idea of enforced exile absolved the emigrant from the charge of desertion in the pursuit of personal gain, and offered an external explanation of the personal agony that emigration commonly involved.

The ambivalence of commentators on the issue of whether emigration was beneficial or would prove ultimately damaging to Ireland continued into the post-famine period. In reporting the continual exodus from the country in alarmist language, newspapers unwittingly created the impression of doom and defeat:

> We regret to perceive that emigration still continues to thin the ranks of our already decimated population. . . . The neighbourhood and town of Loughrea, and the country from thence to Ballinasloe appears to have suffered most severely from this system of voluntary expatriation . . . two out of every three houses [are] closed up, and the inmates gone either to America, the workhouse, or the grave. What extermination has left undone in Connemara, emigration seems likely to accomplish. Day after day the people are slipping away, leaving behind them whole villages untenanted and desolate, so that ere long many portions of this vast and populous district threaten to become so many howling wildernesses.[72]

To then deplore emigration and make a plea to stay to build up the country could only sound helplessly unreal:

> Emigration is draining the country, and is at present one of our national curses . . . he is an enemy to Ireland who advocates or promotes further emigration of her children . . . We advise each Irishman to stay at home and do a man's work towards bettering his own condition and his country's.[73]

Others were resigned to what appeared to be the remorseless logic of the labour market. Ireland, as part of the Atlantic economy, was bound to be subject to the demand for cheap labour from the industrial powers of Britain and the United States. On this understanding, the rate of emigration in Ireland varied only with the level of demand for labour abroad. Writing from Skibbereen, Hugh Loudon reported to Thomas Hewat of the Provincial Bank of Ireland in 1865:

> Emigration. It still continues about 500 having left from this district; it doubtless would have been more but for the civil war in America. So long as labour is so cheap so long *should* emigration continue. What blood letting is to a full man emigration is to a country with a redundant population. The one is relieved by the operation and the other also is relieved. As well might we expect full vitality to continue say in three men doled out only two mens rations as expect anything but the most disastrous results in the present state of things by retaining at home the always increasing population.[74]

Attitudes of despair and a resignation to the working out of economic laws, along with press reporting of such responses, may be viewed as facilitators of Irish emigration.

Closely allied to the power of the printed word and essential for the communication of information about emigration, was the growth of literacy in Ireland. The establishment of the National Schools system in 1831, to promote and finance primary education had, by 1845, produced over 4,000 schools and almost half a million pupils. Illiteracy fell to 45 per cent by 1851 and was probably at a lower rate among the age group 15–40—the most prone to emigrate—and more evident in the less advanced western counties where emigration rates were low. A further bonus for would-be emigrants was the widespread growth of English speaking, fostered in the schools. In 1851, Gaelic speakers formed only about 5 per cent of the population and these were concentrated in the south and west where emigration rates were relatively low. If the purpose of the National Schools was to provide 'an antidote to economic improvidence, violence, and political disaffection' in Ireland, it had the effect of equipping a substantial section of the Irish people for leaving the country.[75]

In an altogether different way the physical passage of emigrants to Britain and overseas was facilitated by the development of transport in the Industrial Revolution. We have seen how the long trek for seasonal harvesters from the western counties to the north-east ports was reduced by the cheap service offered by the

Midland Great Western Railway in Ireland. Many thousands of reapers took advantage of low fares, to avoid a hundred-mile walk followed by the crossing to Scotland or England, before embarking on a further hundred-mile journey in search of work in the harvest fields.

From the 1820s, when steam passenger services began to operate on a regular basis across the Irish Sea, the competition for traffic between private companies and between rival ports brought the fares down for both cabin and steerage customers. By the mid-1830s, competition brought fares below economic levels to the benefit of all passengers. The *Antelope*, in 1833, was taking cabin passengers for a shilling and steerage passengers for sixpence between Belfast and Glasgow.[76] Without doubt, the very cheapness of fares both assisted and encouraged the flow of seasonal and permanent emigration to Britain.

Despite these benefits, the experience of Irish emigrants crossing by steamship from Belfast to Glasgow or from Dublin to Liverpool, has been described as uniformly wretched:

> By all accounts, though, the emigrants' first experience with the sea was particularly miserable. Baggage and livestock had first priority on the Liverpool steamers, and the poor Irish huddled without shelter on the open decks packed shoulder to shoulder, 'holding on to each other, and to anything else they could lay hold on to keep from being washed overboard: one ship's officer admitted crowding 1,400 emigrants on the deck of a single vessel and many passengers had to stand during the entire passage. Accidents were common, safety provisions such as lifeboats were absent or woefully inadequate and during heavy seas the passengers were drenched with cold seawater on decks awash with vomit and 'animal mire'. Seasickness was nearly universal . . . [and] many passengers arrived so ill and weakened they had to be carried ashore.[77]

Although acknowledging the satisfactory arrangements made for cabin passengers, H. S. Irvine writes in similar vein of the plight of deckers, mostly condemned to spend the voyage open to the elements. Only exceptionally in bad weather might they be allowed below deck amongst the cattle:

> Conditions on deck could be frightening. If the boat was at all crowded there was barely more than standing room; the

spray lashed over the deckers; the cold was sometimes so intense that they were frozen to the deck. In such circumstances it was impossible for most of them, during a voyage of ten to thirty hours, to reach water closets or drinking water. In bad weather of course many were seasick, which added to the horrors of the voyage. When cattle were being carried on deck the passengers often had to cluster round the pens, and the 'passengers and cattle were therefore indiscriminately mixed together; the sea and urine pouring on their clothes from the animals; and they stood in the midst of filth and mire.'[78]

Certainly such unpleasant conditions existed but they formed the common experience of emigrants only at the beginning and end of the harvest period, when the decks were crowded with harvesters on their seasonal migration. Bad weather brought the most severe discomfort and represented the greatest danger for steerage passengers. The worst weather was mostly confined to the winter months when there were fewer sailings and much less likelihood of overcrowding. With the onset of the Great Famine and a major increase in the level of emigration, more crossings took place outside the normal spring and summer months. On some voyages, lives were lost and naturally these were fully reported in the press:

> An inquest was held at White-chapel workhouse in London on the body of Mary Collins, aged 45, a poor Irish emigrant brought from the *Duke of Cambridge*, an Irish steam vessel, from Cork. The body of the deceased was in a most emaciated condition and covered with bruises and contusions, as if she had been severely ill-used . . . She was suffering under a strong fever, and, on being undressed, was found to be in a most deplorable condition. There were bruises upon her face and legs and also two large fresh wounds upon her thigh . . . The wounds upon the back of the deceased were very large, and she appeared to have been drawn across some rough surface . . . . Her clothes were ragged and some parts of her body exposed. She was also in great pain, and did not possess the power of standing or sitting . . . Two of the deceased's children were on board with her, and they were also in a state of nudity . . .

The surgeon 'found her lying upon that part of the vessel appropriated for the use of cattle. There was nothing under her, and all her clothing only consisted of a blanket, a ragged gown, and a chemise. She was quite pulseless, and perfectly speechless.' The captain said 'he had a very boisterous voyage and the emigrants had been exposed to the inclemency of the weather . . . He had brought over between 400 and 500, and was in the habit of bringing over a similar number every week. The charges for deck passengers are 2s 6d and 1s 3d. The voyage generally lasted three days, and occasionally during that time the provisions would become short . . . , 'Patrick Collins, the son of the deceased, said his mother was discharged from the workhouse in Skull. They walked to Cork, a distance of 50 miles, and embarked on board the *Duke of Cambridge*. His brother, who was in Greenwich, sent his mother 6s to pay the expenses of the voyage, and his mother was frequently drenched to the skin.' Mr Nash, workhouse surgeon, said 'the deceased died from typhus fever, which had no doubt been accelerated by the overcrowding of the vessel and exposure to the weather.'

The coroner said 'it was to be regretted that this system of emigration was allowed as it caused so many mendicants to be in this country.'[79]

The state in which pauper emigrants arrived in English ports during the famine years prompted hostile comments like those of the coroner in London. These were not confined to the emigrants alone but were directed to the conditions on board the ships. What established the bad reputation of steamship crossings between Ireland and Britain, however, was a truly exceptional incident involving major loss of life.

The tragic story of the *Londonderry*, a 277-ton vessel sailing from Sligo to Liverpool in December 1848 and carrying 177 passengers all due to re-embark for America, was to become a classic in the annals of coastal shipping. On the voyage a storm blew up off the north-west coast of Ireland, the passengers were put below decks and the hatch was secured with ropes. Within a confined space of only 307 square feet, 174 people struggled for lack of air and water. In the storm, the lights went out, the atmosphere became stifling and people suffocated and collapsed, their bodies being trampled on by those left standing in the cramped conditions. Eventually, one man was able to force off the hatch and persuade the crew that people were dying below deck. By the time assistance arrived, 72 passengers had died.

Dr Miller's evidence at the subsequent inquiry likened the incident to that of the notorious Black Hole of Calcutta where only a third of 140 prisoners had died in a relatively larger space. J. E. Handley enthusiastically took up this theme in his treatment of the story in his pioneering study of the Irish in Scotland: 'Into an evil-smelling hold, twenty-three feet long, eighteen feet wide and six and a half feet high, the captain and his crew drove the hundred and seventy-four steerage passengers. Then, like the Bengal nabob's guards, deaf to the entreaties of the prisoners for air and water, they battened down the hatches. In the morning, when the ship reached Derry, seventy-two corpses were taken out and laid on the quay.'[80]

The emotive comparison with the Black Hole of Calcutta and the sympathetic concern of Dr Miller for the emigrant passengers, was countered in subsequent letters to the press by attacks on Irish emigrants as a breed which assumed that all were equally poor and wretched. One of these, quoted by Handley, exemplifies how a tragedy can be interpreted to fit predisposed prejudice, in which everything is explained in terms of the moral degeneracy of the Irish:

> The true cause of the low fares paid, and the miserable accommodation accepted, by the Irish emigrating to this country, is their extreme poverty. They know no better. Those who wish to improve the condition of the Irish must raise the quality of many things as well as the steerage accommodation from Sligo to Liverpool. If men are not to be permitted to endanger their own lives and the lives of their families, by crowding the deck of a steamer, ought they to be allowed to destroy themselves in many ways which are unnoticed because they are so common? Lazy, filthy habits, miserable mud huts, and whisky kill more yearly than have been lost in all the steam-boats that ever were built. If some restraint be not imposed on the Irish immigration into this country, we will soon be reduced to the condition of the miserable beings who fly to our shores.[81]

Just as the emigrant was typically seen as a poor famine victim whose presence in England might lower the condition of the decent English working class, ignoring the diversity of condition among those who left Ireland, so the fate of the *Londonderry* was taken as representative of steamers crossing the Irish Sea. Yet the circumstances of the journey were quite exceptional. The voyage took place in the depths of winter from the only western port with passage to British ports, with sailings only once a week compared with the daily crossings from Drogheda or Dublin. Also the enquiry established that the *Londonderry* was a relatively well equipped vessel, capable of carrying up to fifteen hundred passengers on peak summer crossings. The attendant publicity surrounding the disaster of December 1848 should not obscure the very real benefits bestowed on the great majority of passengers by the development of steamship transport across the Irish Sea. Steamships enabled businessmen, emigrants and seasonal workers to make the journey quickly and cheaply, providing a choice of ports and frequent sailings. If conditions for deck passengers could be very unpleasant, especially in overcrowded boats during the summer months, conditions were usually satisfactory for cabin passengers. The *Superb*, built in 1826 for the Cork-Bristol route, was designed solely for carrying 78 cabin passengers. The cabins had sofas, lockers, a bookcase, and a water closet attached.[82] Most emigrants, however, took the shorter cross-channel passages from Irish ports to Glasgow, Liverpool or Bristol, which usually lasted between 14 and 30 hours and might cost 10d or less. These crossings, albeit uncomfortable or worse, were infinitely preferable to the long and hazardous voyage across the Atlantic that most emigrants rightly dreaded. Nevertheless, even allowing for the infamous 'coffin ships', loss of life was less spectacular than legend has it. The dramatic examples are taken, not as the exception, but the norm.[83]

The desire of groups of harvesters and emigrants to travel together, and the mysterious preference for one ship as against another, often exacerbated the extent of overcrowding, leaving some vessels overloaded and others with only a few passengers. Tickets were not confined to a single sailing, only to the same steamship company, and the authorities had no way of preventing the chaotic late rush on board that was a common practice. This lack of regulation suited the shipping companies, who resisted any effective interference by Parliament and the passengers, some of whom almost certainly evaded payment for their passage, in the rush to board ship. The sense of togetherness among the deckers could make for a convivial crossing, although this too was not without its dangers. Patrick MacGill describes his own experience as a seasonal harvester from Donegal taking the Derry boat to Greenock at the end of the century:

The Foyle was a sheet of wavy molten gold which the boat cut through as she sped out from the pier. The upper deck was crowded with people going to Scotland to work for the summer and autumn. They were all very ragged, both women and men; most of the men were drunk, and they discussed, quarrelled, argued, and swore until the din was deafening.

Little heed was taken by them of the beauty of the evening, and all alone I watched the vessel turn up a furrow of gold at the bow until my brain was reeling with the motion of the water that sobbed past the sides of the steamer . . .

Many of the passengers were singing songs of harvest-men, lovers, cattle-drovers, and sailors. One man, a hairy villainous-looking fellow, stood swaying unsteadily on the deck with a bottle of whiskey in one hand, and roaring out 'Judy Brannigan':

'Oh! Judy Brannigan, ye are me darlin',
Ye are me lookin' glass from night till mornin'.
I'd rather have ye without wan farden
Than Shusan Gallagheer with house and garden.'

Others joined in mixing up half a dozen songs in one musical outpouring, and the result was laughable in the extreme . . .

There were many on board who were full of drink and fight, men who were ready for quarrels and all sorts of mischief. One of these, a man called O'Donnel, paraded up and down the deck with an open clasp-knife in his hand, speaking of himself in the third person, and inviting everybody on board to fistic encounter.

'This is young O'Donnel from the County Donegal,' he shouted, alluding to himself, and lifting his knife which shone red with the blood hues of the sinking sun. 'And young O'Donnel doesn't care a damn for a man on this bloody boat! I can fight like a two-year old bullock. A blow of me fist is like a kick from a young colt. . . . I'm a Rosses man, and I don't care a damn for a man on this boat!'

He looked terrible as he shouted out his threats. One eyebrow was cut open and the flesh hung down even as far as his cheekbone. I could not take my eyes away from him, and he suddenly noticed me watching his antics. Then he slouched forward and hit me on the face, knocking me down.

This was the beginning of a wild night's fighting.

> All over the deck and down in the steerage the harvestmen and labourers fought one with another for hours on end. Over the bodies of the women who were asleep in every corner, over coils of ropes, trunks and boxes of clothes, the drunken men struggled like demons. God knows what they had to quarrel about! When I could not see them I could hear them falling heavily as cattle fall amid a jumble of twisted hurdles, until the drink and exertion overpowered them at last. One by one they fell asleep, just where they had dropped or on the spot where they were knocked down.[84]

MacGill, for all his poetic qualities and burning sense of injustice, was worldly enough to know the value of providing the public with vicarious violence and of reinforcing the stereotype of the drunken, fighting Irishman.

In addition to hazards from drunken brawls on the boats, emigrants to Britain making their first trip, unlike the seasoned harvesters who knew the ropes, might encounter all sorts of tricks from the 'sharpers' in the ports. A mostly rural population made an easy prey for the frauds imposed on them by ticket agents, lodging-housekeepers, porters and a motley crew of huck-sters and hawkers who infested the dockside districts. Commonly emigrants stayed a week to ten days in port before making the crossing to Liverpool. They stayed in low taverns and typhus-ridden lodging-houses where overcharging was universal and robbery commonplace. If emigrants avoided the worst impositions from their own countrymen in Cork or Dublin, they were liable to be parted from their savings by the emigrant trappers in Liverpool, who lay in wait for innocent new arrivals.

EMIGRANT TRAPPERS IN LIVERPOOL

> At the police office yesterday, a pair of miserable-looking creatures were brought up before Mr. Nicol on a charge of defrauding a poor Irish girl of a sum of £10. They were Rosanna and Andrew Dunn apparently husband and wife [who] . . . appeared to belong to the lowest grade of society . . . The girl, who appeared to be about 18 years of

age, came over from Dublin by the steamer on Tuesday last. She states that she has no father or mother alive; and that, as both her brothers were in America and she longed exceedingly to be with them, she broke into the cash box of an uncle who resides in Dublin, abstracted £10 therefrom, and took a passage in a steamer to Liverpool. [The couple were] accosted on the quay by the male prisoner who asked various questions and discovering she was an emigrant said he would take her to 'daycent' lodgings. Later the same day, he asked her to give him the money she had, as he'd look after it. She refused but the next day all three went to a shop but the male prisoner, on pretext of getting some change, went off with her money.[85]

Liverpool magistrates believed that many of those who lived in the city's slums were indeed emigrants bound for America, but cheated out of their passage money and savings by the local 'sharpers'.

This chapter began with the simple notion of the Great Famine and the consequent emigration of thousands of poor Irish to America. What has followed has been a survey of the work of a generation of scholars which has altered our understanding of the context of emigration in the nineteenth century. The Famine itself exercised a far from uniform influence throughout Ireland as variations in mortality rates and levels of emigration indicate. This was primarily because nineteenth-century Ireland was a markedly diverse country in population structure and in economic activity. Even a broad division between the more advanced east and the relatively backward west of Ireland fails to recognise the coexistence of a commercial economy and a subsistence economy throughout Ireland.

Diversity also characterises the range of interpretations of the Great Famine. Two schools of thought have been outlined; one the nationalist view, pioneered by John Mitchel, that successfully pinned the blame for starvation and emigration on the British government, and was summed up in a biting letter to Lord Clarendon, printed in the *United Irishman*:

But the case is this: I assert and maintain that in the island of Ireland there is no government or law—that what passes for 'government' is a foul and fraudulent usurpation, based on corruption and falsehood, supported by force, and battening on blood. I hold that the meaning and sole object of that Government is to make sure of a constant supply of Irish food for British tables, Irish wool for British backs, Irish blood and bone for British armies; to make sure, in one word, of Ireland for the English, and to keep down, scourge and dragoon the Irish into submission and patient starvation.[86]

The other, a revisionist view, draws attention to conflicts within Ireland and to social forces promoting emigration. Both schools of thought provide insights into why Irish men and women looked to emigration as a solution to their problems and, indeed, how they interpreted that experience in retrospect. Specific agents of change—'strong farmers', the Catholic Church, and the nationalist movement—went hand in hand with social and economic change in promoting emigration. Contributing to the mood of despair and defeat surrounding emigration, press reporting, although ambivalent in tone, may be seen as facilitating the loss of population out of the country. The rapid growth of literacy in Ireland, improved in great measure through the insistence on the learning of the English language in the National schools, increased the importance of the printed word and the availability of information about emigration. Certainly, the development of transport, especially of steamship navigation across the Irish Sea, but also including the growth of railways in Ireland, Scotland and England, greatly assisted the physical passage of Irish emigrants to Britain.

In the next chapter, the theme of diversity is continued in a discussion of the migration and settlement of the Irish in the cities of mainland Britain. Irish communities commonly became known as 'Little Irelands'.

2

Little Irelands

*Ireland has revenged herself upon England, socially—by
bestowing an Irish quarter on every English industrial
maritime or commercial town of any size . . .*
(Karl Marx, 1855)

Irish settlers were caught up in the fears and anxieties surrounding the urban crisis that dominated early Victorian Britain.
It was a tragic coincidence that an awareness of acute urban
problems in the 1830s and 1840s occurred at the same time as the
rising tide of Irish immigration into the cities of mainland Britain.
The Irish became a target for denunciation by reformers and
officials alike. As numerous investigations and commissions of
enquiry revealed the alarming scale of urban squalor, crime,
drunkenness and epidemic disease, an explanation was found in
the presence of an alien people. The horrific details uncovered
were in truth part of an old problem. Slums had existed long
before in London and elsewhere but the problems were now
perceived to be of epic proportions.[1] The burgeoning cities lacked
the administrative and legislative capacities to deal with the crisis
and, even if they had been in place, there was no recognition in
contemporary understanding of the economic forces that created
a slum district. What was seen as a social evil was interpreted as
the product of moral degeneracy.

The wretched inhabitants of early Victorian slums were
regarded as outcasts from respectable society and, as many such
districts were labelled 'Irish colonies' or 'little Irelands', the association between Irish immigrants and slum conditions became
established in a crisis atmosphere. More significantly, what was
to prove a temporary condition and one that affected only part of
the Irish community was to carry a stigma that took on a long-
lasting and universal application. The image of the Irish in the

ghetto exerted a powerful influence, fuelling both English prejudice and an Irish sense of injustice. That influence remains a dominant force in shaping modern attitudes on both sides of the Irish Sea. The theme recurs in some recent work on Irish settlement in Victorian cities, depicting an outcast mass of poor migrants, huddled together in squalid ghettos and subject to the hostility and prejudice of the host community in terms of race, religion, politics and employment.[2] Moreover, discussion of anti-Irish racism, depicting the Celt as a sub-human, ape-like creature, allied to Irish appraisals of their own national character, accepting the much advertised features of stupidity, drunkenness and violence, tended to confirm the well-established 'Paddy' stereotype.[3] Taken altogether, this reinforces the contemporary view that Irish fecklessness, allied to the fatalism induced by Roman Catholicism, created a poverty-stricken people destined to fester in the slums of Victorian cities.

Almost certainly this is not the intention of liberal scholars, no doubt moved by the modern problems of racism, religious bigotry and the oppression of ethnic minorities throughout the world. Yet attention focused on the most appalling squalor, the most dramatic incidents and the most extreme examples of hostility and prejudice exhibited against the Irish in the nineteenth century, unwittingly have the effect of not only distorting the scale of the problem but also of lending substance to anti-Irish prejudice.

In order to deepen our understanding of a complex process it is important to review the nature of Irish migration and settlement in the critical middle decades of the nineteenth century. Irish migration developed progressively in the first half of the century, reaching a climax in the famine period 1845–1852. In 1841 the number of Irish-born residents in Britain was over 400,000 and within a decade had risen to over 700,000. By 1861 the Irish-born had reached a peak of 806,000. Thereafter there was a gradual decline to a figure of 632,000 in 1901. Irish settlers formed a higher proportion of the population in Scotland (6.7 per cent in 1861) than in England and Wales (3.0 per cent in 1861).[4]

There were three main emigrant routes—1) the northern route from Ulster and North Connaught to Scotland; 2) the midland route from Connaught and Leinster to the north of England and the midlands; and 3) the southern route, from South Leinster and Munster, often via South Wales or Bristol, to London.[5] Most Irish immigrants came from rural Ireland but they were by no means only the poor and destitute who settled in Britain. The famine Irish made destitute by the destruction of the potato crop in the west mostly took the passage to North America. The Irish in Britain tended to come from the more advanced parts of Ireland, especially from the industrialised north-east. As Fitzgerald succinctly puts it: 'Irish society was not homogeneous, and neither was its emigration.' [6]

The great majority of the Irish who came to mainland Britain entered on a short-stay basis as a first step towards emigration to the United States, Canada or to Australia.[7] Others continued the old pattern of entering and leaving on a seasonal basis, working as harvesters in agriculture or recruited on short-term contracts as navvies or as factory operatives.[8] Significantly, there was no uniform pattern of permanent settlement. The three main areas of concentration were the west of Scotland, the north western counties of England, and London. In addition, there was a wide dispersal and high mobility among the Irish throughout Britain. In both 1851 and 1861 at least 31 towns in England and Wales had a recorded Irish-born population of over 1,000. Some of the towns listed are not normally associated with an Irish presence— Bath, Colchester, Derby, Newport (Salop), Plymouth, Portsmouth, Southampton.[9] Although the Irish were very largely drawn by employment prospects to settle in the larger industrial centres, there were differences in the experience of cities with an Irish presence. The character of Irish migrants attracted to particular towns and at particular periods varied in terms of their county of origin, social class and religious faith. Further variations occurred in the rate of influx and in the density of settlement in Irish 'colonies' or 'ghettos'. In turn, the response of the host community varied in relation not only to the scale of in-migration but to local conditions of employment and was shaped by the context of local religious and political allegiances.

In responding to contemporary fears about Irish immigration it is salutary to review the scale of Irish settlement in the context of the overall pattern of migration and population increase in Britain in the middle decades of the nineteenth century. E. H. Hunt has observed that Irish immigration appeared more overwhelming than it was in reality. Even in the famine decade of the 1840s, immigration accounted for less than a third of the population increase. Before the 1840s and throughout most of the 1850s and 1860s the number of immigrants was roughly balanced by

Britons who went abroad. Subsequently, the scale of emigration from Britain, in which the Irish were prominent, exceeded the level of immigration.[10] At the time, Irish immigration was perceived in simple, alarmist terms, not at all a reflection of the actual scale and complexity of the process.

The rapid growth in population of the great cities of England and Scotland was only exceptionally the result of a major influx of Irish settlers.[11] London had the largest Irish-born population in 1841, some 74,000 or 3.9 per cent of its inhabitants. By 1851, the Irish-born had risen to 108,548 or 4.6 per cent of the total. During the same decade, the population of London increased by 414,000, out of which the Irish formed only 8.3 per cent, and by 1861 the Irish-born had declined slightly to 106,879 or a mere 3.8 per cent of London's population. Far more important numerically, in the additional population coming into the metropolis, were migrants from the rest of the United Kingdom.

The pattern in London was repeated in Liverpool, Glasgow and Manchester, the cities with the highest proportion of Irish-born population in mainland Britain in 1841. The proportion of Irish-born in the increased population of Liverpool between 1841 and 1851 was 38.2 per cent, but less than 1 per cent in the 1850s, and it dwindled to a minus figure during the 1860s, when the numbers of Liverpool Irish declined by more than 7,000. In Manchester, a third of the 68,000 additional population between 1841 and 1851 were Irish-born, while during the 1850s, as the population rose by 36,000, the number of Irish-born people fell by 428. Glasgow, which in 1841 had the second highest proportion of Irish-born inhabitants (16.2 per cent) in mainland Britain, experienced a more modest Irish immigration in the 1840s. The number of Irish-born increased by 15,456, representing just over a fifth (22.1 per cent) of the increased population of Glasgow of 70,000 between 1841 and 1851. In the 1850s and 1860s, Irish-born newcomers formed only 3 per cent and 6 per cent of Glasgow's additional population.

What these figures reveal is that Irish immigration, even in the peak years of the famine period, was responsible for only a minority of increased urban population. Most of the increase was generated by internal migration to the cities from the surrounding rural areas.

This can be demonstrated by reference to the detailed analysis of census enumerators' books by Alan Armstrong in York and by

Michael Anderson in Preston—two medium-sized towns in the north of England[12]. Armstrong has shown that the population of York increased from 28,842 to 36,303 between 1841 and 1851 and, although the Irish-born population rose significantly from 429 to 1,928, it is clear that four-fifths of York's increased population came from Yorkshire (57.7 per cent), the rest of England and Wales (19.7 per cent) and Scotland (3.1 per cent). The dramatic increase in the Irish population of York to 5.3 per cent of its population in 1851, ahead of many other northern towns, still represented only a fifth (20.1 per cent) of the city's increased population in the 1840s. In 1851, the population of Preston, like that of other Lancashire cotton towns, had grown rapidly, having doubled in the previous twenty years. Most of the increased population came from people born outside the town. Between 1841 and 1851 the Irish-born population of Preston increased from 1, 703 to 5,122, representing an increased proportion (rising from 3.4 per cent to 7.4 per cent) of the town's population. The Irish presence continued to expand in the 1850s with 6, 974 Irish-born recorded in 1861, 8.4 per cent of Preston's population. Yet the predominant pattern of in-migration in Preston, as in other towns, was one drawn overwhelmingly from the surrounding area. Over 40 per cent of Preston's inhabitants in 1851 were migrants from a 10 mile radius and only about 30 per cent were drawn from more than 30 miles from their birthplace. The Irish-born proportions of intercensus increases in the population of Preston between 1841, 1851 and 1861 were 18.4 per cent and 13.8 per cent respectively. Thereafter, the Irish-born population experienced a marked reduction. In short, the figures do not support the sense of being swamped by a flood of Irish immigration, conveyed by contemporary writers and reiterated by some modern historians. Far more numerous were the migrants attracted to the towns from their rural hinterlands. As already noted, Irish immigration had its most intense period in the 1840s, then slowed down or went into reverse in the later decades. The flood was more like a tidal ebb and flow, heavier in some places than others, but everywhere being submerged in a broader inrush of migration from the countryside to the towns.

More influential in alarming the host community than the scale of immigration were the apparent levels of concentration of Irish settlement. Frequent references have been made to the Irish living in the worst slum districts of British cities and the terms 'colony' and 'ghetto' have been commonly associated, by contemporary commentators and by modern historians, with an Irish presence.[13]

The most important example in establishing the notorious association between the Irish and the ghetto is identified in Little Ireland, Manchester. As Werly has pointed out, its very smallness 'made it the target of detailed sociological study during the thirties and forties'.[14] While New Town was inhabited by over 20,000 Irish, Little Ireland's population was only 2,000. Nevertheless, Werly takes the descriptions of Little Ireland as evidence of Irish concentration in ghettos, with the supporting testimony of selected witnesses before the commission of inquiry into the state of the Irish poor:

> The physical ghetto consisted both of external and internal features. Black smoke, polluted rivers, unpaved streets, the smell of pig sties, privies, and open sewers, coupled with the filthy, cramped dwellings with their barren, damp interiors, all created a miserable existence for the Irish of New Town and Little Ireland.[15]

Among witnesses in Manchester, Werly cites the evidence of a local pawnbroker, James Butterworth who claimed, 'there are very few Irish with whom the English mix; it is like oil and water'.[16] Interestingly O'Tuathaigh refers to Little Ireland by name, along with the unnamed slums of other cities, as a byword for industrial slum living. 'These were the conditions which appalled Engels, terrified Carlyle and absorbed the attention of a generation of social investigators and commentators from the 1830s to the 1860s.'[17] He argues that the Irish presence in the urban slum continued through to the end of the nineteenth century and beyond. 'Booth's description of the rat-infested Irish ghetto of dockside London at the close of the nineteenth century is as chilling as anything penned in the worst years of the famine influx.'[18]

So we have an image of the Irish in the ghetto that has lasted a century and a half and has been accepted uncritically as a permanent and universal feature of Irish life in the great Victorian cities. In the circumstances, it is worth reminding ourselves of the immediate context in which Little Ireland was discovered and made infamous to a credulous world. Little Ireland was originally given prominence by J. P. Kay in a pamphlet written at the time of the 1832 cholera epidemic. In the foreword to a modern reprint, E. L. Burney explains that the pamphlet was written with a frenzied sense of urgency due to the belief that cholera was liable to become endemic among the urban population.[19] Dr Kay, himself, was secretary to the Special Board for the Board of Health and knew the district well. Moreover, he was well placed to communicate his views in giving extensive evidence before the commission on the state of the Irish poor and before the Poor Law commission in 1838. The pamphlet is interesting, not merely for the horrific descriptions of the living conditions in the poor districts of Manchester but in reflecting the intellectual climate of the day.[20] Kay was undoubtedly a key influence in identifying the Irish presence with the evil effects of squalid living conditions. More significantly, Kay's writing became a source book for many subsequent books on the subject, including Engels' classic work on the condition of the working class in England (where the debt to Kay is freely acknowledged), and also influenced the literary fascination with Manchester indulged in by Benjamin Disraeli, Mrs Gaskell and Frances Trollope. [21]

Kay's tone was highly charged and his association of urban squalor with a lower form of life appealed to contemporary fears surrounding the 'condition of England question'. The belief in the existence of an abyss, a moral cesspit, below the level of respectable society, with the threat of a savage mass rising up to destroy the institutions of civilised society—church, monarchy, parliament and property—was the dominant fear in early Victorian Britain. Little Ireland, physically located below the river level, subject to frequent flooding and blackened by a pall of industrial smoke, provided a perfect symbol to represent this fear. The very language employed by sanitary reformers like Kay moved indistinguishably between physical descriptions of insanitary conditions and a moral condemnation of the slumdwellers living in squalor. What begins with the 'contagion' of disease leads inexorably to the 'contagion' of Irish immigration. As Kay puts it:

> In some districts of the town exist evils so remarkable as to require more minute description. A portion of low, swampy ground, liable to be frequently inundated, and to constant exhalation, is included between a high bank over which the Oxford Road passes and a bend of the river Medlock, where its course is impeded by a weir. This unhealthy spot lies so

low that the chimneys of its houses, some of them three storeys high, are little above the level of the road. About two hundred of these habitations are crowded together in an extremely narrow space, and they are chiefly inhabited by the lowest Irish. Many of these houses have also cellars, whose floor is scarcely elevated above the level of the water flowing in the Medlock. The soughs are destroyed, or out of repair: and these narrow abodes are in consequence always damp, and are frequently flooded to the depth of several inches, because the surface water can find no exit. The district has sometimes been the haunt of hordes of thieves and desperadoes who defied the law, and is always inhabited by a class resembling savages in their appetites and habits. It is surrounded on every side by some of the largest factories of the town, whose chimneys vomit forth dense clouds of smoke, which hang heavily over this insalubrious region.[22]

Despite the suspicion that the district had a bad reputation before the presence of Irish settlers, the Irish as a race served as a convenient explanation for urban squalor and depravity:

Ireland has poured forth the most destitute of her hordes to supply the constantly increased demand for labour. This immigration has been, in one important respect, a serious evil. The Irish have taught the labouring classes of this country a pernicious lesson . . . Debased alike by ignorance and pauperism they have discovered, with the savage, what is the minimum of the means of life, upon which existence may be prolonged . . . As competition and the restriction and burdens of trade diminished the profits of capital, and consequently reduced the price of labour, the contagious example of ignorance and a barbarous disregard of forethought and economy exhibited by the Irish, spread.[23]

Of its kind this represents a fair parade of ill-considered prejudice. Within a few years many of Kay's assumptions were discredited by more sober analysis. Not least the fear of contamination, both in terms of 'Irish fever' and from a culturally inferior race, was shown to be untenable. A devastating refutation of popular prejudice was made by Dr Lyon Playfair in his report on the sanitary condition of large towns in Lancashire in 1845. He began:

In Liverpool I found that an impression prevailed, not only with its authorities, but also with the public generally, that the excessive mortality of that town was attributable to the migratory character of a large portion of its population, and not upon the structural arrangements or physical causes of disease in the town itself . . . In other towns in Lancashire similar opinions prevail as to the effect of a migrant population.[24]

Not to put too fine a point on it, the assumption made was that the Irish brought fever with them from their native land which had the effect of inflating the death rates recorded in Liverpool and Manchester to be, unenviably, the highest in the country. After undertaking his own investigations, which included a statistical analysis of age specific mortality, Playfair concluded:

The migratory population of Liverpool is a much more healthy class than the residents of that town. That the migratory population consists generally of adults. That the deaths occurring among such a population must give an appearance of longevity to Liverpool, to which it is not entitled. That the proportion of the population to deaths is elevated by migrants, and that Liverpool is thus rendered apparently more healthy than it really is.[25]

Popular prejudice was shown to be fallacious but the damage was done by the legitimacy already conferred by Kay's influential pamphlet. Also, those responsible for the appalling sanitary conditions of Liverpool and Manchester, who included employers with property interests and local officials responsive to their political influence, found it easier to blame the Irish than to face the problems of their own making.

Of course what lent credence to the association of the Irish and slum conditions was the undoubted reality that *some* Irish migrants did live in *some* of the most squalid conditions in cities like Liverpool and Manchester, both before the famine migration and for many years afterwards. From that association, the image of the 'ghetto Irish' emerged and with it the package of fears among the host community. Specifically Irish habits—the diet of potatoes, sleeping on straw and allowing the children barefoot in the streets—were identified and deplored as potentially contaminating influences.[26] Fears of the Irish lowering wages generally, and therefore bringing living standards down among the resident labour force, were commonly expressed. The legendary Irish habit of illicit distillation of spirits and heavy drinking was a further source of anxiety. Drinking was itself commonly associated with public disorder and what, it was maintained, was unwisely spent on drink left insufficient for the barest essentials of domestic comfort and decency.

Prejudice, once launched on a tide of righteous indignation, comfortably ignores its own contradictions. If the Irish were accused of living apart in the worst slum conditions, it was difficult to see how they were able to exercise such a malign influence on the decent English and Scots who were regarded as living outside the Irish 'ghettos'. Similarly, the accusation that the Irish would only work a few days in the week, sufficient to provide for their low standards, is difficult to reconcile with the praise from employers about their industry and adaptability.[27] English contempt for the potato diet of the Irish would not command the universal support of modern nutritionists, a judgment which may confirm Playfair's conclusion that Irish migrants as a body were healthier than the resident population of Liverpool and Manchester.

An explanation of the conflicting observations and opinions to be found among witnesses before the inquiry into the state of the Irish poor lies in the partial nature of individual responses. All referred glibly to the Irish as a homogeneous group although specific reference is made to labourers, skilled craftsmen and respectable tradesmen. Further distinctions included parents born in Ireland retaining Irish customs and the children assimilating with the practices among the host community. Not all the Irish were ravaged by drink. The twin benefits of temperance and education had rescued some Irish men and women just as they had affected the working class as a whole.

This variety of condition among Irish migrants is echoed in an analysis of the population of St Bartholomew's, reputedly the worst area of Liverpool in 1841.[28] Just over half the population were recorded as Irish, a condition that qualifies St Bartholomew's for the hallowed phrase as a district 'chiefly inhabited by the Irish'. Within an area covering twelve streets of varying length and population, only five streets actually had a majority of Irish and these varied significantly in number and in levels of overcrowding. Two streets, Midghall-Lane (containing eight houses and seven cellars) and Stockdale (containing eighty-six houses and twenty-five cellars), had populations that were 90 per cent Irish. Three streets, Banastre, Oriel and Cherry-Lane, had Irish populations of 60 per cent, 72 per cent and 59 per cent respectively. Average household size was highest in Midghall-Lane at 16.4 persons per household where seven out of eight houses were inhabited by the Irish but the numbers involved were very small. Stockdale was next highest with a comparable figure of 11.7 persons per household extending over eighty-six houses. These undoubtedly represented the worst conditions in the district and they were naturally associated with an Irish presence. What is equally significant is that the Irish who inhabited these two streets represented only about a fifth (21.8 per cent) of the Irish in St Bartholomew's. Almost four-fifths of the Irish lived alongside the English, Scots and Welsh and in comparable and unexceptionable conditions in terms of household size in the rest of the district.[29]

A further consideration following the concentration of the Irish in particular districts and streets was that it made the Irish presence appear more pronounced than it was numerically. In the case of the notorious Avon Street in Bath,[30] where in 1851 1,284 people lived in eighty-four houses and the average household size was 15.3 persons, the 230 Irish-born inhabitants, although less than a fifth of the census population, lived in close proximity in the street. Of the fifteen Irish household heads, seven were adjoining each other and most of the households were situated at one end of the street known locally as the Catholic end. In one common lodging-house thirty-eight out of the fifty-eight inhabitants were Irish-born.[31] This practice of huddling together can be explained in terms of native loyalties and the bonds of kinship but was also characteristic of recent migration and settlement. Irish lodging-house keepers often specialised in helping new migrants become established.

Essentially two patterns are discernible. One is the concentration of Irish in particular streets and courts in some of the worst parts of Victorian cities, living a life apart. The other, rather more predominant but rather less highlighted, is of the Irish living alongside the English, sometimes in a majority, sometimes in a minority, yet in conditions similar to their neighbours and offering opportunities for assimilation. Added to these two patterns and subjecting them to qualification over time is the transitory nature of Irish migration and settlement. It seems probable that the most dramatic examples of the Irish living in urban squalor, symbolised by Little Ireland in Manchester, were unrepresentative of Irish settlement in Britain.

Yet it is clear from the more detailed studies of specific Irish communities that the validity of such terms is suspect. Lynn Lees, in her study of mid-Victorian London, argues that poor Irish migrants were not ostracised or locked into urban ghettos but were mostly relegated to the side streets and back alleys of their neighbourhoods.[32] They lived close to the English and European immigrants but retained a separate physical and cultural identity. Interestingly, Lees found that the Irish were present in every census district of London.[33] Although commonly identified with notorious streets and with some of the vilest slums of London, many Irish lived in ordinary working-class districts, and a few middle-class professionals or lower middle-class clerks and teachers lived in predominantly English areas. Very high concentrations of Irish settlers, forming over 50 per cent of the population of a district, were comparatively rare and where they occurred it was in the back alleys and courts, tucked away behind the commercial streets. These were just the areas of squalid housing that attracted the attention of sanitary reformers. Understandably, the Irish who lived quietly in equal numbers and in lower concentrations in predominantly mixed centres of population went unnoticed. In addition to this varied pattern of settlement, the London Irish were a highly mobile population, moving from the riverside districts to the south and also returning to the traditional Irish quarters of central London, wherever there was a demand for unskilled labour.[34] It is clear that social class and employment opportunities were more decisive factors than mere ethnicity in determining the pattern of Irish settlement in London.

Some of the assumptions commonly made about the Irish presence in Victorian cities require qualification. It is misleading to view the migrant Irish as a homogeneous ethnic group. The 'Irish' label ignores not only the class differences already noted but also the importance of religious allegiance and the near-tribal loyalty of Irish men and women to their county of origin. In the process of 'modernisation' of Ireland since the late eighteenth century, there was a marked disparity in economic development between Ulster and Leinster, on the one hand, and the relative backwardness of Connaught, on the other. The incidence of the

Great Famine was also by no means uniform in its devastation. Paradoxically, the readiness to migrate in the famine period was created by economic progress among farmers, shopkeepers and artisans as well as by starvation and poverty among cottiers and landless labourers.[35]

The work of Lynn Lees on the London Irish is echoed by John Papworth on the Irish in Liverpool. Papworth has identified a concentration of Irish-born immigrants into seven wards in 1841, located principally in the north and west of the city of Liverpool. After 1851, a shift in population occurred in the outlying districts of St Anne's and Scotland wards. Two patterns are discernible among the Liverpool Irish. There existed both a concentration and a dispersal of Irish settlers. This conclusion is similar to the one reached by Lees about Irish settlement in mid-Victorian London. Significantly, Papworth calculates that only 50 per cent of the Irish-born lived in enumeration districts with a high concentration of Irish population. These areas were situated in the docks, to the north and south of the town centre with a major cluster stretching from the centre outwards, through Exchange, Vauxhall and Scotland wards. Although these were recognised as 'Irish' districts, they rarely contained more than 50 per cent Irish population. Only exceptionally did the Irish presence exceed half the population, in a few streets. Also, as in the St Bartholomew's district, accompanying the Irish concentration in certain districts was a dispersal of the Irish population to areas of medium and low concentrations, like St Anne's and the two Toxteth wards. Papworth concludes that the terms 'ghetto' and 'colony' were not applicable to the Irish in Liverpool. While the 'Irish' districts represented homogeneous social areas, characterised by large numbers of unskilled workers living in poor housing near their place of work and supported by social centres such as Irish pubs and the churches, the Irish, although they lived in areas with some of the characteristics of a ghetto, could not be legitimately described as living in 'Irish' ghettos.[36] Here, as Papworth observes, the question of scale is crucial. At the street level, the perception of the Irish presence may have been alarming to the host community. At the level of the parish, township or county, in the way official figures were represented in recording only the Irish-born, there appeared to be less reason for concern.

Differences within the Irish community need also to be recognised. There was no single Irish identity among the Irish population. Within Irish communities, Connaught men and the Orange men from Ulster were despised by their fellow countrymen.[37] The Irish loyalty to family name, county of origin and to their religious faith remained a frequent source of conflict between Irishmen in Britain, and although it was common to equate Irish and Catholic together, the Catholic Church (while a great strength and support for many) catered for only a minority of settlers.[38] Furthermore, Irish communities were subject to high mobility, often over short distances but nevertheless involving a high turnover of different families.[39] Determined not to fester in Irish ghettos, alienated from the host community, it was the common experience of many poor Irish families to move frequently and to adapt speedily to changes in the labour market. Constant movement and the changing composition of the Irish presence invalidate the permanent label attached to 'Irish' districts.

In contrast to patterns of settlement, reconstructed with hindsight, the framework of contemporary responses to the influx of Irish migrants was shaped by fears that were powerful and immediate. A common theme in comments at the time was the belief that the Irish would lower standards among the decent English working class. It was shared by such different spokesmen as the socialist Friedrich Engels and the Tory Lord Ashley:

> For when, in almost every great city, a fifth or a quarter of the workers are Irish or children of Irish parents who have grown up among Irish filth, no one can wonder if the life, habits, intelligence, moral status—in short, the whole character of the working class assimilates a great part of the Irish characteristics.[40]

With equal certainty could the future Lord Shaftesbury, the great philanthropist and champion of the oppressed, proclaim:

> Was it not found that where the Irish appeared wages were lowered, respectability disappeared, and slovenliness and filth prevailed?[41]

Part of the fear of the host community lay with the advent of major cholera and typhoid epidemics in the 1830s and 1840s which provoked a fervent hostility to Irish migrants as disseminators of killer diseases. Hard-pressed officials were tempted to use the Irish as a scapegoat in the face of epidemics that were beyond their effective control. J. V. Hickey has shown that the medical officer of the Cardiff Union identified the main cause of the increase in disease as the 'immense invasion of Irish destitute labourers, navigators and others, who had been brought over to this town by public works', and the majority of cases of fever 'may be said to have been imported direct from Skibbereen and Clonakilty'.[42] Public officials and the local press represented public hostility to Irish settlers: 'We are accustomed to associate notions of filth, squalor and beggarly destitution with everything Irish from the large number of lazy, idle and wretched natives of the Sister Island who are continually crossing our paths'.[43] This was characteristic of the response in many cities to what was often known as 'Irish fever' but it is instructive in gauging the extent of hostility to the Irish to find examples of a more tolerant attitude to Irish immigrants in Newcastle-upon-Tyne. Faced with the same coincidence of epidemic disease and an Irish presence in the Sandgate area of the city, Dr Robinson, in making a thorough investigation of the causes of the epidemic in 1846–7, did not even mention the Irish. Again in 1853, when cholera raged in the city, the local press saw it as an issue of public health, the cause of the malady being unknown. Even though 350 lives were lost in the parish of St Mary's in a single month, the Irish were not singled out for public attack. Interestingly, as R. J. Cooter points out, the only body of people who tried to implicate the Irish in the epidemic were the outside commissioners for the Board of Health. Cooter concludes that almost all the available evidence on the Irish in the north east fails to point to any consensus of opinion that the Irish lowered the Englishman's 'superior prudence', morals, drinking habits or living conditions.[44]

Why was there a contrast in attitudes to 'Irish fever' in Cardiff and in Newcastle? Two further studies, of the Irish in York and in Bristol, suggest possible answers. Frances Finnegan identifies a change in the character of the migrants in York as the rate of settlement increased during the 1840s. Before 1846, 'there was little to distinguish York's small pre-Famine Irish community from the rest of the population'.[45] In 1841, the Irish were distributed throughout almost every parish in the city, with concentrations in the poorest and most unhealthy quarters, Walmgate, Hungate and the Waterhouses. Although particular streets and courts exhibited a strong Irish presence, the Irish formed a small percentage of York's poor. The York Irish were represented in every social class and were employed in a wide variety of occupations.

The extent of inter-marriage between the Irish and the host community suggests that there was no distinctive or beleaguered ethnic minority but rather a group that experienced a fair degree of assimilation. However, post-Famine immigration changed the situation of the Irish community in York. The Irish population (Irish-born and their children) increased from 781 (2.7 per cent) to 2,618 (7.2 per cent) of the population of York between 1841 and 1851. In this period, the newly arrived migrants concentrated in the poorest area, notably the four Walmgate parishes, extending their hold over particular streets and yards. With the arrival of post-Famine immigrants, the social structure of the Irish community experienced a substantial change of character. The percentage of persons in Class II and Class III (dealers and skilled occupations) more than halved and the percentage in Class IV (partly skilled occupations) more than trebled. Subsequently little occupational mobility took place and a decline occurred in the level of mixed marriages.

David Large, in a study of the Irish in Bristol (based on the 1851 census), found that there was no 'little Ireland' in the city and, although there was a tendency to settle close to the docks and Floating Harbour in the heart of the city, the Irish were well distributed throughout the city parishes and were as likely to be found in wealthy Clifton (580 Irish) as in poor St Augustine the Less (475 Irish).[46] Large concludes that while the Irish concentrated in particular streets and courts, they were also widely scattered throughout the city and spanned the whole range of social class groups. In 1849, the Irish were to be found in cholera-ravaged streets but not all the unhealthy spots included Irish inhabitants. Significantly, in a city with the third highest mortality rate in England, the Irish were not blamed for the incidence of epidemic disease.

The different response to Irish settlement identified in York and in Bristol reflects the character and scale of migration during the famine years and was also influenced by the nature of the local labour market. Whereas York experienced a sharp rise in the numbers of Irish migrants, Bristol experienced a very gradual increase in the number of its Irish-born inhabitants. Also, whereas most of the new migrants arriving in York were poor Irish from a variety of places, including the decaying textile areas of Mayo and Sligo, the Bristol Irish were predominantly from County Cork, Dublin, Waterford and Limerick and, representing a wide

variety of trades, they were more easily absorbed into the variegated labour market in Bristol.

The character and scale of migration and the local conditions
in terms of employment opportunities may also explain the
sporadic violence and disorder that occurred in some cities but
not in others. It is evident also that the political and religious
character of a city and the policy adopted by certain police forces
towards the Irish community were additional factors in sparking
off riots and other incidents that were the cause of public
disquiet.

Irish disorder in Bradford has been explained in terms of a
predominantly Roman Catholic migrant force, of whom many
were Gaelic-speaking from the west of Ireland, settling in a
staunchly Protestant city.[47] The Bradford Irish lived in highly
concentrated communities and gained a reputation for inter-Irish
feuds and clashes with the non-Irish population. In local police
reports, the Irish were singled out for special attention. A similar
pattern has been identified in Leeds.[48] The majority of Irish
migrants came from Dublin or the western counties and 83 per
cent of them settled in three poor wards in the city. The familiar
charge of drunken, violent behaviour and a fierce resistance to
arrest was made against the Leeds Irish, and public anxiety supported police supervision of the 'Irish quarters'. Within the Irish
community, sectarian conflicts and disputes over loyalty to
different Irish counties were characteristic of incidents of disorder. In Manchester, the traditional distillation of spirits and
Sunday morning gambling allied to the regular Saturday night
brawling, associated with the Irish presence, were the subject of
local police activity.[49]

Bradford, Leeds and Manchester are examples of places where
police reports identify particular forms of crime and disorder as
an 'Irish' problem. To accept this diagnosis may be to take the
perspective of the police at face value. A further perspective on
'Irish' disorder and crime is suggested by Roger Swift in a study
of the Irish in Wolverhampton[50]. He records the concentration of
Irish in Caribee Island, a district of insanitary and squalid housing,
and the familiar propensity of the Irish to court the displeasure of
the police through illegal distillation and sale of liquor in 'wabble'
shops. The shops were singled out for special treatment with an
aggressive, paramilitary form of policing, deliberately aimed at
suppressing the Irish population. In support of this contention,

Dr Swift argues that other poor districts of Wolverhampton were not subjected to the kind of discriminate policing directed at the Irish quarter. The appointment of Chief Constables with experience of military style policing in Ireland, a policy also followed in the neighbouring county of Warwickshire, appeared to have a clearly designed intention of suppression attached to it.[51] The high proportion of prosecutions made against the Irish population was part of a policy of increasing the general level of convictions to impress the ratepayers as to the efficiency of the borough police force. Irish 'disorder' was being highlighted as a means of justifying the size of the police force.

An absence of serious disorder or conflict represents the reverse side of the coin in the pattern of Irish settlement observed in Bradford, Leeds, Manchester and Wolverhampton. Dundee is an example of a city 'remarkable for its moderation and restraint towards the Irish'.[52] Yet Dundee experienced a very rapid increase in Irish migration and as high a proportion of Irish settlement as any other Scottish city. In 1851, the Irish-born population of Dundee was 18.9 per cent, slightly higher than the comparative figure for Glasgow. Irish migration to Scotland was also on a larger scale in relation to the national population than Irish migration to England.

Walker argues that only the Catholic Irish settled in Dundee so there was a marked absence of the sectarianism between Catholic and Protestant Irish that occurred in Glasgow. Moreover, the Irish in Dundee were predominantly female and established a reputation as good workers, earning ready promotion in the expanding jute mills in the city. In the middle decades of the nineteenth century, Dundee was a rapidly expanding frontier town, attracting Highlanders and the rural population of Angus in addition to Irish migrants. These groups were not rigidly segregated and there was an absence of a distinctive Irish ghetto in Dundee. Also, Dundee was a staunchly Liberal town with a proud belief in religious toleration. The local press did not share the anti-Irish and anti-Catholic prejudice that Handley identified as the general attitude towards the Irish in Scotland.[53]

A further example of a relative absence of conflict is the case of the Irish in Hull.[54] As a mill town and a port, Hull attracted Irish migrants from Lancashire and Cheshire and they were probably more acclimatised to English conditions than newly-arrived migrants in Liverpool. In 1851, the Irish-born population of Hull represented just over 3 per cent of the total, and thereafter they formed a declining proportion of the city's inhabitants. Mostly employed in the mills and on the docks and concentrated in three areas of the town, the Hull Irish always remained a minority in employment and settlement. As a predominantly Roman Catholic population, they were also distinctive as a religious minority.

By all accounts, housing conditions in Hull at mid-century were appalling. The 1849 cholera epidemic claimed 1,860 deaths, one of the highest rates of mortality in the country. The Irish were identified as living in the poorest areas and being prominent in local disorder. The level of crime in Hull was distorted by the number of Irish vagrants committing offences to obtain a bed for the night. A further potential cause of friction lay in Hull's long tradition as a nonconformist stronghold with its leaders proclaiming a well-developed puritanism.

Yet it is striking that there was no real conflict when the conditions and climate of opinion appeared to favour an attack on the Catholic Irish. The principal reason seems to have been the presence of a few key individuals in Hull, who occupied positions of authority and influence. Most important was E. F. Collins, from 1841 the editor of the *Hull Advertiser* and a man who gave Hull twenty years of outstanding public service. Collins transformed the *Advertiser* from a Tory to a Radical journal. He championed the cause of good housing, attacked religious bigotry, and ended the deportation of Irish paupers. In the field of public health reform he was supported by another Irishman, the local surgeon Edward Owen Daly. Also, the crucial post of Chief Constable of the Hull Police was held from 1836 to 1866 by Andrew McManners who was drafted in from the Metropolitan Police. The presence of Irishmen in positions where sensitive handling of opinion and policy were essential ensured that the Irish in Hull were not made the subject of scapegoat abuse as in some other cities.

As regards Bristol, public order could not be taken for granted in a city which had experienced the worst riots in England in 1831,[55] Also in the 1830s, the slavery question was the subject of bitter electoral battles and violent mobs were hired to support rival candidates in the city.[56] Furthermore, Bristol was a highly devout and staunchly Protestant city, recording one of the highest levels of church attendance in the national Religious Census in 1851.[57] The potential existed in Bristol for the display of religious bigotry and hostility to Irish Roman Catholics that was all too evident in some other British cities. Another potential source of conflict arose from the poor sanitary condition of much working-class housing in Bristol and in the alarmingly high level of mortality rates in the city, the third highest in England during the 1840s, after Liverpool and Manchester.[58] Overcrowding in densely populated riverside districts persisted into the 1840s long after the cholera epidemic in 1832. Fear of 'Irish Fever' in Bristol would not have been surprising in the 1830s and 1840s at a time of rising Irish migration.

Despite such an inauspicious background, Bristol did not feature as a centre of major Irish incidents or experience bitter conflicts between the English and Irish populations. Earlier it was observed that the character and scale of Irish migration, the density of Irish settlement, and the range of opportunities within the local labour market were positive factors in the process of easier assimilation in Bristol. Equally, just as aggressive policing appears to have provoked disorder in Irish communities in other cities, so the well regulated Bristol police force (modelled on the Metropolitan Police) contributed to the improvement in public order in the city.[59] Certainly, there was little disorder in Bristol during the Chartist period (1836–48) against a background of Chartist incidents at nearby Bath, Trowbridge and Devizes.[60]

Newspaper reports provide a window on public attitudes to Irish migration and settlement during the famine years. The ambivalence of English attitudes to the Irish is revealed in the combination of religious bigotry and benevolent charity that feature in reported incidents involving the Irish. It is also clear that anxiety was increased by alarmist references in some newspapers to 'hordes' of Irish vagrants 'flooding' into certain cities. In a temporary atmosphere of panic, magistrates were more likely to adopt a harsh stance against Irish people charged with begging. Similarly, the atmosphere surrounding the restoration of the Catholic hierarchy in England reinforced anti-Catholicism in the early 1850s. Yet, these were essentially temporary influences and calmer attitudes prevailed once an atmosphere of crisis had subsided. More enduring was the influence of editorial bias which coloured the reporting of particular incidents as specific religious or nationalist interests were defended in the provincial press in England and Ireland. Press reporting was filtered through a framework of self-interest to appeal to existing prejudice.

In one sense, the way in which the Irish were reported in the provincial press of the nineteenth century did much to reinforce popular beliefs that drunkenness, violence and disease were somehow peculiarly 'Irish'. The press image of Ireland and the Irish in the Bristol region came in part from a virulently anti-Catholic newspaper, the *Bristol Times*, whose anti-Catholicism was sharpened in the early 1850s during the controversy over the restoration of the Catholic hierarchy. Yet despite its religious prejudice, the *Bristol Times* was not aggressively anti-Irish. In the famine and immediate post-famine years it made no open attacks on the Irish, such as appeared in the High Tory and strongly Protestant *Stockport Advertiser*, which rhetorically asked its readers in May 1852,

> What is it that so often disturbs the peace of the borough, increases our rates and saps the very foundation of all our charitable institutions, but popery embodied in Irish mobs, paupers and fever patients?[61]

In the *Bristol Times*, the Irish were presented as figures of fun, with their 'brogue' parodied in police court reports,[62] and as the butt of jokes in the 'Varieties' column, but the practice of reprinting news from other provincial papers did link the Irish with violence, for they were frequently reported as sectarian rioters, as the perpetrators of murders, or as the instigators of 'dreadful affrays' between gangs of navvies. At the local level the image of a drunken, violent 'Paddy' was fostered by the fact that Irish Bristolians featured most often in the *Bristol Times* in reports of proceedings at the police court, commonly for offences in these categories.

The overwhelming majority of men and women with Irish names who appeared before the Bristol magistrates in the years 1847–48 and 1851–52 were not specifically identified as 'Irish' in the press but the *Bristol Times* evidently had no clear policy on this. There was presumably no need to spell out the national origins of Daniel O'Brien, John O'Connell and a 'woman and girl named Hogan' who were all charged in November 1851 for various incidents of assaulting each other, assaulting the police and 'inciting the mob to rescue'[63] but Irish offenders with non-Irish names were sometimes clearly labelled as such. On occasions, too, the 'Irishness' of a Barney Kelly or Catherine Regan would be emphasised by references to them as 'a son of Erin', 'a native of the green isle' or a 'Patlander'. Because there was no Little Ireland in Bristol, Irish disorder in places like Marsh Street or Lewin's Mead had to be pointed out to readers of the *Bristol Times*, if they were to differentiate it from the drunkenness, violence and attacks on the police (usually arising from attempts to resist arrest) which were fairly commonplace events in what were 'rough' working class districts.[64] In fact, only one incident was actually reported as 'An Irish Scrimmage' (in 1851)[65] although in the late 1840s a drunken brawl in Lewin's Mead, which involved about twenty people and took nearly half a division of police to quell, was described as 'a regular English and Irish row'.[66]

An archetypal case of the drunken Irishman was Jemmy Donovan who made a regular appearance before the magistrates in Bristol but was treated with affectionate tolerance in the columns of the *Bristol Times*:

> JEMMY DONOVAN AGAIN!
>
> This well known character appeared before the bench this morning for nearly the hundredth time, charged with being drunk and incapable of taking care of himself.
>
> P. C. 27 duly proved the fact of finding Jemmy in a riotous state of inebriation on the Quay, about twelve o'clock on Saturday night.
>
> Mr. Rogers.—You are here again, Donovan; now what have you to say to the magistrates?
>
> Donovan.—Please your honours, now, be so kind as to let me go back to Stapleton where I come from; I'll promise you I'll never come to trouble your honours any more if you will be so kind.
>
> The Mayor.—We fear it's no use to try you. However, it is impossible the public can be annoyed by your repeated outbreaks, and we shall now order you to find sureties; in default you will be sent to your old quarters, the Bridewell.
>
> Donovan.—I don't care where you put me, so long as you put me somewhere; but I should like to go back to Stapleton, if you please.
>
> Mr. Phippen.—You will be prevented from committing these outbreaks in Bridewell; you will have no chance of getting beer there.

Donovan.—Very true, your honour, but beer don't agree with my head, although I am very fond of it—(*laughter*).

Mr. Phippen.—Nobody doubts that, Jemmy; but you should avoid getting too much.

Donovan.—I like it well enough when I'm drinking it, but when it's gone it don't agree with me at all—(*laughter*).

The Bench decided upon requiring Jemmy to find sureties, and he was committed in default.[67]

Whilst deploring Donovan's persistent drunkenness, the magistrates considered his case sympathetically. Here was a clear example of English ambivalence towards the Irish.

Whatever degree of toleration existed in the city towards the resident Irish population, the local response to the Famine was a mixture of sympathy for the plight of the Irish in Ireland and suspicion towards the vagrant Irish who were seen to be coming in increasing numbers to Bristol. In the early months of 1847 the *Bristol Times* gave extensive coverage to all aspects of the Famine. As well as reporting on conditions in Ireland and on national charitable efforts, it published a list of subscribers to the Bristol Irish Relief Fund which eventually totalled £9,000.[68]

The paper also published letters from Anglo-Irish residents in some of the worst-hit areas, like Skibbereen, County Cork, appealing to Bristolians to send money direct to Ireland.[69]

The writer of one letter was evidently aware that the humanitarian response to the famine was likely to be tinged by middle-class attitudes to the poor and by some suspicion of the Irish. Writing from Tyrawley, County Mayo, the author made it clear that charity would be practised with discrimination and that funds would not be misused: 'Every case is subject to strict personal investigation before relief is afforded, and in this county the people are too heart-broken and miserable to think of buying fire arms.'[70]

As famine migration to the mainland increased, so fear of being overrun by hordes of fever-ridden, starving Irish spread throughout the country. Although there is no evidence of a massive influx of vagrant Irish into the city, readers of the *Bristol Times* would have been well aware that their numbers were rising; more and more frequently, offenders before the magistrates were identified as Irish, charged with begging, stealing bread, or applying for relief while in possession of money. Alarmist reports from

other parts of the country probably heightened the fears of
Bristolians. It was claimed that nearly one million poor Irish had
flooded into Liverpool in the first fourteen weeks of 1847;
Warrington and other towns around Liverpool were 'crowded
with them' by April.[71]

The following month, under a stark headline 'THE IRISH', the
Bristol Times reported that 500 men, women and children had
recently landed at Newport, South Wales, where they had been
granted temporary relief but then ordered out of the town.[72] It
was not only the sheer volume of immigration which provoked
hostility to the Irish in the famine years but also the fear of fever.
The Irish were often associated with fever in press reports but
not always blamed specifically for it. An article on 'The Famine
Fever' published in the *Manchester Guardian* in July 1847 was
mildly optimistic, in stating that 'the health of the town, or rather
of its Irish immigrants, is greatly improved'.[73] The link was also
made in a *Bristol Times* report on the 'very considerable' amount
of fever in the city in May 1847, which was noted to be especially
prevalent in 'those quarters occupied by the poor Irish' even
though, as we have seen, there was no 'Irish quarter' in Bristol [74]
and the Irish were not singled out as scapegoats.

Indeed, public concern in Bristol seems to have been mainly
about vagrancy rather than fever. This concern showed itself in
numerous complaints to the magistrates about vagrants roaming
the streets, which came 'from all parts of the city' and were
accompanied by demands for some action from the authorities.[75]
Increasingly, the Irish became the targets for particular attention
from the police, which culminated in fifteen men, women and
children, 'principally Irish', being brought up 'for lying about the
streets' in the summer of 1847. They were closely questioned
individually and those who satisfactorily 'accounted for being
out' when the police round-up took place were discharged but
'one or two' were imprisoned for short terms, without any specific
charge apparently being made against them.[76] The magistrates
sent some individuals back to Ireland at the ratepayers' expense
but a member of the Committee of Managers of St Peter's Hospital
tried to set up a more ambitious repatriation scheme, by arranging
with one of the steam packet companies to ship 'a large number
of Irishmen' back to their country of origin. The scheme was only
a partial success, for when sailing time arrived more than twenty
people who had agreed to go 'could not be found'.[77]

The acute crisis of famine immigration had passed by the early 1850s but the press still carried reports of many destitute Irish crowding into British cities.[78] That events of the preceding years had firmly fixed the Irish in the collective English mind as a 'problem' was demonstrated in October 1852 (when remarkably few cases came before the police court) when Bristol magistrates attributed the decline in 'ordinary police business' partly to a fall in unemployment but mainly to 'the cessation of immigration of Irish into the city, as most of their disorderly cases were formerly supplied from the Irish'.[79]

Yet as the fears aroused in the famine years subsided, there is evidence of a growing sympathetic awareness of the implications of massive depopulation for Ireland's future. In reporting the numbers of Irish leaving for America or the colonies, the *Bristol Times* made it clear that it was not only 'the lowest scale of humanity' which was fleeing Ireland but that migrants included middle-ranking farmers, people with some capital, the young and the enterprising.[80] A *Bristol Times* reporter wrote about 'The Exportation of Girls from the Union Workhouses'[81] and told his readers that it had been explained to him that the Guardians 'were only too glad "to get rid of their livestock" . . .'[82] He described, in comic terms, the departure of girls from the workhouses of Ennis, Corofin and Killadysert as they were sent off from Clare to Limerick for 'shipment' to the colonies, but he concluded on a serious and not unsympathetic note. There was, he wrote, 'something sad' about a country which had lost one to two million of its population in a decade having to see 'so many candidate wives exported away from young Irishmen who could not afford to marry, to Australians and colonists who could; for Ireland now comes under the category of those countries which Southey said, must be truly miserable, "where it is imprudent to marry, and a family is a misfortune".' [83]

In the *Bristol Times* there are also examples of sympathy towards Irish immigrants who were in one way or another exploited when they reached the mainland. They could be easy prey for a variety of tricksters. The 'Emigrant Trappers' of Liverpool[84] had their counterpart in every port and some of the con-men were themselves Irish, like Daniel Mahoney who was one of the 'touters' who infested the packets as they docked at the Cumberland Basin in Bristol.[85] The experience of a young Tipperary girl, who arrived in Bristol from Cork in April 1852, was probably not untypical. Agnes Heman intended going on to London and emigrating further if she 'could not get on decently' there but before even disembarking at Bristol she was accosted by a middle-aged couple who successfully duped her. The woman, discovering that Agnes came from 'County Tip', claimed to be from a neighbouring county and offered to put the girl up while she stayed in Bristol but, in the event, the couple robbed her of all her luggage and savings.[86] Although the case against the pair was not proved, the magistrates expressed sympathy and concern for Agnes Heman. They gave her money from the Poor Box to support herself in Bristol and, at her request, arranged a free passage to her home some seventy miles from Cork City. There was a similar response to the case of Anne Murphy, one of 'several' young women brought over from Belfast to work in the Great Western cotton mill at Barton Hill, Bristol. When trade became slack Anne Murphy,'as one of the youngest hands', was laid off and it was in circumstances of 'extreme distress' that she had stolen a shawl from Catherine Riley and pawned it. The bench was highly critical of the factory manager for importing labour but failing to provide continuous employment for the girl, or in some other way providing for her. Although she admitted the offence, the magistrates discharged Anne Murphy and gave her two shillings from the Poor Box.[87]

These instances of sympathy, and others like them, occurred in the 1850s, not at the height of the famine influx when the Irish were widely perceived as a faceless, threatening mass. The fact that the Famine coincided with a period of food scarcity and trade depression on the mainland was a complicating factor, which had important implications for English-Irish relations. As Pauline Millward has shown, it added another dimension to the complex tensions between the English and Irish in Stockport, which eventually erupted into violence in the notorious Stockport Riots of 28–30 June 1852.[88] Millward points out that there is little evidence to support the claims that the Irish in Stockport were an economic threat to the indigenous working population, but she acknowledges that they were certainly seen as such, because the peak of Irish immigration was reached in 1848 when a 10 per cent wage cut was enforced. A multi-causal explanation is the most appropriate for the Stockport Riots, as Millward emphasises, but a limited survey of contemporary reporting shows that the provincial press tended to present the disturbances in simplistic, mono-causal terms, according to their editorial bias. The *Bristol Times* first reported the events by reprinting an excerpt from the *Daily News* in which the riots were described as 'a quarrel between the Irish Catholics and English Operatives', originating in the proclamation against Catholic processions.[89] Although the religious element is clearly stated, the use of the term 'English Operatives' does imply that there was also conflict over work, but when the *Bristol Times's* own correspondent filed a report he made no mention of this angle. Instead, he stressed the religious causes—and blamed the Irish—by defining the disturbances as 'serious rioting . . . [between] . . . Roman Catholics and Protestants . . . arising out of the insolent and aggressive conduct of the former'.[90] *The Tablet*, a Catholic paper, also presented the riots as an outburst of religious intolerance but, not surprisingly, denounced the Derby Proclamation as the cause which had provoked them.[91]

A similar line was taken in the *Cork Examiner* but in this paper the news from Stockport was used as a platform from which to urge Irish Catholics to support Liberal candidates at the forthcoming election.[92] The partisanship of the authorities was criticised in some sections of the English press but criticism was particularly vehement in the nationalist and Catholic *Galway Packet*. In a passionately written editorial, headlined 'The Hurricane of Fanaticism', the riots were roundly condemned but the disturbances were not ascribed solely to the 'brutal proclamation', for it was acknowledged that they owed something 'to the influence of Irish immigration in lowering rates of wages'.[93] In contrast to the restrained comment of a *Manchester Examiner* and *Times* reporter, who merely noted that 'several of the special constables took an active part in the destruction of property',[94] the editor of the *Galway Packet* condemned the authorities wholesale. Their conduct, he declared, 'could not be better illustrated than by the production of the prisoners they had seized, who were to a man, Irish. The English mob had nothing to apprehend at the hands of their allies, fellow countrymen, and fellow-fanatics—the police and special constables.[95]

The differences in emphasis in the reporting of the Stockport Riots clearly show how editorial bias could shape the reading public's view of contemporary events and perhaps influence their future behaviour too. The anti-Catholic *Bristol Times* presented the disturbances as purely sectarian violence provoked by Irish Catholics, and thus it reinforced the anti-Catholicism of many of its readers. The Liberal Catholic *Cork Examiner* used the religious dimension of the riots for political ends: it deliberately played on Catholic sentiments by describing the sacrilegious attacks on chapels and schools in horrific detail and then urged its readers to defend the faith by voting Liberal at the next election. The nationalist and Catholic *Galway Packet* skimmed over the details of the violence as being too awful to dwell on, thereby leaving it largely to its readers' imagination to speculate about the atrocities committed against the Irish Catholics. It also slightly distorted the news by stating that the prisoners were 'to a man' Irish (when in fact they were overwhelmingly but not exclusively so) and the editor couched his justifiable condemnation of the Stockport authorities in such terms that, by implication, the English in general were damned for their anti-Irish 'fanaticism'. So a little more fuel was added to the blaze of anti-English feeling in Ireland.

A partisan press reinforced existing positions. It was more a process of rallying the faithful than of attempting to convert the uncommitted. More significantly, the variety of stances adopted in the provincial press, in England and Ireland, called into question the blanket assumption commonly attributed to the English and Irish about each other. Not only were there different perspectives on each side of the Irish Sea but important differences of view within both Irish and English opinion.

From an Irish nationalist perspective, there was an overwhelming sadness and air of defeat at the loss of population, described as the brightest and best of the Irish peasantry, during the famine years. An acute sense of loss was mixed with anger and resentment over the 'injustice' of feudal laws and the 'oppression' of English colonial administration. The famine added to the long-standing bitterness of many Irish people against England. As a means of coping with a deep sense of grief for the loss of kith and kin, the myth of Irish 'exile' was harnessed to the dream of a free Irish nation.[96] The impressive scale of money sent back to Ireland from the United States, in the aftermath of the Famine, kept alive the idea of a nation in exile and fostered ambitions of 'getting on' by getting out of Ireland.

> Looking back in 1862, it was argued that since the famine years, the population that has remained in Ireland is deteriorated. The best educated have emigrated during the last

fifteen years . . . A progressive decrease in population and in the production of wealth is a sign that something is not right in the legal and social condition of the country. The legal conditions under which the peasantry live extract almost all the produce of the land from them, leaving only potatoes and turf to the cultivators. The consequence is that with the slightest climatic change the peasantry have nothing to fall back on—famine, eviction, assassination become the normal conditions belonging to the tenure of land in Ireland.[97]

Other voices in Ireland were eager to please their English governors in endorsing the fashionable philosophy of 'self-help'. In the same year the *Irish Times* took delight in the figures compiled by the Emigration Commissioners: 'The most remarkable fact ever recorded in history, probably, is contained in the following words:— "The remittance sent home by emigrants to their friends in fourteen years amounted to upwards of twelve millions sterling." What a tale of industry, thrift, and love of kith and kin is here!'[98]

In contrast to Irish perspectives, the classic English perspective, buoyed up by economic prosperity and colonial ascendancy, can look uncomfortably close to an attitude of racial superiority:

We say that a little pride is pardonable to an Englishman as he turns his globe, and notes, as they pass under his hand, all these rich and fertile countries coloured 'with one brush' . . . The truth is that a prosperous hive will throw off swarms, especially if the bees feed on northern flowers. There is that old distinction between the Teuton and the Celt . . . Your Celt cannot colonise. He can seize an Algeria or a Cochin China—no one better; or impelled by hunger, he can leave Limerick and Cork in hordes to seek food in the far West; but he is not a founder of nations.[99]

The English who emigrated to the colonies, invariably in search of opportunities denied to them at home, were cast in the role of empire builders—bold, creative and adventurous. The Irish who migrated to Britain or America, in search of a better life, were usually described as the most ignorant and wretched of the population. Mid-Victorian English imperialism combined a blend of apparent contempt for the Irish with a fear of the French. Ireland, of course, was regarded, with its Celtic and Catholic ties with France, as a potential back door for a French invasion of England.

Yet this was not the sole mentality in England. Imperialism was a sectional creed and held to be morally untenable by men such as John Bright, who dismissed the Empire as a form of out-relief for the aristocracy. Equally important was the deep-felt humanitarianism of Victorian social reformers and the romantic affection for continental nationalist heroes like Garibaldi and Kossuth. A few Englishmen championed the cause of Ireland. Prominent among them was the Quaker philanthropist, James Hack Tuke, who visited the west of Ireland at the height of the famine and became involved in relief work for the starving population.[100] Another visitor to Ireland was the English writer Thackeray who spent three months in Ireland in 1842 and published his impressions in *The Irish Sketch Book*. In Cork City, he became entranced by the wit and vivacity of conversation and the extraordinary degree of literary taste and talent amongst the Irish.

Thackeray commented: 'I think, in walking the streets and looking at the ragged urchins crowding there, every Englishman must remark that the superiority of intelligence is here, and not with us.'[101] Yet he later observed: 'All round the town [of Muckross] miserable streets of cabins are stretched. You see people lolling at each door, women staring and combing their hair, men with their little pipes, children whose rags hang on by a miracle; idling in a gutter. Are we to set all this down to absenteeism, and pity poor injured Ireland?'[102] In these observations, Thackeray was representative of many Englishmen in their response to the condition of Ireland and its people.

English attitudes to the Irish have to be understood in the context of the many contemporary issues with which they became entangled. It is possible to see the Irish as victims of bigotry, superstition and fear and serving as scapegoats for apparently insoluble problems. Ireland and Irish migrants may also be seen as providing opportunities for benevolent work and missionary zeal on a heroic scale.

English attitudes to the Irish were, as Sheridan Gilley has argued, essentially ambivalent—a mixture of admiration for the qualities of military valour, family loyalty and capacity for industry with, at the same time, disapproval of Celtic lawlessness, drunkenness and idleness: 'The English invoked the good points or the bad according to their temperament, moment or mood.'[103] Gilley effectively answers the racist charge of Professor Curtis as oversimplified and one that is not sustained after 1870. He endorses

Jackson's view that the period of English concern about the Irish as a 'social problem' was confined to the years 1800 to 1860. Thereafter, English attitudes to Irish immigrants were 'passive and unconcerned'. Increasingly, the Irish merged into the crowd in British cities.

Some reservations, in relation to Gilley's scholarly case, may be expressed about the assertion that Irish immigration represented a net liability after 1834. This assumes that English disapproval of Irish disorder was based on 'social fact'. Yet Gilley himself has demonstrated that the 'Paddy' stereotype was created by a mixture of the Irish self-image and English attitudes. If 'Paddy' rested on a basis of social fact, the facts in question were gleaned from the discriminatory reporting of Irish brawling that shaped the English idea of the Irishman in England. Today we recognise the same negative images perpetuated in the British press in relation to Asian and West Indian immigrants.[104] As to the supposed ill-effects of a culture based on casual labour upon the mores of the English working class, such an assumption takes at face value and as a social reality the contemporary fear expressed by middle-class observers. It is much more likely that the casual labour which formed a substantial base of the mid-Victorian labour force produced a hand-to mouth existence among all manual workers, whether English, Welsh, Scots or Irish. The Irish 'fondness' for casual labour was more a matter of necessity for a predominantly unskilled migrant force.

Referring back to figures cited earlier on the dispersal of Irish settlers, it is doubtful whether in many cities in England or Scotland the Irish were sufficiently numerous or concentrated to exert a malign influence on the host community. They were merely an easy target, and once the label had been applied in Liverpool and Glasgow it was accepted as universal for the Irish presence in Britain. Hostility was bound up with a host of other issues. Coincidentally, Irish peak migration occurred at a time of seemingly insoluble problems—overcrowding, epidemic disease, unemployment and disorder; the poor Irish (the only visible Irish), became convenient scapegoats. Long-standing fears of Roman Catholicism and of French invasion, fears played on for political purposes, threw suspicion on the Irish as an alien people.

In surveying the work of the last twenty-five years on the Irish in Britain, a number of key themes emerge. The label 'Irish' is continually employed for convenience but does less than justice to the lack of homogeneity among the peoples of Ireland, including the men and women who migrated to Britain, North America and to Australia. Added to a variety of condition, religion and expectations among Irish migrants were varied patterns of migration and settlement throughout the world. More specific to Britain was the temporary nature of the panic and alarm induced by Irish immigration in mid-Victorian cities and the sporadic nature of outbursts of anti-Irish feeling. English and Scottish attitudes to the Irish presence were complex and ambivalent. The variety of experience and response to Irish migration in Britain was rooted in the specific conditions that obtained in the different communities in which they settled. Important influences on Irish relations with the host community were found in the leadership available and in the prevailing local political, religious and economic climate. New patterns will be identified later, but they are likely to reflect the pluralistic experience of Irish men and women that varied with time, place and circumstances.

Lastly, in comprehending Irish quarters or 'Little Irelands', the subject has not only moved forward but come full circle. As early as 1963, E. P. Thompson observed: 'If they were segregated in some towns, the Irish were never pressed back into ghettos.'[105]

In opposing this view, Werly cited the case of New Town and Little Ireland in Manchester as evidence that the 'Irish of that city did live within two clearly delineated ghettos'.[106] In the 1830s and 1840s, the idea of a Little Ireland served as a symbol for a generation of polemicists, social investigators, and men of letters in attacking industrial capitalism and urban degeneracy.[107] It was a product of creative imagination and contemporary ideology. In our own time, the image of the Irish in the ghetto has endured, appealing to historians looking for an oppression model for the emigrant Irish.[108] Now there is sufficient evidence to show that as many Irish settled outside distinctive Irish quarters as settled in them. This is less potent symbolically than the ghetto but it helps to explain the complexity and variety of response among the host community in Britain.

There is further evidence of complexity and ambivalence amongst the host community in the field of employment. The impact of the Irish in the British Industrial Revolution is also a subject of long-standing debate among historians. These issues are examined in the next chapter, 'Irish Labour'.

3

Irish Labour

There are two reasons why there are so many Irish in
Manchester: first the gentlemen of Ireland, seeing the poverty
of the natives, entered into subscriptions to send them out of
the country to any place . . . Secondly, the capitalists have
sent out false reports that they wanted hands, in order to
induce Irish to come over that they might accept lower wages.
I am at a loss to know whether the Irish gentlemen or the
English capitalist has done more for the destruction of the
working classes, both of England and Ireland.
(Richard Sheridan, hand-loom weaver. 1836)

Witnesses before the commissioners on the state of the Irish
poor in 1836 present a bewildering array of contradictory
evidence on the influence of Irish migrants in Britain. The Report
itself has been hailed as one of the most impressive essays in
sociology among the blue books of the 1830s.[1] Most of the witnesses were drawn from the major centres of Irish settlement in the
north-west manufacturing towns, the midlands and in Scotland.
Northern industrial employers were especially prominent but
the views of Poor Law officials, doctors, farmers, clergy and a
few operatives were also represented.

From a wide range of independent voices, two themes are
discernible. One represents a hostile view that condemns the
moral condition of the poor Irish, and carries grave forebodings
on the lowering of standards that would surely follow the
presence among the decent English and Scots of 'a less civilised
race'. The other acknowledges that there might be a social cost
from large-scale Irish immigration but this was outweighed by
the economic advantages brought by cheap Irish labour. The long-
term importance of the report lies in its influence on subsequent
debate amongst historians about the impact of Irish immigration
on British society. A much quoted source, it has, with the Bible,

the singular merit of supporting, through selective reference, completely conflicting interpretations.

At the root of the stereotype model was the fear of the Irish as a cheap labour force, initially attracted by higher wages than those available in Ireland, but willing to work for lower wages than those paid in Britain. It was feared that the presence of large numbers of Irish migrants threatened to lower the standard of living, and so the moral condition, of the native working class.

There is no doubt that the expectation of higher wages was well founded, not merely for adults, but the employment prospects for children could also materially improve the household economy of potential migrants. The statement of Samuel Holme, builder of Liverpool, provides a clear example:

> I had a conversation last week with an Irish labourer, named Christopher Shields: he said that the reason of his leaving Ireland was, that in the county of Wexford, his own county, he could only get 6d. a-day and his own meat: that at one time he rented a small cabin with a potato patch, and worked for the landlord. He then got 1s. a-day but the landlord charged him £3 a-year for his holding. He told me that there was a general impression among his countrymen that if they came to England their fortunes would be made, wages are so much higher here. He told me that he could get his clothing as cheap here as at home, and generally all the things he wanted. He now gets 16s. a-week. He stated likewise that it was a great inducement to them to come here that they can get situations for their children, which they could not get at home. He told me likewise that he could more easily get his children educated here than in Ireland. This man lives in a cellar, He will never return to Ireland: he has no wish to go back. [2]

Taking into account the additional earnings of his children, Christopher Shields would have probably received in the city of Liverpool three times the income of 6s a week that he could earn in County Wexford. Nevertheless, this economic incentive for Irish migrants was perceived to be potentially harmful to the host community. The 1836 Report echoed the views of many witnesses in identifying the dangers inherent in rural migration to the city:

The Irish who migrate to Great Britain come to a considerable extent from the country, or at least from villages and
small country towns. In Scotland and England, however,
they settle exclusively in towns, and for the most part, in
very populous towns, as London, Manchester, Liverpool,
Glasgow, Edinburgh, Leeds. The change from the more
simple, regular, and tranquil life of the country, to the varied,
troubled, and stimulating life of towns, appears to be in
general hurtful to the morals, if it takes place after youth.
There is a constant influx from the country into towns, the
population of which is increased more by immigration than
by new births: and the persons who swell the population of
the towns are of two classes, either those of a more adventurous character, who think that they possess qualities above
the ordinary standard, which they can bring to market to
the best advantage in towns, or those who have by some
misdeed forfeited the good opinion of their neighbours,
and seek to escape notice among the crowds of a city.[3]

These fears about Irish migration were of course equally applicable
to rural-urban migration within mainland Britain. Irish migrants
merely represented a more visible minority among new urban
settlers. Roman Catholic clergy were prominent in deploring the
character of Irish migrants and in claiming a deterioration in
their moral conduct. The Rev. Peach of Birmingham spoke for
many of his faith in stating:

A great many Irish are here because it would not be safe for
them to remain in Ireland, having been engaged in disturbances and breaches of the law. Irish priests, with whom I
have talked, had the same opinion and thought, that the
scum of the Irish came over.[4]

Dr Scott, the Roman Catholic bishop of Western Scotland, resident
at Glasgow, argued that for a considerable number of Irish,
migration meant a lowering of moral standards:

In my opinion the change of abode does not in general
produce a good effect on the moral character of the Irish
who come over to this country. I must, however, distinguish
between those who appear to have been very immoral
before leaving Ireland, and those who immigrate to this
country, generally ignorant, but moral in their conduct. I

am sorry to say that the last mentioned class . . . is not the most numerous one. Those whose morals are corrupted before they come to Scotland, generally become worse in this country, because they seem to throw off all restraint, and soon learn that their pastors here cannot exercise the same control over them in correcting their faults as the Roman Catholic clergy do in Ireland. I have ever observed that the more these ignorant moral people mix and associate with the lower orders of the Scotch in large towns, the more their morals are deteriorated.[5]

All this must be taken as opinion rather than evidence, and shows the threat migration posed to the authority of the clergy in exercising social control over a mobile population. A major concern was the belief that the presence of the Irish set lower standards of comfort and diet for the local population to imitate.

A key witness before the commissioners in 1836, Dr J. P. Kay was an articulate spokesman of what became an orthodox view, and the man who identified 'Little Ireland' in Manchester as the classic Irish ghetto. Kay provided a very full testimony which was amply endorsed in the report. One of his central arguments recognised the tension between the economic benefits and the social costs of Irish immigration:

Under the present restrictions on the commerce of the country it is of the utmost importance to the successful employment of capital that manufactures should enjoy an unlimited command of labour, without which it is a serious question whether the commercial position of the country could be maintained in its competition with foreign rivals, and therefore the immigration of the Irish has been of service to the trade of this town . . . But the effect of the colonisation of a barbarous race on the habits of the people of this country must be considered apart from the economical questions, and, provided the trade of the country did not require the importation of cheap labour from Ireland, the moral condition of the labouring classes of this country might be more easily ameliorated if unaffected by the example of the Irish with whom they are now mingled.[6]

The 1836 Report also noted the evidence of the Rev. Malthus before the House of Commons Committee on Emigration in 1827, where he predicted a lowering of wages in England and the undermining of the superior prudence of the labouring classes. He also predicted that the Irish might have the 'pernicious effect of introducing the habit of living almost entirely on potatoes'.[7]

Central to this belief, in a lowering of standards, was the a priori assumption that the Irish were used to a lower standard of living, and were therefore more content to accept lower wages than the native English and Scots. Athough the Irish in Britain received higher wages than they were used to in Ireland, it was argued that they did not spend their money on improving their diet or domestic comfort, but on the consumption of spiritous liquor.[8]

From the whole of Kay's influential testimony, it is clear that the alarm generated by the presence of Irish immigrants in the northern industrial cities provided a vital platform from which to present a major programme of social reform. Kay was astute enough not merely to rehearse a catalogue of woe, but to suggest remedies to the established government of the day. New building enactments and sanitary legislation would ensure that squalid housing of 'Little Irelands' would no longer be tolerated. A reformed municipal police force would inspect the gin shops and low taverns to restrict drunkenness and disorder. Police supervision of such places would also combat the breeding of crime and revolutionary conspiracies among an ignorant mob, whose passions were easily inflamed by the consumption of alcohol. A reform of the Poor Law would encourage greater mobility of labour throughout the country, and thereby place less reliance on the heavy migration from Ireland.

More positively, Kay did not see the Irish as irredeemably lost, but merely at a less advanced stage of civilisation. He recognised 'no intellectual inferiority among the Irish'. Consequently, he could see obvious merit in the promotion of a system of education and the provision of rational leisure, such as well-regulated drama, as powerful moral agencies to raise the condition of the Irish poor.

It is difficult to avoid the conclusion that Kay used the opportunity of the enquiry into the state of the Irish poor to alarm the authorities into an acceptance of his own agenda for reform. In this sense, the presence of the Irish in Manchester offered a convenient degree of urgency to a more widespread fear about the degraded state of the English working class. It was not so much a concern for the plight of the Irish migrants, as fear of the temptations they might pose for English workers. The dominant issue in the 1830s was the condition of England, and the Irish were regarded as a subversive influence in a potentially dangerous situation—that is, dangerous to the interests of the propertied classes.

The evidence of other witnesses may be understood in similar terms—how an Irish presence affected their main preoccupations. Clergymen were most absorbed with fears of lax religious observance and the moral condition of their congregations. Employers, among whom there were some who denied that wages were lowered by Irish workers, were content to receive a supply of cheap labour from Ireland.[9] Conversely, English hand-loom weavers like Richard Sheridan, quoted at the beginning of the chapter, were convinced that as wages were lower than formerly, the importation of Irish labour, with passage paid by Irish landlords, was the obvious cause of their plight.[10]

The issue of whether Irish immigration had the effect of lowering wages in Britain has wider implications for economic historians interested in the Industrial Revolution. Arthur Redford's pioneering study, *Labour Migration in England*, written in 1926, accepted unquestioningly the evidence of the 1836 Report, along with that of other contemporary accounts:

> The main social significance of the Irish influx lay in its tendency to lower the wages and standard of living of the English wage-earning classes. This clash of social standards had been clearly foreseen by the Committee on Emigration in 1827. 'Two different rates of wages and two different conditions of the labouring classes cannot permanently co-exist. One of two results appears to be inevitable: the Irish population must be raised towards the standard of the English or the English depressed towards that of the Irish. The question appears to your Committee to resolve itself into the simple point whether the wheat-fed population of Great Britain shall or shall not be supplanted by the potato-fed population of Ireland.[11]

Alongside this gloomy economic prognosis was an equally depressing social scenario which appeared to be confirmed with the great rush of 'famine-stricken and diseased Irish peasants to Great Britain in the years following 1846':

The disastrous social effect of the Irish influx was, however, already apparent in the 'thirties. Much of the evil arose from the lower standard of living general in Ireland, which was transplanted by the immigrants into their new environment. The Irish in Great Britain always lived in the cheapest houses: families were often to be found sharing house with several other families, and they retained their native practice of keeping pigs in the house. With this lower standard of living went a lower efficiency as workmen, and a worse moral tone. The Irish were less provident, and more given to drunkenness; they were slovenly, careless, and stupid. On this account they were not usually put in charge of power-driven machinery, and were necessarily given the lower-paid work. They formed a submerged class, always tending to drag down their neighbours to a lower level of living. 'Where they are a majority they banish providence, temperance, and quiet from the neighbourhood in which they reside.'[12]

Redford's assumptions about lower standards, taken uncritically from contemporary accounts, rested on simple associations between the poor Irish and urban slums. Such assumptions, as the previous chapter demonstrated, command less certainty today.

For modern economic historians, a key question is whether Irish immigration had a significant effect on the contentious issue of the standard of living in the first half of the nineteenth century. Did the Irish have a measurable impact on real wages in Britain? Redford's view that the Irish presence did have the effect of lowering wages was followed by J. H. Clapham in the 1930s and reaffirmed in the 1970s by Sidney Pollard.[13] The 1970s also saw the beginnings of a revisionist challenge to the long-standing consensus. E. H. Hunt began to question a reliance on 'a substantial body of literary evidence which suggests that immigration reduced wages rates . . . but no quantitative assessment of these influences has been possible'.[14]

By 1981, Hunt was arguing that the importance of Irish immigrants to the Industrial Revolution, in terms of being a highly mobile, adaptable and, above all, a cheap labour force, was based on false assumptions. He attacked the various arguments put forward by J. A. Jackson, J. E. Handley and E. P. Thompson, on the indispensability of Irish labour to the progress of the

Industrial Revolution.[15] Hunt proclaimed that the evidence to support what he called 'the indispensability thesis' was drawn from manufacturers engaged in a 'fairly blatant piece of special pleading'.[16]

It was convenient for employers to draw on the supply of labour from Ireland but this did not mean that Irish labour was indispensable. Immigration from Ireland occurred at a time of rapid population growth, and the British economy was characteristically prone not to labour shortage but to a labour surplus, especially among the large pool of unskilled workers to which most Irish immigrants contributed. Secondly, the mobility of Irish migrants was not unique. As we have already observed, it formed only a part of the general migration from rural areas to the cities. Hunt cites the case of the 1851 census in Birmingham which showed that well over half the population of that city, aged twenty and above, had been born elsewhere, and in the city of Bradford, the Irish formed less than a fifth of the number of native migrants.[17] Thirdly, the assumption that only the immigrant Irish would perform some of the hardest and roughest kinds of work, because the native population avoided dirty and dangerous jobs, cannot be substantiated. Some of the essential tasks of industrialisation, the building of canals for instance, had been completed before large-scale Irish immigration took place. These jobs were performed, outside the areas of Irish settlement, by the English and the Scots.

Hunt concludes that 'the main influence of Irish immigration upon wages and employment fell upon less prosperous parts of Britain that the immigrants themselves shunned'.[18] Moreover, the economic advantages of immigrant labour, however marginal, accrued to the northern employers while a considerable part of the economic and social costs fell upon native workers.

The revisionist case has been developed more fully in an article by Jeffrey Williamson which attempts to quantify the impact of the Irish on British labour markets during the period 1820 to 1860. This is not merely revisionist history but revisionist economic theory, so it is not the most accessible material for a general reader. Nevertheless, its importance to a broader understanding of the presence of the Irish in Britain invites the attention of a wider audience.

Williamson picks up a point made by J. P. Kay, as a witness before the Poor Law Commission in 1835, that Irish immigrants would crowd out the potential native-born migrants from the southern counties.[19] The same point drew comment in the 1836 Report on the State of the Irish Poor, where it was concluded that 'the demand for labour in the manufacturing districts of the North of England would, in part, have been satisfied by a 'migration from the South.'[20] Williamson calculates that the proportion of Irish immigration into non-agricultural employment had the effect of crowding-out native labour: 'when the Irish immigration rate reaches its peak in the 1840s, the rate of immigration from British agriculture reaches its trough, indeed an enormous fall from 0.51 per cent per year in the 1830s to 0.21 per cent per year in the 1840s. Furthermore, when the Irish immigration rate picks up after the 1810s, the rate of immigration from British agriculture falls off with a decade lag. In both the short run and the long run. Williamson argues that there does appear to be some suggestion of Irish crowding-out.' [21]

How serious was this effect of Irish crowding-out on the British economy? In examining this question, Williamson rehearses some well-known characteristics of Irish migrants to Britain. As an overwhelmingly unskilled labour force with a high rate of illiteracy, the Irish had very little impact on skilled labour and settled predominantly in the unskilled, urban labour market. Although Williamson confirms the concentration of Irish settlement in the major cities of Britain, he also identifies the trend of Irish dispersal away from the largest centres. In 1841, 52.1 per cent of the Irish-born population lived in Britain's seven biggest cities when these cities formed only 17.9 per cent of the British population. Yet when, by 1861, the figure of 17.9 per cent had risen to 20.6 per cent, the proportion of the Irish-born population had fallen to 42.4 per cent. This is further evidence of the temporary shock of Irish immigration which created most alarm in the ports of entry and in a few key manufacturing centres in the 1830s and 1840s. In the longer term, and on a broader scale, the problem of absorption was much less acute.

The Irish, along with native rural migrants, were predominantly adult. In 1851, 74.4 per cent of Irish immigrants in Britain's cities were adults, and in 1861 83.4 per cent of the Irish were aged 20 and over, compared with a figure of 54.7 per cent for the non-Irish urban population. Although a poor and unskilled labour force was especially prone to unemployment and reliance on poor relief, where obtainable, the age selectivity of Irish migrants meant that the burden of dependency of young and old was necessarily smaller. This probably had the effect of reducing the social cost to the host community in that a higher proportion of Irish migrants were able to make a direct labour input into the economy. How significant that was depended on how much Irish income was sent back in the form of remittances to Ireland. It was probably less important than remittances from the United States sent to pay the passage money for crossing the Atlantic.[22]

A central question, posed by Williamson, is the size of the Irish labour force in relation to the total British labour force. Williamson argues that only 3.5 per cent of the British population in 1851 was Irish, and he dismisses the point raised in the literature that the Irish share in the cities was 6.9 per cent or that the Irish proportion of certain occupations was very much higher. Critical to his case is the assumption that the labour market in Britain was not highly segmented and that wages were not linked between various regional labour markets. Perhaps there is an element of wishful thinking here, in the interests of applying a macro-economic model without having to account for the wide regional wage differences that existed in Britain.

Nevertheless, Williamson bravely attempts to establish a model of exogenous Irish immigration to Britain, and to calculate Irish labour participation rates over the period 1787 to 1871. Inevitably, given the reliance on imported Third World data and the inadequate detail on Irish immigration to Britain before 1851, there is a degree of speculation built into the model. The results, however, merit serious consideration. Yearly rates of growth of the Irish population in Britain, including the children of Irish-born parents, are estimated as follows:

1787–1821	6.7%
1821–1831	4.7%
1831–1841	3.7%
1841–1851	5.4%
1851–1861	1.0%
1861–1871	-0.4%

A predominantly adult Irish-born population had a higher labour participation rate than was the case for the British population as a whole. Consequently, the Irish share of the British labour force rose from 3.4 to 8.8 per cent in the period 1821 to 1861. Significantly, Williamson shows that the impact of Irish labour was greatest during the period of rapid industrialisation. Indeed, during the 'Hungry Forties' almost a quarter of the increase in the British labour force was recruited from Ireland.

The question posed by Williamson is: how fast would the British labour force have grown in the absence of the Irish? Adopting counterfactual techniques, he estimates that over the four decades from 1821, the British labour force would have grown at a rate 0.15 per cent less, while during the critical 1840s, it would have grown at a rate 0.26 per cent less. The key message is that 'Irish immigration mattered little to British development over these four decades'.[23] The labour force growth rate would have declined by more than the rate of population growth—a decline in the unskilled labour force of from 1.4 to 1.22 per cent per year. But such a decline does not account for lagging real wage gains during the Industrial Revolution. British incomes, it is argued, were little affected by Irish immigration, and they were affected differentially according to social class. Unskilled labour suffered marginally from Irish competition, while all others gained a little, landlords and employers especially.

Williamson's findings are thoroughly revisionist. He challenges the long-established view that Irish labour played a critical role in holding back a rise in living standards and in boosting industrialisation in Britain. He claims that Irish immigration did have the effect of inhibiting rural out-migration among the native-born and assumes that Irish labour was a perfect substitute for native labour within Paisley mills, the Liverpool docks, in railway construction or in Mayhew's East London. In other sectors of the labour market, especially at the point of entry and critically in the short term, Irish migrants were not perfect substitutes and suffered accordingly, with higher unemployment and lower wages. Yet in the long run, Irish mobility spread the problem of absorption across the whole of the British economy.

The implications of these findings are momentous. If the level of Irish immigration was 'simply too small to matter much, given the impressive absorptive capacity of the British economy', then several other conclusions follow.[24] Without the Irish, agriculture as a labour intensive industry would have suffered far more than industry. The emigration rate from agriculture would have been almost double what it was in the 1840s, and the level of wages in the rural south would have risen as a result of competition in a situation of labour shortage. Industry, to the extent it was reliant on cheap Irish labour, was inhibited from greater innovation in labour substitutes. The presence of unskilled Irish workers probably had the effect of widening inequality between all workers. It is also possible to speculate with Williamson that the availability of cheap Irish labour had a marginal influence among the native British in creating a greater propensity for capital accumulation and acquisition of skills. This, in turn, increased the capacity of the British economy to absorb more Irish migrants.

Whilst acknowledging the quality of Williamson's research, some tentative qualifications to his thesis may be offered. By admission, the data on early nineteenth-century immigration is imperfect, and there is a reliance on twentieth-century Third World data on labour participation rates which must be, at the least, speculative. Moreover, Williamson's method of surveying the impact of Irish labour on the total British labour market depends on doubtful assumptions about the structure of the labour market in the middle decades of the century. In many respects, Britain was still a series of regional economies both in terms of capital investment and in the normal pattern of short-distance migration. The assumption that agricultural labourers in the south would have moved to northern industrial towns in the absence of Irish migrants begs the question why they failed to move north as agricultural labourers, virtually doubling their wages, at any time during the century. Emigration was perhaps a more attractive proposition to them but Wiltshire agricultural labourers were deeply sceptical of better prospects elsewhere and firmly wedded to local practices. Professor Mingay recounts the story of an American farmer Frederick Law Olmstead, who visited England in 1850 and tried to persuade Wiltshire labourers to give up their poor wages and conditions, and emigrate to the United States. All his arguments were rejected once it was discovered that on American farms there was no free allowance of drink.[25]

Canon Girdlestone found the same conservatism among his labourers in north Devon. When in 1866 he began to organise the migration of labouring families to northern industrial towns, he found that some had never been more than a few miles away from their parish and believed that Manchester was somewhere overseas. To ensure that they arrived at the right destination, they had to be consigned to the railway company and labelled like so many evacuee children of a later generation. As Mingay points out, for migration to take place, it needed someone local to give a lead and make the necessary arrangements.[26]

The high mobility of the Irish tends to obscure the conservative nature of patterns of movement among Irish migrants. Migration across the Irish Sea was not random, but followed clearly defined routes, and local ties were often maintained in settlement patterns in British cities.[27] There was also a conscious attempt to retain skills no longer in demand in Ireland. Textile workers are a well-documented group who made a successful transference to British textile towns in Yorkshire and Scotland. Others responded to the demand for labour in expanding industries, and adapted successfully to new occupations in mining or sugar-refining.[28] Yet others were less fortunate. Irish shoemakers, tailors and hand-loom weavers, all found themselves competing in already overcrowded labour markets, and suffered unemployment and poverty as a consequence.

What is striking about Irish migration and Irish labour at this time is its marked diversity of experience. Not only the occupation but the place of settlement was of vital importance in determining wages and conditions.[29] Therefore, a general model identifying Irish migrants as a uniform, unskilled body, while providing some interesting answers to major economic questions about the impact of Irish labour on the Industrial Revolution, may nevertheless be misleading about what actually happened to the Irish workforce.

In turning to examine the Irish experience in various sectors of employment, a far from uniform picture emerges. There were at least three categories of employment where Irish labour made a distinctive mark and which differed significantly from one another. Even within these categories there was an apparent diversity of experience.

A first category could be described as itinerant workers who did not settle permanently in Great Britain. The 1836 Report identified three kinds of such migrants. These were seasonal workers, drovers of cattle and pigs, and beggars and vagrants seeking alms. The first and most numerous of these were seasonal workers who came over for the corn and sometimes for the hay harvest. For the most part they came from the western and mountainous counties of Ireland and landed at Glasgow, Liverpool and Bristol. From the wages earned during the harvest period, they often paid the rent on their holdings back in Ireland. Mostly they came alone, but those who brought wives and children sent them begging around the country and arranged to meet them before returning home. As a group they were praised for their public behaviour and economic value: 'Their conduct is in general orderly, their habits remarkably frugal and sober, and they appear to give satisfaction to their employers.'[30]

By contrast, Irish drovers, who belonged to a higher class than seasonal labourers, nevertheless enjoyed a reputation for disorderly and drunken behaviour. They were employed in the extensive trade in livestock between Ireland and the major ports in main-land Britain. Unlike the seasonal harvesters, who were generally described as sober and well behaved, drovers were dubbed as 'uniformly drunken' and 'very troublesome' on board the steam packets.[31] In the ports their boisterous behaviour attracted the attention of prostitutes anxious to relieve them of the substantial sums of money they carried with them:

> Margaret Taylor and Mary Ann Lawrence were charged with robbing Robin Tobin of £70. The prosecutor is an Irish cattle drover from New Ross, near Wexford: he was picked up by the prisoners and taken to a house in Morris's Court: he went to bed with both women, fell asleep, and next morning found his companions and his money gone . . . [£47 in notes was found on Taylor and some silver on the other, and both were committed] . . . The brother of the prosecutor, only a month ago, was robbed of £110 in a brothel in Host-Street, but though the fact was well known to the prosecutor, the first time he comes to Bristol, he falls into the same snare and gets plundered in the same way.[32]

Also making regular but shorter crossings all through the year from Belfast to Glasgow, were Irish hawkers bringing poultry, eggs, bacon and other provisions to sell in Britain. These were not to be confused with the class of beggars and vagrants, who moved between Ireland and Britain, and took up the trade of hawking as the occasion warranted whilst wintering in the poor quarters of British cities.

The driving force for seasonal workers was to earn as much money as possible while on the mainland, and to spend as little as possible so as to accumulate enough to pay their rents in Ireland. In practice, this meant walking from the western counties to northern or eastern ports, employing all kinds of tricks to evade payment on the steam packets, never paying more than 5s per head, and living in barns and outhouses once they arrived at the harvest fields, to avoid paying the cost of accommodation. In 1825, a Warwickshire farmer was paying Irish labourers 12s a week, with a quart of beer a day and a dinner on Sunday and sometimes on Thursdays. Piece-work earnings were 15s a week but if there were too many Irish harvestmen, wages were as low as 8s a week. These rates were lower than those paid to English agricultural labourers at the same time.[33]

From Warwickshire, these Irish labourers followed the harvest to Staffordshire.[34] Others would stay beyond the harvest season obtaining work as hod-men or as porters about the docks and settle permanently in England. A few of those who returned to Ireland made arrangements to give their earnings to one of their party whom they agreed to meet again later, and they then applied to be returned as paupers, so saving the expense of the return fare. Most, however, paid their way back.

Earnings varied according to the season and to where harvest work was done. In Lincolnshire earnings might be as high as £10 to £15 but elsewhere each man might receive from £4 to £7. When the fruits of their labours were safely deposited in Ireland, the banks made special arrangements to cope with the rush of business. Mr Guinness, a director of the Bank of Ireland, gave evidence in 1836 'that the Irish reapers, on their return from England, come in such numbers to the Bank of Ireland to exchange their gold for notes, that it is necessary to make a regulation that they should attend early, before the press of business commences, and thereby, prevent inconvenience to the public.'[35] Here is an image to conjure with alongside that of the poor, starving Irish emigrant. David Fitzpatrick has calculated that Mayo's 10,000 migratory workers sent home £100,000 annually in remittances between 1876 and 1880.[36]

The experience of Irish migrant agricultural labourers may be reconstructed, in part, from a Lincolnshire study by Sarah Barber.[37] The Irish began to come over in large numbers to the county in the 1840s. By 1844, some 800 a day were arriving at the town of Stamford and made for the local Catholic Church. This offered a convenient meeting place and initial shelter, and the priest provided local intelligence on accommodation and the state of the harvest. In the first half of the century, there was little apparent organisation among Irish migrant workers apart from travelling together as a body for mutual protection. If they happened to arrive too early, they remained in the neighbouring towns of

Lincoln, Stamford or Boston. When the railways were established, specially chartered cattle trucks brought five hundred Irish at a time into the towns. The fare from Liverpool to Lincoln was 5s.

The good prospect of employment on large farms, and high summer wages, attracted a large migrant Irish labour force to Lincolnshire. In the second half of the century, seasonal harvesters became better organised under a gang system. In early summer, the Irish ganger would write to the farmer asking how many labourers he wanted, and would then organise the gang accordingly, usually from among his friends and relatives. Such organisation produced a better regulated and better paid labour force, earning the same wages as English labourers. Those outside the gang system were taken on at the hiring fairs and often continued with the same farmer for many years. Surviving letters suggest that personal contact was a very important part of the relationship.[38]

Gangs of labourers lived rough in barns or, on the larger farms they were lodged in 'Paddy Houses' made of brick. This arrangement suited both farmers and their Irish workers who wanted little or no expenditure on accommodation to eat into either profits or wages.

Seasonal migration was on a significant scale for the harvest in Scotland. Some six to eight thousand harvesters came to Scotland each year in the 1820s and, according to J.E. Handley, by the mid–1840s, the Clyde steamers carried this number in a week. Over the season some 25,000 Irish reapers came to work in Scotland.[39] From 1841 an attempt was made to calculate the size of this annual migration and to register the counties of origin in Ireland. Seasonal workers used four main ports, Dublin and Drogheda to Liverpool, and Londonderry and Belfast to Glasgow. Connaught, and County Mayo in particular, furnished the greatest number making the journey via Liverpool. Ulster, and notably County Donegal, headed the list of seasonal workers en route to Scotland. Predictably two-thirds of those whose ages were obtained were between the ages of 16 and 36.[40] Fitzpatrick has pointed to the concentration of seasonal migration from seven Irish counties, showing how it operated as an adolescent phase, often as a prelude to permanent emigration later in the life cycle, when the transfer of farm occupancy between generations was taking place.[41]

Handley has commented on the sympathetic response of the Scots to the privations of Irish reapers. 'Their privations and fatigues during the season of harvest work are unexampled, and could only be borne by Irishmen. We regret to observe, however, that these poor fellows, immediately upon their arrival in town, are attacked by a set of harpies who attempt to fleece them by disposing of sundry articles of clothing, but more especially glittering pieces of jewellery, at prices inconceivably beyond their real value . . . The police should keep a sharp eye on these tricksters, and not allow them to prey upon the poor reapers, who, sure enough, deserve our best sympathies and protection.'[42] An earlier letter commends their attitude to employers and says that their skill as reapers surpasses the Highlanders and other Scots at harvest work. 'Irishmen have uniformly shown the warmest gratitude for any kindness and attention shown them . . . they work more willingly and labour harder'.[43]

A witness who watched their passage through Glasgow describes the return of Irish harvesters in terms of admiration and a respect for the dignity of labour:

> Much has been said and written about the indolence and improvidence of the Irish peasantry and labouring class, but when they have a motive and inducement and fair return for their labour, there is not a more laborious, hardworking and persevering class of men to be found anywhere. Many of these men travelled far on foot before reaching the sea-port in their own country where work was to be had, ever labouring hard and living very sparingly, in order that they might scrape together £2 or £3 to take home with them to provide food for father and mother or wife and little ones during the winter. And it was very interesting to notice the changed appearance of the men on their return home six, seven or eight weeks later, according to the time harvest-work was to be had. There was no change in their outward appearance. The garments were the same, only a little more worn and patched, but there was in general a more manly, independent look about them than they had on the day of their arrival—perhaps, in most cases, without a copper in their pockets; and now, coming down Jamaica-street in small groups, about the time of the sailing of the boats, with to them, abundance of money, hard wrought for, and every penny carefully saved, wearied and footsore. Yet cheerfully they tramped down the street and along the

quay, scarcely looking in at a shop window, and even resisting all the attractions of dram shops, it being a very rare circumstance to see any of them the least touched with liquor. No doubt these men had their faults and failings . . . but if they were a fair sample of the industrious peasantry of Ireland they could put to shame many other nationalities who think themselves very much their superiors.[44]

E.J.T. Collins has placed the pattern of Irish seasonal migration into a wider context.[45] He distinguishes between the cottiers from western Ireland who formed the largest single category, and the 'internal' migrants who moved from the pastoral south-west to the arable south-east of Ireland, and then sometimes migrated further to Britain. Other workers involved in temporary migrations, who were mostly from the east of Ireland, were building workers and other labourers drawn by contract work or the demand fluctuations of the trade cycle. In Britain, the 'brawny Leinsterman' and the 'scrawny Connaught mountaineer' might work alongside each other in the harvest fields. Other recruits to harvest work were drawn from the major cities. Irish building workers from Edinburgh were employed as seasonal harvesters in Berwickshire in the 1830s. Great numbers of the London Irish left the capital for the hay season, the hop season or the harvest and returned when they were over.[46] From the 1860s, a similar out-migration of the Irish from Leeds, Manchester and Glasgow featured among the harvest workers in the surrounding areas.[47] In addition, Irish handloom weavers, tramps and vagrants swelled the numbers engaged in seasonal work in agriculture.

Given the complexity of so many migratory groups, it is not surprising that the official figures on Irish seasonal workers underestimated the scale of the Irish labour input into agriculture. Officially Irish seasonal migration declined from 60,000 in the early 1840s to 20,000 in the late 1880s and to 15,000 before 1914. The decline in Scotland was the more dramatic. Between 1840 and 1880 the number of Irish seasonal workers entering Scotland fell from 25,000 to less than 4,000. In England the numbers probably kept up until the 1870s. By then the supply of labour was beginning to dry up anyway. Renewed famine in Connaught was followed by further emigration to North America, which at last broke the fragile subsistence economy of the cottiers and small farmers, who had been sustained by seasonal migration to

Britain. High mortality and the continued drain of emigration combined over time, to produce labour shortages in the southern counties of Ireland.[48]

Collins, drawing on an EEC study of migrant labour, which concluded that immigrants increased real output and redistributed real income in favour of employers, finds a similar pattern with Irish seasonal workers in nineteenth-century Britain.[49] Employers' opportunity costs were lower for seasonal workers. For instance, housing costs, which might normally involve the provision of cheap cottage accommodation or room in the farmhouse itself, were negligible when migrant workers lived in barns or out-houses. There was no expense in subsidising labour in the winter months, nor the burden of poor rates when migrants came for temporary work and usually left their dependants in Ireland. The farmer gained because he got his harvest in without enduring the full labour cost. The seasonal workers gained through higher wages which often went to pay the rent on a small plot in Ireland. As against these advantages, itinerant labour had to endure the cost and inconvenience of travel over hundreds of miles. A social cost was also paid by the towns where large numbers of migrant workers congregated. Complaints about begging, drunkenness, noisy and boisterous behaviour were made against Irish seasonal workers in the towns, in contrast with conduct usually described as sober and frugal.[50] The Irish, in turn, may be said to have endured a further social cost in the form of occasional hostility from the local community, especially in the first half of the century.

Incidents of violence between Irish seasonal harvesters and native agricultural labourers appear to have been less serious than those that took place in urban and industrial areas. What is striking about the documented cases is that they involved rival migrant labour as often as the resident labour force. As early as the 1820s in Scotland, Irish reapers had begun to oust the High-landers from their old stance at the Cross of Glasgow, and by the 1830s Highlanders were almost completely supplanted by Irish reapers in the Lothians and in Roxburghshire.[51] In Cheshire, a fight took place in the early 1830s between Irish labourers and Welsh, Lancashire and Cheshire labourers over competition for harvest work. The fear of the Irish as cheap labour led the Cheshire men to beat them and steal their sickles and to use all means to prevent their coming.[52] Other conflicts occurred in towns between the Irish and town labourers wanting harvest work. In Scotland

and in northern England the practice of contracting casual labour at the hiring markets in towns, rather than at the farm gate, brought about the direct competition, in a potentially explosive situation, of a large gathering of migrant labour. Most of such incidents appeared in the 1830s and 1840s, and some, like the incidents of arson in the Swing Riots of 1831 in Lincolnshire, became caught up in other grievances.[53]

In view of the differential costs and benefits, it is perhaps not surprising that the most favourable comments on Irish migrant workers emanated from farmers, who were often supported by local newspapers. The least favourable comments and actions came from native workers, who saw the Irish as unfair competition, tending to lower wage rates and threatening their livelihood. Of course wages were influenced by a number of factors: the competition for labour from industrial employment which increased agricultural wages in the northern counties, the level of prices for arable crops—cereals, especially—which fluctuated with the quantity of the harvest and, from the 1870s, the competition of cheap, imported wheat from North America. The visible presence of Irish seasonal workers, if coinciding with reduced wage levels for any other reason, made them an easy explanation and target for abuse.

Yet the economic arguments point the other way. Far from posing a threat to native agricultural workers, seasonal labour was not only indispensable to gather in the harvest but ensured a greater level of employment for local labour throughout the rest of the year. If, as a contemporary estimated, the harvest season generated five times the amount of work, and five times the number of hands required, compared with the other ten months of the year, a normal situation of underemployment was temporarily transformed into one of chronic labour shortage.[54] Even with inter-county migration and the longer hours worked by resident agricultural labourers in south-east England, three times the normal amount of work was available at harvest time. The labour for such work was indispensable to the farmer, who could not afford any delay. If foreign labour was not brought in, some two-thirds of the harvest would be lost, a situation which would not be repeated. Farmers would grow only the crops they knew they could harvest, and if necessary, they would reduce their workforce by two-thirds accordingly. Thus, the English labourer would suffer from a loss of employment during the other ten months of the year, as the amount of fieldwork was correspond-ingly reduced.

The main source of temporary labour to assist in gathering in the harvest was among labourers in the towns. The supply of hands from the towns had been steadily reducing in the first thirty years of the nineteenth century, as urban wage rates moved ahead of those in agriculture. If Irish migrants had withdrawn and agricultural wages went up at harvest time, this would have had the effect of enticing town labourers into competition with agricultural labourers. Indeed when the number of Irish seasonal workers began to fall in the late century, and wages began to rise, accompanied by a further rural migration to the towns, their place was taken by Irish labourers resident in the towns, who still retained their migratory traditions and a taste for rural life.

Textiles was a second important category of employment for Irish migrants in Britain. As with seasonal harvesting, the Irish who took employment in the cotton and woollen cloth industries were retaining their work skills gained in Ireland. The decline of rural textiles in the northern and midland counties from the late eighteenth century to the 1820s, prompted an exodus of Irish migrants to textile centres in Scotland, Lancashire and Yorkshire. Migration of this kind may be explained as a deliberate attempt to continue in the same kind of employment by a transfer to areas where there was a demand for labour in Britain.

Several examples demonstrate the decline of industry in Ireland accompanied by a migration of labour to specific manufacturing centres in Britain. The Dublin silk trade, which was a principal industry in the early nineteenth century, was badly affected by the relaxation of protective duties in 1824–6, and Dublin silk manufacturers found themselves losing out to the competition in Manchester and Macclesfield. Consequently, Dublin silk weavers experienced great distress and many moved to Lancashire and to Cheshire in search of work.[55] Also the Irish cotton trade was killed off by the introduction of steam power, so by 1830 it was no longer viable. At the same time, mechanisation and expansion of cotton manufacture in the west of Scotland and in Lancashire drew substantially on Irish immigrant labour. The mechanisation of the Belfast linen industry had the effect of undermining the domestic industry in the northern and midland counties of Ireland, so encouraging migration to Scotland.

Identifying the county origins of Irish migrants in British cities also links decaying textile districts of Ireland with booming textile centres in Britain. Lobban's study of Greenock revealed that 44.3 per cent of the female workers in the textile mills in 1851 were natives of Ireland, who had acquired their skills in the Ulster linen industry.[56] C. Richardson has traced the principal movements of Irish migrants to Bradford from Queen's County and the western counties of Mayo and Sligo. As late as 1840, Mount Mellick and Mount Rath, the main towns of Queen's County, were centres of cotton and woollen manufacture. Also linen cloth manufacture had been extensively carried out on a domestic basis since the mid-eighteenth century, supplementing a subsistence agriculture in the cabins of the poor in Mayo and Sligo.

Over a third of Irish migrants arrived in Bradford from other textile towns in Lancashire and Yorkshire. The rapid growth of textiles in Bradford offered good opportunities for employment to the migrant Irish. The number of mills increased from five in 1810 to over eighty in 1844, and to more than 200 by the late 1860s. An expansion of textiles on this scale was matched by an increase in employment in construction, coal mining and engineering. Booming towns like Bradford provided employment, not only for women and children in the mills, but also for men in the building and coal mining industries.[57] The transformation in the potential earnings for the whole household provided an important incentive for the migration and settlement of Irish families in particular industrial centres.

In times of labour shortage, or of industrial dispute, some employers turned to Ireland to supply hands. James Taylor, of Newton Heath Silk Mill, Manchester, explained the process, as a witness before the commission in 1836:

> I employ 190 Irish in my mill out of about 500, as winders of silk: they are chiefly boys and girls from seven to twenty years of age. Their wages vary from 2s to 13s but most of them get from 3s 6d to 7s 6d; they are paid by the week. . . . I consider the Irish as of great value as a check on the combination of the English.
>
> The moment I have a turn-out and am fast for hands, I send to Ireland for ten, fifteen, or twenty families, as the case may be. I usually send to Connaught, and I get the children, chiefly girls of (I suppose) farmers and cottiers. The whole

family comes, father, mother, and children. I provide them with no money. I suppose they sell up what they have, walk to Dublin, pay their own passage to Liverpool and come to Manchester by the railway, or walk it . . . The communications are generally made through the friends of the parties in my employ. I have no agent in Ireland. I have sent a man over once or twice for this purpose, and he found me sixty or seventy hands. I should think that more than 400 have come over to me after they had learnt their trade.[58]

Taylor's evidence has been taken as support for the notion of the Irish as strikebreakers, a form of cheap labour, and as a threat to the standards of English operatives.[59] Information on whether Irish wage rates were lower is by no means clear cut and, at best, was practised by some employers only during temporary periods of high immigration. What is clear is that Taylor's need for additional hands met a ready response among poor families in the western counties of Ireland. The migration of the family unit to Manchester was made possible, not only by juvenile employment prospects, but also by the prospect of work for adult males in other industries such as building. Taylor, himself, describes how the Irish had an exclusive hold as bricklayers and he employed them to build his own mill. Significantly, once new skills had been acquired Taylor's Irish workers improved their employment prospects and moved to other jobs. The constant turnover of labour meant that individual migrant families were not inevitably trapped into a permanent condition of low-paid work.

The habit of thinking of Irish migrants as victims, continuously exploited by unscrupulous employers or grasping landlords, and harassed by hostile police and public officials, is enduring. It is founded on good evidence but it may be argued that it represents only a partial truth. Redford cites the case of the famous cotton strike at Preston in 1854, when employers imported Irish hands as blackleg labour. At the end of the strike, some of the children, who had been imported from a Belfast factory, were discharged and shipped back to Dublin as paupers.[60] Such instances represent Irish labour as passive victims of oppressive treatment.

Hand-loom weavers probably represent not only the best known casualties of industrialisation but, by association, Irish hand-loom weavers are the classic example of Irish labour depicted as victims. Manchester employers, serving as witnesses before the commission in 1836, provide the background on their circumstances. As Peter Ewart stated:

> About thirty five years ago there was a great influx of Irish to supply the extraordinary demand which existed at that time for hand-loom weavers; that was the first great immigration of Irish into Manchester. A good many also came about the same time on account of the rebellion . . . Many also came over in order to live on their friends and relations till they can get employment. The Irish are very kind and hospitable to each other,and assist one another very much in sickness and distress.[61]

This last comment, echoed by a number of witnesses, was seen rather as a sign of weakness than as a virtue. By the standard of the rugged individualism admired by Manchester employers, communal values were deplored.

James Aspinall Turner had about 500 looms in fancy work in the Manchester area, half of them wrought by Irish weavers. Wages were, on average, 9s 6d a week but lower for calico weaving. The weavers took the work out and did it in their own homes. It cost about £2 to set up a loom and its appurtenances, which made for an easy entry into the trade. Turner admitted that wages were lower than formerly and blamed this on the numbers of Irish who had depressed them.[62] In other words, they were the authors of their own misfortune. The very distressed conditions of hand-loom weavers in Lancashire in the 1830s meant that only the most desperate remained in the trade. A high turnover of labour ensured that these individuals, both the English and the Irish, did not suffer the decline in income that was the experience of the class as a whole.

Other critical points were made by John Potter, who testified that the Irish are more given to combination, and are more intractable than the English, and, also, they are fond of creating a disturbance for its own sake:

> It is a notorious fact, that in the small hand-loom weaving mills where many Irish are employed, there have been more turnouts than in others. I believe that several small hand-loom weaving mills have been given up in consequence of the mutinous disposition of the Irish weavers. There have

been several instances where they have beaten their masters and overlookers.[63]

The adverse comments of witnesses before the Commission on the Irish Poor in 1836 were reinforced in special reports on hand-loom weavers in 1840. Arthur Redford, whilst recognising a difference in the kind of labour available to Irish migrants in the Lancashire and Scottish cotton industries, noted that the main Irish influx into textiles was composed of hand-loom weavers. Moreover, as the distress among hand-loom weavers became acute by the 1830s, it was increasingly understood as an 'Irish problem'. Redford very accurately reflects the emotive language of contemporaries informed by a sense of crisis:

> The effect of this general decline of the Irish textile manu-factures in the early nineteenth century was to send into Great Britain a *swarm* of handloom weavers, of whom the Lancashire and West Scotland cotton districts bore the chief burden. The Irish handloom weavers, as already seen, formed a considerable proportion of the *burden of pauperism* in Manchester by the end of the Napoleonic wars: and their numbers throughout the Lancashire cotton district increased very rapidly during the next thirty years.[64]

Quite understandably, the focus of contemporary concern and of modern historians has been the areas of highest Irish settlement, north-west England and the west of Scotland, and, within those areas, the most distressed sector of the labour force. However, as Dr Bythell has shown in his modern study of hand-loom weavers,[65] Redford almost certainly overestimated the level of Irish penetration in the Manchester area, and in Scotland there was a varying experience in different cities with a varying effect on both the living and working conditions of Irish weavers. It is clear that the picture of uniform distress was created in a crisis atmosphere and it fails to encompass the diversity of conditions revealed in specific studies.

A contrasting picture of the experience of Irish textile workers in Scotland is presented by Brenda Collins. Far from seeing Irish migrants as passive victims, Collins argues that they were able to influence the social and economic structures of two Scottish cities where they settled. She found a continuity of experience among Irish migrants to Dundee, but not in Paisley, in the first half of the nineteenth century. Migration was not simply an economic imperative for the retention of work skills; the specific destination was influenced by the ability of individuals and families to bring their cultural traditions into urban life.[66]

More than a third of the Irish in Dundee, in 1851, originated in Cavan and Monaghan; 70 per cent came from Leitrim, Fermanagh and Sligo; 15 per cent from Donegal, Tyrone and Londonderry; and 12 per cent from King's County. In Paisley, in 1851, almost 70 per cent came from the northern counties of Donegal, Tyrone and Londonderry. What all possessed in common was the tradition of domestic cloth production within the context of a landholding society. The family operated as a complete production unit, combining spinning and weaving with agricultural work, and employing the women and children of the household.[67]

Emigration occurred when both sources of livelihood—textiles and farming—suffered severe losses, culminating in the disastrous potato crops of the mid–1840s. From Cavan and Monaghan, it was a rational choice to move via Drogheda to Dundee. In the 1830s and 1840s, Dundee became the leading centre of production for coarse linen, and the trading links established between the two towns spread information about better prospects and conditions available to Irish migrants.

Less specific, and occurring at an earlier period, migration from north-west Ireland to Paisley was part of the general movement to the Glasgow region via Londonderry and Belfast on low-cost steamships. Irish migrants in west Scotland moved around in search of employment. A general prosperity, based on the exclusively Scottish shawl-weaving trade in the 1820s, brought employment opportunities for the Irish in Paisley, across a range of ancillary textile processes, such as bleaching and dyeing, and in construction work. The decline in the shawl trade in the 1840s restricted the flow of Irish migrants during the famine decade and the old family unit of production was abandoned as Irish labour became integrated into the local economy.

The Irish presence, and particularly the Irish concentration in the textile industry in Dundee, was such that the traditional family unit of production could be maintained. Significantly, 60 per cent of Irishmen employed in Dundee in 1851 were hand-loom weavers, compared with only 6 per cent of Scots migrants and 12 per cent of non-migrants. The participation of children continued even after weaving moved from the domestic sphere into hand-loom weaving factories. Weavers preferred to employ their own children below 13 years of age, when full-time mill employment was possible, in the task of winding the weft yarn on to bobbins. In 1851, some 30 per cent of Irish children, aged 9 to 12 years, were employed in this way.[68]

Collins demonstrates the importance of the family unit, including the earnings of children or the saving on employing outsiders, by reference to family structure: 'Over half the families of Irish-born weavers in Dundee were clustered in the life-cycle stages where the ratio of dependents to income earners would be greatly altered by the children entering work.'[69] Over 70 per cent of sons and daughters aged over 15 years were employed in weaving or millwork, and each family had an average of two working children or young adults. Textile towns provided employment opportunities for young people living at home, so preserving the coexistence of adolescent and adult children at home that had been a feature of domestic linen production in Ireland.

Young single girls and widows were drawn to employment opportunities in Dundee. Most female textile workers were single and most of them were aged 15 to 24. By moving from Ireland to Dundee, the work changed from a domestic to a mill setting. Commonly, young girls migrated in sibling groups of two to four, and many lodged with Irish families. More than half of Irish female textile workers lived in lodgings. Widows, who were hard-pressed to maintain a family, were also likely to migrate to textile towns. Almost a fifth of all Irish household heads were widows in Dundee in 1851, and nearly 70 per cent of them were in life-cycle stages crucially dependent on textile work. In fact, widows had a higher figure of co-residing and working adolescent children (just under 3) than other Irish households. In addition to the children's earnings Irish widows frequently took in other lodgers. The constant flow of new immigrants meant that widows possessed considerable flexibility in sustaining income as the children left them.

The Dundee case is particularly interesting in showing how the expansion of the linen and jute industry provided 'the greatest possibility of advancement to migrant families because they could exploit the age and sex divisions of the textile labour force according to their household membership patterns'.[70] Collins goes on to argue that Irish migration into Dundee influenced the subsequent development of the linen and jute industry. It continued to be dominated by young adult women. Moreover, the females employed in the mills were the daughters of male hand-loom weavers. Given this family structure, there were advantages to manufacturers in retaining hand-loom weaving production for longer than it survived elsewhere in Britain.

Further evidence to support the contention that Irish migrants were not always passive victims is found in W.A. Walker's portrayal of Dundee's jute mills in the later nineteenth century.[71] Walker describes how, with a female-dominated industry, traditional male/female roles became reversed. Men became dependent on women's earnings and the behaviour of millworkers was more like that of working-class men. They were described as 'over-dressed, loud, bold-eyed girls' who had a reputation for uproariousness in the city streets. Mill girls, confident from earning more than husbands or brothers, were often able to overrule the male element at home. In such circumstances, female labour was regarded as the best recruiting-sergeant in Dundee. Half the men who joined the army were driven to enlist by the successful competition of their mothers and sisters. In other respects, women workers assumed the dominant role in the workplace. In the Mill and Factory Operatives Union, women trade unionists outnumbered men by four to one.[72]

It is clear that one of the problems that arises from dividing the labour force into discrete categories of workers is that the labour experience of individuals was not restricted to one sphere of employment. This was particularly evident in the case of Irish immigrants, who were a highly mobile labour force. As already observed, Irish labourers might serve a turn as bricklayers, seasonal harvesters, weavers, colliers or in whatever capacity work was available.

Another dimension for men with wives and children was found in the availability of employment for all members of the household of an age to be gainfully employed. This proved a major attraction of family migration to textile centres, where employment opportunities were available for women and children, and where men might find employment in building, mining or in a range of assorted trades. Such a variety of employment available in one place was a major incentive for Irish migrants to settle. Not only was the family unit preserved and some at least of the traditional household economy continued but there was a significant improvement in total household earnings.

A third group, normally regarded as isolated by the nature of their work, were railway navvies. A number of myths grew up surrounding railway navvies, and the Irish presence among them lent credence to the lurid press reports of the day. These featured accounts of grotesque violence and depravity on an alarming scale. The bad press given to navvies in the middle decades of the nineteenth century has been exposed in a number of studies, following the pioneering work by J.E. Handley and Terry Coleman.[73] The transport historian, Dr David Brooke, has explored the reputation of navvies, which extends back at least to the canal building era of the eighteenth century. Navvies were portrayed as savages, quite outside the pale of respectable society. Dr Brooke cites the example of a macabre incident on the London & Birmingham line, where a ganger organised a raffle in which the corpse of a fellow worker was the prize. Violent assaults on the police by 'lawless and furious men were commonplace' and when the navvies celebrated pay day with what were called 'randies', these were depicted as orgies of drunkenness and debauchery in the company of an army of lewd female camp followers.[74]

On closer investigation, the reputation appears to be based on a few sensational incidents that received maximum publicity. These served to establish a universally bad character for railway navvies, closely associated with the stereotyped image of the wild, reckless, hard-drinking Irish labourer. Even though the Irish remained a small minority among railway construction workers, 'Paddy' and the 'navvy' became synonymous in the public mind. Interestingly, J. H. Treble estimated that only 10 per cent of navvies were identified in the 1841 census as Irish by birth.[75] Indeed, there was a reluctance on the part of many English contractors to hire Irish navvies for fear of trouble with the native labour force. With mostly indigenous labour employed on railway construction in the south of England, Irish navvies were largely confined to the north and to parts of Scotland. For instance, J. A. Patmore found that 26 per cent of a navvy gang numbering 239, employed in Knaresborough in Yorkshire in 1851, had been born in Ireland, almost the same proportion who were born within 12 miles of the town. Like the English navvies, the Irish lived alongside textile workers. Some of the women folk of the navvies were employed in the linen industry and in local agriculture. Most navvies, however, were young, single lodgers, living in overcrowded conditions. Navvies as a group appeared to experience the worst levels of overcrowding in the town, and this included English as well as Irish navvies. Social class and the itinerant nature of the work appear to have been more important than ethnicity in determining living conditions.[76]

This appears to contradict the image of navvies living in shanties (rough, temporary shacks) alongside the railway workings. In reality, only a minority of navvies lived in such conditions, in the remoter parts of Britain away from urban centres. Dr Brooke found that only 26 per cent of railway navvies in 1881 lived in some form of temporary accommodation.[77]

A common charge made against Irish navvies was the familiar one of undercutting the wage rates of the native labourers employed in railway construction. Contractors attempted to separate the Irish navvies, where possible, in order to prevent trouble between them and the English and Scots navvies. Hostility to the Irish appears to have been associated with the perception of economic fears rather than because of racial or religious prejudice. However, once riot and disorder broke out, racial abuse was included in the grim catalogue of violent behaviour.[78]

The worst episodes of anti-Irish disturbances took place in 1846, the year of 'railway mania'. The very rapid pace of construction in the mid–1840s meant a major expansion in the total workforce from 9,000 to 100,000 men in England and Wales alone.[79] In the circumstances, employers took on any hands they could get, some of whom were drawn from the pool of the outcast and semi-criminal population of neighbouring towns. Added to this, the flight of poor Irish labourers into Britain, even before the worst of the famine years, created another source of recruitment. J. H. Treble appears to argue that the intention of contractors in separating English and Irish navvies was not merely to reduce the risk of disorder breaking out, but may also have been a way of imposing lower standards of pay on the Irish. If this was the case, it was not always effective as the disturbances at Swinton, Penrith and Lockerbie demonstrated. Here the Irish were employed on separate sections of line, and rumours of undercutting sparked off attacks on the Irish by the English and Scots.[80]

Perhaps not surprisingly, Irish navvies who found themselves on the receiving end of brutality and taunting complained of racial hatred directed against them:

It is impossible to describe their [English] animosity towards us: after abusing us, they often assemble together in large numbers, with all kinds of weapons, to drive us from the work—it makes no odds whether we are Catholics or Protestants—to be Irish is offence enough—we are all treated alike.[81]

In most instances the Irish, being in a minority, were vulnerable to the physical assaults made upon them by the English and Scots navvies. Commonly this resulted in the withdrawal of Irish labour. At other times, revenge was taken for atrocities and a form of tribal warfare broke out, encompassing labourers from further afield. Dr Brooke describes the infamous case in 1846 of a dispute between an English ganger and an Irish navvy who came to blows on the Lancaster and Carlisle line, near Penrith. Rumours spread and a band of Irish made an assault on the ganger, while within hours the huts of Irish workers were being destroyed at Yanworth, near Penrith. In their turn, a great number of Irish, armed with 'knives, billhooks, pistols, pokers, sticks, clubs, pitchforks, hammers and other weapons', arrived to defend their fellow countrymen, and were only persuaded against a revenge attack by an appeal from the magistrates, who promised to pay off those who wanted to leave and to protect those who stayed.

Three days later, English navvies were summoned from as far away as Shap, Orton and Kendal, and up to 2,000 men marched on Penrith:

> great numbers had knocked or sawn heads off their pickaxes and taken the staves as cudgels, others took their spades, some carried the bars of iron used in blasting the rocks and one detachment had mounted a red handkerchief upon one of the wooden rails, by way of a 'bloody flag'. The mob swept through the Irish lodgings leaving a trail of misery and destruction. Order was eventually restored by the Westmoreland & Cumberland Yeomanry Cavalry under the direction of the local magistrates.[82]

The worst incident had been an assault on Mclevi's lodging-house, Penrith. One by one, the Irish were driven out to be beaten, 'the same as they would beat a rat'. The magistrates and railway police took an even-handed approach in rounding up suspects and in trying to get the Irish re-started on railway work south of Penrith.

Similar incidents took place on the Edinburgh & Hawick and the Chester & Holyhead lines. Persistent trouble was almost entirely confined to lines where the Irish were prominent in the workforce and represented a visible target for the suspicions of Scots and English troublemakers. Particular incidents captured the headlines and tended to reinforce the reputation of navvies for riot and disorder.[83] These incidents were usually associated with bouts of excessive drinking, something for which the Irish were notorious.

However, the heavy drinking was all of a piece with other forms of arduous physical labour and was institutionalised by the custom of long payment at the end of the month and the infamous 'truck' system. Dr Brooke puts the sporadic disorder in which navvies were involved on a relatively modest scale compared with the Reform Riots of 1831, or the anti-police resistance in Yorkshire in the 1840s. He concludes that 'given his physical attributes and the huge potential for destruction inherent in the numbers of men involved . . . the navvy was an irresolute and unheroic rioter'.[84]

From a broader perspective. one might emphasise the common elements amongst Irish, English and Scots navvies. Treble poses the question whether navvies felt isolated, even outcast from civilised society by their brutalising and dangerous work. Patrick MacGill, Irish navvy, poet and writer, provides a personal view from his own experiences in Scotland:

> the men who braved this task were outcasts of the world. A blind fate, a vast merciless mechanism, cut and shaped the fabric of our existence. We were men flogged to the work which we had to do, and hounded from the work which we had accomplished. We were men despised when we were most useful, rejected when we were most needed, and forgotten when our troubles weighed upon us heavily. We were the men sent out to fight the spirit of the wastes, rob it of all its primeval horrors, and batter down the barriers of its world-old defences. Where we were working a new town would spring up some day; it was already springing up and then, if one of us walked there, 'a man with no fixed address', he would be taken up and tried as a loiterer and vagrant.[85]

Navvies shared a common experience of danger and privation, and were united by a sense of injustice and exploitation.

Sustained by high wages when contract work was available, navvies created a rough camaraderie which was greater than the racial antipathies that surfaced during the years of railway mania.

Apart from Royal Commission reports and studies that have illuminated the experience of particular groups of workers or the occupational distribution of individual towns, two major surveys conducted in 1872 and 1892 make a valuable contribution to our knowledge of the condition of Irish labour. Dr Alan O'Day has edited a series of weekly newspaper articles entitled 'The Irish in England', written by Hugh Heinrick, that appeared in the *Nation* in 1872. John Denvir's *The Irish in Britain*, published in 1892, included a similar survey at the end of a long historical account.[86] For our purpose, the value of the two works is that they provide unusual detail on the Irish in communities both large and small, throughout all the regions of England, and in Denvir's case in Scotland as well. Both are written from an unashamedly partisan commitment to faith and fatherland. Irish virtues are enthusiastically proclaimed and the numbers of Irish are almost certainly exaggerated. Nevertheless, there is real value not only in the detail provided but in having an Irish perspective to set alongside the heavy reliance on British sources and British opinion. Moreover, through reference to these two works, a number of themes may be explored which extend the discussion from the earlier sections of this chapter into a more general conclusion.

Heinrick and Denvir both provide ample evidence on the wide diversity of experience among the Irish who settled in Britain. Heinrick found very contrasting conditions facing the Irish in London. He found an English priest who echoed Henry Mayhew's testimony to the purity of Irish street-sellers. Despite being surrounded by the most degraded of the English poor, festering in vice, Irish coster-girls remained chaste. The extent to which Irish virtue remained unsullied was thought to be a marvel, but it had to be admitted that 'there are thousands—tens of thousands of the Irish people in London alone who are lost—lost irretrievably.'[87] Poverty and drink were seen as the twin evils that led them to degradation and destruction. Ironically, whereas English commentators in the 1830s had feared the contamination of the poor Irish coming into their cities, here was an Irishman in the 1870s, deploring the threat to the virtuous Irish immigrants of the immoral English. Perception is all important:

The young girl fresh from Ireland is forced, from her poverty, on arrival into positions most detrimental to her safety. The lower middle-class, the small shopkeepers—often devoid of religion and morals—or the still lower and more demoralised Jews of Spitalfields and Whitechapel, are the chief employers of the unsophisticated Irish girl when she first arrives in London. She is strong and willing, goes for low wages and not over fastidious in matters of food and accommodation, and hence she becomes the prey of the mercenary and immoral classes I have pointed out. In multitudes of cases the end is as might be anticipated. The virtuous Irish girl is ruined. She is degraded in her own estimation, and sinks into lower depths still, till, in the end, the bright and blooming Irish girl who left her native village as pure as the breeze on the heather of her native hills, with the benediction of the old priest who counselled and guided her from childhood on her head, and the fond wishes of generous friends and devoted parents following her in the land of the stranger, sinks broken-hearted and lost beneath the burden of her sin (verily, indeed, more sinned against than sinning), her young spirit sullied and defiled, her young life trampled out in the triumph of vice in its never-ending heartless procession.[88]

Certainly this describes the real-life experiences of many unfortunate young Irish women in Victorian London, but it also reflects the anxiety of an older, rural and religious culture being undermined in the freer and more secular world of British cities.

Denvir takes up the same theme, quoting an 'eminent Irish dignitary of the Church in London' to the effect that an intermixing with the English population had produced 'an undoubted moral deterioration—even among those of purely Irish descent—during the past twenty years'.[89] At the same time, Denvir was more optimistic in describing the condition of Irish dockers in London. He estimated that the Irish had established a near monopoly among the stevedores, 'the skilled workmen' among the dock labourers. Nevertheless, it was a precarious living, subject to very real dangers. To provide against disability, the London Irish organised a 'Friendly Lead' as a form of benefit society based on licensed premises where something had to be spent 'for the good of the house', but this practice had recently been discontinued by the League of the Cross, a temperance organisation founded by Cardinal Manning.[90]

A sense of progress is also evident in Denvir's reference to the myth of the bulk of the Irish living in 'Irish quarters'. If it was the case formerly, it was not so now. 'Those who are compelled by circumstances to live in undesirable surroundings do not, perhaps, constitute one-tenth of the whole. As in other large towns these quarters are gradually disappearing. You find that our people are now spreading all over London, and in much healthier localities than formerly'.[91] Denvir also claimed that in the days of patronage, it was practically a case of 'no Irish need apply', but with a fair field and no favour, since the introduction of competitive examinations, Irishmen were bound to come to the front. This applied, in particular, to the civil service, among Customs officials, and to a large Irish contingent in the Government Ordnance Survey. According to Denvir, fair progress was being made. It was not uncommon for substantial shopkeepers and wholesale traders to have risen from the ranks of costermongers, while Irishmen were represented in every profession and calling in the capital—doctors, clergy, lawyers, actors, writers, painters and musicians.[92]

If London had the largest numbers of Irish, Liverpool had the highest proportion of Irish people of any town in England and was where, as Heinrick claimed in 1872, there lived 'a larger proportion of Irishmen who have risen to position and influence. Here one meets with Irish merchants and Irish manufacturers— Irish doctors and Irish lawyers—Irish tradesmen and businessmen of all classes—Irish priests and Irish teachers—to be counted by the score. . . . Indeed, everything considered, the Irish people in Liverpool have attained to a degree of prosperity and power eminently creditable to their industry and force of character— eminently discrediting to the actions of the insolent libellers who deny that the Irish people possess the qualities essential to material success.'[93]

Heinrick estimated that about one-fifth to one-sixth of the Irish of Liverpool were above the ranks of unskilled manual labour. Among these were a large class of some 3,500 stevedores, master-porters and warehousemen—who 'require a high order of intelligence as well as trained adaptability to their duties. So important is this class, and so essential to the daily requirements of the mercantile affairs of Liverpool, that a dispute with the merchants, ending in a suspension of work, would, for the time being, upset the whole commercial economy of the town.'[94] Heinrick also lauded Irishmen occupying official positions in the Customs, Excise and Post Office, as being of superior intelligence and integrity.

Virtues of another kind were found among the dock labourers, who offered the only commodity they had—'strong arms, broad shoulders, and brave hearts that are cheerful and jocund in the midst of toil'. A sentimental account celebrates the physical strength of Irish labourers, yet also mourns the inevitable loss of manly vigour brought on by heavy work:

> The whole line of docks, extending nearly six miles, swarms with Irish life. The leading men in the sheds—the first in many of the warehouses—the strongest men at the wrench— the most enduring in the stifling ships hold or the laborious and exhaustive sack-carrying, are Irishmen. There is, in truth, a marvellous amount of Irish power to be seen in the Liverpool Docks. The faint-hearted and the weakly endure not long: they are crushed out to make room for the resolute and strong—men full of heart and energy, who laugh at labour. But these in their turn become worn out, many by excessive toil, more by hard living combined with hard work. Many drop into easier positions when unable to bear the severest toil. Others pass into the hospital to linger and die.[95]

The irregularity of work, and the casual and intemperate habits that went with it, took a heavy toll in waste of life and great mortality. Corn-heavers and corn-carriers could expect from ten to twelve years; coal and salt-heavers nearly the same; working at the winches, jigger work, five years; general labour, fifteen years. Few could last after the age of fifty, and many lingered on in employment as bag and cotton menders or as watchmen. The Liverpool Docks wore out men more rapidly than work in the furnaces and in the mines.

Twenty years later Denvir tapped a similar vein in surveying the Irish in Liverpool. 'Irish intellect and Irish courage have, in thousands of cases' brought our people to their proper place in the social scale, but it only too often happens that adverse circumstances drive the great bulk of them to the hardest, the most precarious, and the worst paid employments in the English labour market.'[96] All too often a sentimental memory of 'home', and the neighbourly welcome to fresh emigrants from Ireland, had the effect of drawing newcomers into the same miserable conditions as the friends who had come over previously. Yet the Irish of Liverpool, Denvir claimed, also showed a remarkable aptitude for dealing. 'The steady Irishman, with a good wife, is frequently able to save enough to open a marine store, a coal yard or a small shop. By degrees he gets on, for, as a rule, our people are more quick-witted in bargaining than even the Jews— the difference being that Moses sticks to all he gets, while Pat's often too generous nature frequently lets go easily what he has won so hardly.'[97]

Here Denvir is clearly in the realm of fancy, and wishful thinking is evident in his claim that the success of Irish dealers in Liverpool shows that under the care of a native government 'ours would develop into a great commercial people'.[98] Yet in another sense Denvir correctly showed how the Irish moved up in small business, in classic immigrant fashion, when other areas of advancement were closed. He described the process of starting out as a general dealer with a few shillings of capital:

> He becomes a collector of rags, old ropes, bones, old metal, rabbit and hare skins, and other apparently waste materials, for which trade has its uses. Sometimes, he gives ready money for his purchases, sometimes he adopts the barter system, and gives, in exchange, crockery, or other articles useful in a household; and in this way, realises a double profit. By dint of pinching and screwing he is able to leave the hawking to others and to set up what is termed a 'marine store', where, instead of trudging about in search of trade, the trade comes to him. Along with this, in consequence of the barter system, many of these marine store dealers develop large businesses in china and crockery ware, hardware of every kind, fur, wool, and every conceivable article of trade and commerce.[99]

The great diversity of condition, among the Irish in London and Liverpool in 1872 and 1892, was repeated in the reporting of Irish communities throughout Britain. Heinrich noted how the Irish in Newcastle-upon-Tyne, who numbered over 30,000 by birth or descent in 1871, prospered in employment as dockers, in the mines, in iron foundries and as labourers in public works. The Irish were also prominent in Gateshead, Hebburn, Garrow, Wallsend and Howden, so that within ten miles of Newcastle, there were an estimated 83,000 Irish, making the fourth largest Irish settlement in England, after London, Liverpool and Manchester.[100] Furthermore, the Irish had become better accepted in the northeast than elsewhere. 'There is no town in England where labour has more resolutely maintained its rights, and none where the Irish labourer has more completely gained his recognised place in the ranks of his fellow work-men.'[101] Twenty years later Denvir had the same message. The Irish in Newcastle prospered as artisans in shipbuilding, ironworks and chemicals at a time of unprecedentedly good conditions.[102]

Both writers showed that the condition of the Irish was materially better in places where employment was available for women and children as well as for men. This applied to some of the Yorkshire cloth towns, like Keighley and Wakefield, where women and girls worked in the mills and men worked in the collieries or blast furnaces in the district.[103] Heinrick found wages were relatively good in the Yorkshire towns of Bradford and Halifax and, as a result, the state of the Irish population was satisfactory. As ever, the one prevailing vice was drunkenness, one of the pitfalls of life in the major cities.[104] Denvir also noted how the Irish were often better off living in smaller communities in Scotland. In Lanarkshire, where the Irish were employed in the collieries and blast furnaces, he was struck by the neatness of the cottages in places like Carluke and Carfin, where the one-storeyed cottages were made more cheerful by the small gardens at the front and back. These made a favourable contrast with the closes and wynds in which many Irish lived in Edinburgh, Glasgow and Dundee. In Airdrie, Denvir noticed that a number of 'our people' had attained tolerably good positions as shopkeepers and traders, and the number of Irish publicans and pawnbrokers was a feature of many Scottish towns.[105]

By contrast, Heinrich saw as degraded the general condition of the Irish in places as diverse as Hull, Burton-on Trent, Kidderminster and Nottingham, with low pay for dock labour, brewing, and in the carpet-making and lace-making industries.[106] Other contrasts, identified by Denvir, were found in the general character of Birmingham as compared with conditions in Liverpool and Manchester. In Birmingham, although the Irish-born population had fallen from 9,341 in 1851 to 7,086 in 1881, those who remained along with their offspring, had assimilated well. Birmingham was famous for its hod-carriers in the building industry at mid-century, and their sons were mostly found among the artisan class and making fair progress in various occupations. Their daughters still found employment in the manufacture of metal goods in Birmingham's workshop-based economy.[107] The Birmingham Irish, as also the London Irish, intermixed and intermarried with the general population to a far greater extent than was the case in Liverpool, Manchester and other northern towns. Denvir regretted the intermixture of Celt and Saxon as liable to produce a loss of faith, nationality and political force, thereby weakening the Irish community. However, this intermixture almost certainly followed on from the more variegated economy of Birmingham which was dominated by small-scale workplaces, compared with the larger-scale employment to be found in mill towns, coal towns or ports.

In assessing the level of conflict and hostility experienced by Irish labour in Britain, the overwhelming impression is that the frequency and ferocity of disturbances over employment had subsided from the peaks of sporadic violence that occurred between the 1830s and 1860s.

Looking back to the 1850s, Denvir quotes A. M. Sullivan's description of the Black Country where, in response to an Irish influx into Staffordshire, English miners 'rose up against them and tried to expel them by fire and sword. Many were killed, many were murdered in the works at night of whom no word was ever heard or trace ever found.' His informant said: 'If we went into a public-house to drink, and that an Englishman came in, we were struck dumb; if he asked for our pipe and didn't get it, he'd pull it out of our mouth. We dare say nothing, for there was neither law nor justice for an Irishman. Many changed their names. We got reckless, too, and used to drink and fight and riot, and would have gone wild and savage outright if it wasn't the mercy of God sent us a priest.'[108] In visiting the Black Country in 1872, Heinrich commented on the improvement in the relationship between the Irish and the English in the coal and iron mines. 'At one time, and not so long since both here and in Lancashire the English "pitmen" refused to permit the Irishmen to work in the mines, but now, in this district at least, differences of nationality rarely occasions a dispute, and prejudice never operates so as to shut out Irishmen from sharing in the mining labour of the district.'[109]

One of the handicaps faced by the Irish in the Black Country was that many newly-arrived immigrants could speak no English. However, towards the end of the century, the spread of educational opportunities and the more tolerant spirit that prevailed enabled Irish youth to become apprenticed to a trade, whereas a generation before they had been shut out.[110]

In conclusion, two general themes have emerged from this survey of Irish labour. First, Irish men and women experienced a wide diversity of conditions and attitudes in the labour market in Britain. That experience was shaped by their county of origin, the circumstances of migration, and the place of settlement. Labour experience was by no means uniform even in the same industry, and as towns differed in their economic structures, so the reception given to Irish labour correspondingly varied from place to place. Towns where employment was available for whole families—men, women and children—provided a better standard of living for Irish migrants. Where the Irish settled in centres of decaying industry or in declining trades, they were less fortunate. The Irish were found on the margins of the labour market dependent on the lowest wages and facing the worst conditions. They were also found establishing a near monopoly of certain kinds of employment, as stevedores in the docks or as bricklayers in the building industry. Predominantly members of the unskilled labour force, the Irish were also represented in many trades and professions. Moreover, within a generation of the famine migration there was less violent hostility to Irish settlers, and there was a degree of upward social mobility and assimilation into the host community.

Secondly, the surviving evidence available to historians of the Irish in Britain is written largely from the vantage point of the English and Scots, and the dominant voices are those of employers, clergymen and officials, who possessed a set of values formed by their place in the social structure and the particular interests they were concerned to defend. If they were anxious and fearful about the native working classes, they were naturally more alarmed by what they saw as a less civilised and unskilled immigrant force. In troubled times the Irish were a ready scapegoat for disorder, violence or industrial disputes. In these circumstances, it is not surprising that the Irish received a bad press when trouble broke out. Yet even in the absence of trouble, the Irish were judged by a set of values that were alien to them, and these perceptions by the host community have become so incorporated into our thinking that they have set the agenda for modern historians.

It is instructive to set alongside each other the Irish perceptions of Heinrick and Denvir on the one hand, and those of most English commentators on the other. The Irish emphasis is on faith, virtue, manliness, on a sense of community and nationality, and the Irish in Britain were celebrated according to how well they lived up to these qualities. To an Irishman, there was something awesome about the power of Irish labour in the Liverpool docks. Yet, judged by English standards of individual responsibility, a disdain for manual labour, and a craving for upward social mobility and respectability, the Irish labourer remained an inferior being from an inferior race. The fact that the Irish lauded qualities that were deplored by the English reinforced the stereotype of 'Paddy' as an ignorant, drunken and violent fellow, to be deeply embedded in our common culture. However, the essential diversity explored in the condition of Irish labour in this chapter suggests that the image disguised as much as it revealed about the working experience of Irish men and women in nineteenth-century Britain.

In the next chapter, the religious culture of Catholics and Protestants in Ireland is explored as a prelude to describing the experience of Irish migrants to Britain, who encountered not only sectarian hostility but an increasingly secular society.

4

Catholics and Protestants

The Protestant minister is in general a holy man, whom
God has not overwhelmed with work: he has twenty or so
thousand francs [£800] income, forty parishioners, and a
small gothic church, which is built at the top of the park.
The Catholic priest has a small house, a much smaller dinner,
five or six thousand parishioners who are dying of hunger and
share their last penny with him; and he fancies that this state
of things is not the best possible one. He thinks that if the
Protestant minister had a little less and the poor Catholic
population a little more, society would gain by it, and he is
amazed that five thousand Catholics are obliged to pay
twenty thousand francs in taxes to support the religion
of forty Protestants.
(Alexis de Tocqueville, 1835)

Ireland

The very high level of attendance at places of religious worship in modern Ireland, north and south, sets the Irish apart
from much of Western Europe, whether by comparison with
Catholic or with Protestant countries. Irish piety can be traced
back to Ireland in the nineteenth century, when the religious
divide became politicised so that religious and political allegiance
became closely bound together. Protestants, both Church of
Ireland and the dissenting denominations, Presbyterians, Baptists
and Methodists, increasingly became identified with the maintenance of the Union with Great Britain. Catholics, who formed
the overwhelming majority of the people of Ireland, progressively
identified with the nationalist aspiration of separation from
Westminster rule.

Since the introduction of the Penal Laws in the seventeenth century, Roman Catholics laboured under severe restrictions in civil rights and in the ownership of property.[1] The Protestant ascendancy was planted in Ireland to exercise political control over a turbulent people and to convert the native Irish to a Protestant allegiance. By exercising a monopoly of landownership, dominating the judiciary, and suppressing or excluding the Catholic majority from public office, British policy provoked a seemingly perverse rejection by the Catholics of what were seen as alien laws and an alien religion. In closely aligning British interests with the exclusive needs of the Protestant community, British governments fostered a deep hostility among the Irish Catholic population.

A conversation between the British economist, Nassau Senior and Mr Revans, Secretary of the Irish Poor Law Commission, recorded by Alexis de Tocqueville, the French writer, who visited Ireland in 1835, neatly summarises the political context of religious parties in Ireland:

S. The spirit of party is very strong in Ireland?

R. To a point that it would be almost impossible for you to conceive. It would take a foreigner ten years to understand the parties. Party spirit pervades everything, but particularly in the administration of justice. To tell the truth, there is no justice in Ireland. Nearly all the local magistrates are at open war with the population. Moreover, the population has no idea of public justice. In Ireland nearly all justice is extra-legal. Unless Englishmen are sent to serve as judges, it will remain the same there. The jury system is almost impracticable in Ireland.

S. Why do the Irish have such a great hatred for us?

R. Above all because we have always sustained the Orangemen, whom they consider as their oppressors.

S. Of what is the Catholic party composed?

R. Of nearly all the people. But very few wealthy and educated men are met with in this party, which has always been oppressed. That is a great misfortune.[2]

Commonly, Protestant Englishmen were suspicious of Roman Catholicism, not only because of ancient association with treachery in league with foreign powers, but also because of profound objections to the doctrines and practices of the Church.[3] The novelist, Thackeray, when visiting Ireland in 1842, commented on the strong attachment of the people to their religious faith, but in a tone of lofty condescension and disapproval of what was regarded as barbarous and superstitious. With no little trepidation, he visited the Ursuline Convent at Cork to be confronted by the awesome presence of nuns, 'in their mysterious robes and awful veils. . .':

> Here I was in a room with a real live nun, pretty and pale—I wonder has she any of her sisterhood immured in *oubliettes* down below; is her poor little weak, delicate body scarred all over with scourgings, iron-collars, hair-shirts? What has she had for dinner to-day?—as we passed the refectory, there was a faint sort of vapid nunlike vegetable smell, speaking of fasts and wooden platters; and I could picture to myself silent sisters eating their meal—a grim old yellow one in the reading desk, croaking out an extract from a sermon for their edification.[4]

Thackeray's fevered imagination conjured up a host of sinister spectres that were drawn from the stock-in-trade of popular Protestant novels. Yet he was almost certainly mistaken, not merely in indulging his prejudice but in overestimating the influence of the Church in the pre-famine period.

D.W. Miller, using data collected by the Commissioners of Public Instruction in Ireland in 1834, shows that religious observance varied significantly between Irish-speaking and English-speaking districts and, moreover, was much lower throughout Ireland than modern practice would suggest.[5] He contrasts the attendance rate in the diocese of Kilmacduagh, centred on the town of Gort, adjoining Galway Bay, where 75 per cent of the population still spoke Irish as late as 1851, with an entirely English-speaking area of County Wexford, bordering the Irish Sea. The level of attendance in the Gaelic-speaking western district ranged between 25.1 and 31.7 per cent, whilst the English-speaking eastern district recorded a figure of 71.9 per cent of the population attending mass on a typical Sunday. Although extreme cases, these two examples were representative of a general trend that revealed Catholics to be more faithful in attendance at mass in English-speaking rural areas than in the Gaeltacht. Generally, attendance rates in the former were in the 30–60 per cent range. These compare with attendance rates varying between 20–40 per cent in Irish-speaking districts.

Even these broad generalisations conceal considerable diversity of practice. Miller found that adjoining Catholic parishes in County Louth recorded figures of 67.8 and 36.1 per cent attendance rates. Rural areas also differed from the towns, where a pattern of more universal mass attendance was beginning to show up. Derry, Drogheda, Clonmel, Kilkenny and Waterford recorded very high attendance figures, varying from 73.8 per cent to almost 100 per cent. Yet the four largest towns in Ireland, Dublin, Cork, Belfast and Limerick, appeared to have much lower attendance rates, ranging from 40 to 60 per cent. A possible explanation lies in the Church's difficulties in providing sufficient clergy to meet the needs of the population, once town sizes rose above 25,000. Certainly Belfast had only one priest for every 4,000 Catholics, and shared the problem of lower attendance common to industrial cities in Britain.

Miller concludes his analysis of attendance figures by arguing that native Irish culture did not sustain modern Irish piety. Traditionally, the advance of the English language and the whole process of economic and social modernisation of Ireland have been viewed as a threat to the religious faith of the people. He dismisses the explanations of inadequate numbers of priests and the long journeys demanded of the laity across mountain or bog in the far western districts. Even where such factors did not operate, as in Valentia Island, off the coast of Kerry, where virtually all the 2,703 Catholic inhabitants were concentrated in an area of 6.2 square miles and were served by one centrally-placed church, only a third of the people attended.

By way of further explanation, Miller distinguishes between the canonical and customary aspects of Irish peasant religion, and shows that religious customs were often accompanied by 'high spirited revelry'. An absence of clerical direction allowed unorthodox forms of devotion and an unbridled use of secular amusements. In some cases, the clergy successfully transformed old Celtic practices into a Christian form, but many remained unaffected by the teachings of the Church. A famous example of the christianising process is the Croagh Patrick pilgrimage in County Mayo which originally celebrated the Celtic Lughnasa festival to mark the beginning of the harvest season.

Thackeray, while staying for a few days in Westport in 1842, recorded the strange amalgam of penitence and acute suffering in the pattern at Croagh Patrick. The steep ascent of Ireland's

holy mountain, barefoot to the three 'stations', and the perambu-
lations around the heaps of stones, seven, fifteen, and a further
seven times, praying on their knees at each turn, left the wretched
penitents 'suffering severe pain, wounded and bleeding in the
knees and feet, and some of the women shrieking with the pain
of their wounds'.[6]

Thackeray did not actually witness the proceedings but took
the details from an informant who clearly supplied the information
a Protestant Englishman wanted to hear. This did not prevent
Thackeray's indignant outburst:

> Fancy thousands of these bent upon their work, and priests
> standing by to encourage them!—for shame, for shame. If
> all the popes, cardinals, bishops, hermits, priests, and
> deacons that ever lived were to come forward and preach
> this as a truth—that to please God you must macerate your
> body, that the sight of your agonies is welcome to Him, and
> that your blood, groans, and degradation find favour in His
> eyes, I would not believe them. Better have over a company
> of Fakeers at once, and set the Suttee going.[7]

Although the priests were clearly in control of the penitents
processing up and down Croagh Patrick, traditional merriment
took over, once they arrived at its foot. For those able to enjoy
them, there was music, dancing, love-making, booths selling huge
biscuits, doubtful-looking ginger beer, cauldrons full of boiling
water for tea and others for cooking legs of mutton. Thus traditional celebration of the start of the harvest season continued
alongside the Christian processions in the name of St Patrick.

Miller suggests that the customary and canonical sides of
Irish peasant religion coexisted happily enough in that some
nominal participation in canonical practice was thought necessary for the enjoyment of customary celebrations. Contemporary
accounts of travellers in Ireland could easily exaggerate the
religious devotion of the peasantry. Alexis de Tocqueville in 1835
was told by the parish priest of Newport-Pratt, County Mayo, of
the regular confessions of his ten thousand flock, but the weekly
attendance at mass in the 1834 census was relatively low, ranging
from 16.5 to 38.7 per cent of the population.[8]

The customary elements within Irish peasant religion were
bound up with the agricultural seasons, starting with St Brigid's
Day (the ancient festival of Imbolc, 1st February) and St Patrick's
Day (17 March), the beginning of sowing, through to Lughnasa

(1st August), the beginning of harvest, and Hallowe'en (31 October), the return of cattle from summer grazing. Magical rites and superstitions were bound up with these festivals. The use of good luck charms, like St Brigid's crosses, woven from rushes, accompanied by festive celebration with much drinking and dancing, formed an essential part of pre-famine culture. Saints' days' celebrations or patterns and pilgrimages were central to communal life. Thousands flocked to the most popular sites, such as Lough Derg in Donegal, often in search of cures from holy wells or the scene of spectacular miracles. There were some 3,000 known holy wells throughout Ireland, often pre-Christian in origin, and accommodated by the Church by the addition of a cross and a saint's name.[9] The fusion of Christian doctrines and magical superstitions was most evident at times of crisis. Fear of the spread of the cholera epidemic in June 1832 prompted reports that the Virgin Mary had appeared in person, to distribute tokens that would protect people from the disease.[10]

The epic scale of the lost harvests in successive years during the Great Famine brought a consequent loss of faith in traditional beliefs. The apparent failure of charms and magical rites to prevent the starvation and death of perhaps a million souls, and the emigration of a further million, explains why the old forms and customs began to die away. Sir William Wilde lamented the loss of traditional beliefs and practices:

> the festivals are unobserved, and the rustic festivities neglected or forgotten . . . The pilgrimages formerly undertaken to holy wells and sacred shrines for cures and penances have been strenuously interdicted . . . The fairies, the whole pantheon of Irish demigods are retiring, one by one, from the habitation of man to the distant islands where the wild waves of the Atlantic raise their foaming crests, to render their fastnesses inaccessible to the schoolmaster and the railroad engineer . . .'[11]

The clergy were able to fill the void left by the loss of faith in traditional magical rites. A reformed Catholic Church, subject to what Professor Emmet Larkin has styled a 'devotional revolution', helped the rural peasantry to come to terms with the harsh realities of post-famine Ireland.[12] If the threat of starvation receded after 1850, despite the renewed famine in the west in the 1870s, there remained the important struggles for land reform and for a national Irish identity. The clergy allied themselves with the peasants' fight for security of tenure, and although leading church-men condemned the worst excesses of the Fenians and the Land League, the Church remained at one with its people in advocating their cause.

The 'devotional revolution', presided over by Cardinal Cullen, the leading churchman in Ireland in the mid-nineteenth century, was made possible by a sharp improvement in clerical discipline and a greater clerical presence among the Catholic population. The Church insisted on a more regular discharge of canonical duties and succeeded in winning acceptance for the full panoply of devotional exercises. Larkin draws a distinction between the ratio of priests to population before and after the famine. In 1840, there were some 2,150 priests ministering to 6.5 million Catholics, a ratio of 1:3,000. By 1900, there were some 3,700 priests for a population of 3,300,000, or a ratio of 1:900 Catholics.[13] The famine and the subsequent emigration over the next half century helped the Church to exercise a closer control over the faithful. This was in contrast with a worsening ratio of clergy to people in England, where all the Churches struggled in vain to cope with a rapidly expanding and increasingly urban population.

Broadly, the analysis proferred by Miller and Larkin serves as useful guide to the national developments as affecting the Catholic clergy and the Catholic peasantry in Ireland. The importance of the famine in the erosion of traditional folk magic, and the 'devotional revolution' that transformed the Church, are viewed as key influences in the modernisation of religious practice in the nineteenth century. However, from the standpoint of assessing the religious outlook and practice of Irish migrants to Britain, this broad analysis may be qualified in a number of ways.

First, it is quite clear that the process of modernisation that included the use of the English language, the decline in the belief of Celtic magic, and the changing patterns of marriage and fertility, was more advanced among urban than rural communities and in the east of Ireland as compared with the south and western counties. Lynn Lees quotes the evidence of travellers and early folklorists, in suggesting that the persistence of a world view based on magic was closely linked to social status, language, and area of residence.[14] T. Crofton Croker recorded that traditional beliefs in fairies still existed in the southern counties in the 1820s.[15] Others witnessed an increasing scepticism about the belief in fairies during the 1840s and 1850s. Jeremiah Curtin records a

Dingle farmer recalling his boyhood when nine out of ten men believed in fairies, but by the 1880s only one in ten believed in them.[16]

Clearly the results of a complex process of social change affected different social groups and different regions. By the 1860s in Limerick, the modernisation process had reached the children of prosperous farmers, who were taught the orthodox Catholic religion, and their parents dismissed the tales of fairies and witches as imaginary or fanciful. Yet the uneducated poor, whilst attending mass, still retained a belief in the magic of charms and a fear of evil spirits.[17] Kerby Miller argues that the Irish Catholic world view was so deep-seated that while some of the forms may have disappeared, the fatalism that stemmed from ancient Gaelic culture remained as part of the culture of exile that the emigrants took with them abroad.[18] This mentality was not confined to the early nineteenth century but persisted, well into the twentieth century. Miller cites the example of the autobiography of a labourer in post-war Britain, who reported that to many of his fellow navvies, Cromwell and the Penal Laws were still held responsible for Ireland's contemporary problems and their own need to work in Britain.[19]

Perhaps the key factor was the survival of the Irish language in which traditional folk tales naturally circulated. The rich oral literature of Irish folklore did not translate easily into English. Whereas the English language ushered in a new outlook for three-quarters of the population, the continued importance of the Irish language in parts of Kerry, Clare, Galway and Mayo, where three-fifths still spoke Irish in 1851, preserved not only the oral tradition but the traditional beliefs in magic and superstition. Indeed, the belief in fairies continued well into the twentieth century in parts of the northern, western and southern counties of Ireland.[20]

Secondly, the revival of orthodox Catholicism was not uniformly felt throughout all sections of Irish society, nor was the Famine such a decisive watershed as D.W. Miller has claimed. Elizabeth Malcolm sees the Famine coming at the end of a process that had been under way for some time. She argues that the Church had been suppressing patterns in the early 1800s and had successfully reduced the number of holy days from 30 to 10 by 1830. From the 1790s to the 1840s, before the Famine and before the period of Cullen's leadership, the clergy were in the forefront of those destroying the old religious practices.[21] Moreover, Sheridan Gilley has pointed to the greatest impact before 1840, as among the urban middle class and more prosperous farmers, from whose sons were drawn the new recruits to the priesthood and religious orders. After the Famine, these social groups prospered, freed from the burden of maintaining the two million poor Irish who died or emigrated. By 1860 a more disciplined and reinvigorated Catholic Church, led by Cullen, was able to impose an orthodox doctrine upon all Catholics in Ireland. These developments had an important influence upon the emigrant Irish. As Gilley explains, the chronology was quite crucial: 'The transformation of the Irish background suggests that migrants were better schooled in a revitalised Ultramontane and "modern faith" in 1840 than in 1790, and in 1890 than in 1840, so that the later the date of their emigration, the more likely they were to carry their religion over into their new surroundings.'[22] By implication, following Gilley's point about chronology, it mattered where migrants moved from, whether Irish or English-speaking, urban or rural areas, whether migrants were literate or not, and from what layer of society. The religious outlook of migrants to Britain was likely to be determined by a mixture of all these factors.

Those who migrated to Britain before 1861, the peak year of the Irish-born living in Britain, probably took with them many of the traditional folk beliefs and superstitions, perhaps mixed with varying degrees of Catholic orthodoxy. The chronology of migration points to the balance being in favour of magic and superstition rather than orthodox belief.

Another part of the religious baggage emigrants took with them to Britain was the legacy of the sectarian divide in Ireland. The upsurge of new sectarian tensions has been traced to County Armagh in the 1780s.[23] With roughly equal numbers of Protestants and Catholics in south Ulster, economic rivalry over land-holding and in the production of linen textiles, was expressed in sectarian conflict. While the principal restrictions on the ownership of land were being removed in the Catholic Relief Acts of 1772, 1778 and 1782, and a greater license was given to Catholic clergy and to Catholic schools, the laity found new opportunities for an improved economic status in linen manufacture. By the 1780s, Protestant weavers in Armagh had suffered a declining status, losing their independence as producers and being reduced to the condition of a rural proletariat. To compensate for their declining position, they formed secret societies like the 'Peep of Day Boys' which made violent attacks on Catholic neighbours, over whom they had enjoyed a traditional superiority. Recent studies point to the particular circumstances of south Armagh in the origins of sectarian violence but, from the 1790s, such violence was to spread throughout most of Ireland.[24]

The Protestant 'Peep of Day Boys' were countered by the Catholic Defenders. Where there were fewer Protestants, as in north Leinster and Connaught, secret societies focused on economic issues: tithes, taxes and occupation of the land. In Ulster, sectarianism was caught up in the struggle between the radical movement and the established government. Inspired by the French Revolution, Catholic Defenders forced an alliance with the United Irish society in 1795. In the same year, Protestants organised themselves into a new force, the Orange Order, to protect their political and economic supremacy. The militant and plebeian Orange Order was regarded, initially, with distaste by the landed gentry, but as the United Irishmen and Defenders were seen as a growing threat, Orangemen were used to counter this threat—of internal disorder and foreign invasion.

Many of the United Irishmen were northern Presbyterians, allied to the Catholics in the common cause of parliamentary reform, but the violence that accompanied the 1798 Rebellion exacerbated sectarian divisions. Irish Methodists publicised sensational accounts of Catholic atrocities at Gorey and Wexford, which had the effect of turning Methodism towards an allegiance to Church and King. Thereafter, at times of Catholic pressure, as in the emancipation campaign in the 1820s, Methodists cited 1798 as a reminder of Catholic persecution of Protestants.

Methodists launched their own crusade with the establishment of the Methodist Mission in 1799. Granted special privileges as itinerant preachers, three Gaelic-speaking missionaries were enjoined to travel throughout the country converting Catholics, in the belief that wholesale conversion was the only path to a peaceful Ireland. The message was delivered in the conviction that the Gospel was the sole means of true enlightenment for 'a deluded and morally corrupt people'. The mission field of Ireland was claimed to offer a divinely ordained opportunity to rescue three million people from ignorance and superstition.

By 1816, there were 21 missionaries operating throughout Ireland, supported by the Wesleyan Missionary Committee in

London. David Hempton describes the amazing traffic of gospel men crossing over the Irish Sea. Irish evangelicals came to England in search of financial aid, recounting terrible persecutions and claiming wonderful successes.[25] Many other societies swelled the missionary ranks with preachers and an avalanche of religious tracts pouring into Ireland. Between them, the London Hibernian Society and the Hibernian Bible Society distributed over 400,000 Testaments and Bibles from 1806 to 1823, while the Religious Book and Tract Society for Ireland claimed, in 1823, to have issued 1,160,000 tracts and 86,000 books since 1819.[26] The sectarian divide that re-opened in the 1780s in Ulster, under the strains of industrial dislocation, was deepened by the onslaught of English evangelicalism in the early 1800s. Buoyed up by economic and military success in the Napoleonic Wars, evangelicalism assumed the certainty of a divine mission to convert Catholic Ireland.

By the 1820s, sectarian hatred had intensified. The earlier missionary euphoria had given way to a defensive mania. Scaremongering letters to English Methodists predicted the massacre of all Protestants in Ireland. The spectre of Catholic Emancipation threatened to destroy the Protestant Church. In the event, far from converting Catholic Ireland, the Methodist missionaries prompted a Catholic resurgence in the early nineteenth century. Although, the revival of Irish Catholicism may be viewed as part of a wider, Ultramontane movement throughout the century, it possessed its own native characteristics that were shaped by the political and economic dependence on Britain.

Among the Catholic poor of rural Ireland, anti-Protestant feeling was reinforced in the recurrent agrarian disorder of the first half of the century. The tithes levied on agriculture to support the Protestant Church of Ireland remained a bitter grievance up to 1838. The suppression of agrarian disturbance by a largely Protestant Yeomanry, county police and regular army, produced a continual resentment against brutal treatment and partisan justice. The work carried out by the military inevitably made for unpopularity. Not merely the search for illegal arms among suspected rebels, or the recourse to violence when challenged by an impoverished peasantry, but also the seizure of illicit stills and the distraining of goods for non-payment of rent or tithes— all these reinforced sectarian bitterness.

Faced with an oppressive system of government in which Irish people were grossly under-represented, a system of landownership which condemned the labouring poor to a bare subsistence, and an alien, Protestant Church that taxed the great majority of Catholics, it is little wonder that millenarian ideas flourished among the Catholic lower classes. Since the Middle Ages, a belief in the imminence of Christ's second coming to overthrow the oppressor and to deliver the faithful had been a common response among door societies in times of upheaval and deprivation.[27] The prophecies of Pastorini, the most famous millenarian of the time, had a powerful appeal during the typhus epidemic in 1817, and again during the threatened famine of the early 1820s. Pastorini encouraged Catholics to believe that the Protestant Churches would be totally destroyed in the year 1825, three hundred years after the persecutions by Protestant reformers in 1525. The Book of Revelations had foretold that after 300 years of tormenting the faithful, the locusts from the bottom of the pit would be annihilated. Other prophecies held that a general massacre of Catholics in Ulster by the Protestant clergy would be followed by a league of Catholic nations forming to stamp out heresy in Ireland and throughout Great Britain.

Donnelly matches the regional extent of Pastorini's influence with the areas where Ribbonmen flourished in 1819 and 1820. They were strongest in Roscommon, and east Galway, spreading to Mayo, Clare, King's County and Westmeath. From the west midlands, the movement spread to Munster. The geographical spread of millenarianism, which incorporated economic grievances and a militant sectarianism, is suggested in the following apocalyptic rallying cry:

> Ye sons, arise and take up arms, and join if only three remain; they shall have from Dingle to Carrick-on-Suir as a property to be happy with; tear Orangemen and Protestants to pieces; dethrone King George, and his own soldiers shall rebel and join the rebels.[28]

Pamphlets printed in Dublin and Cork were distributed by pedlars and itinerant schoolmasters throughout the south and west. Other, simpler versions of Pastorini's prophecies were converted into the form of popular ballads to become part of a sectarian folk culture. A spirited rendering of 'We will wade knee-deep in Orange blood and fight for liberty', sung in a public house in Rathkeale, County Limerick in 1824, not surprisingly attracted the attention of the local police, but was a public manifestation of a widespread belief in deliverance.[29] Such rebel songs were also a response to the'Protestant triumphalism', celebrated in Orange Order marches where loyalist tunes like 'The Boyne Water' and 'The Protestant boys' often provoked violence and disorder.

It seems that where there were fairly equal numbers of Protestants and Catholics, as in Limerick and Tipperary, there was a greater likelihood of head-on violence. In the Rockite burning of Glenasheen, near Kilmallock in 1823, the sectarian attack was directed against German Palatinates who had settled in the early eighteenth century. When faced with Catholic animosity, many emigrated from Limerick in the 1820s. Those committing such attacks faced serious consequences, if caught. The police maintained a strict supervision of traditional gatherings, breaking up country dances, scattering mourners at wakes, and clearing pubs by the use of bayonets. After dark, a curfew was imposed as in a state of emergency, with transportation the likely punishment for offenders. As in the troubled industrial districts of England, the authorities employed informers and spies in an attempt to stir up trouble and to bring out the ringleaders. The importation into the disturbed districts of southern Ireland of great numbers of Protestant soldiers who marched to fill the Protestant churches on Sundays, further intensified sectarian feeling.

In turn, murderous threats were issued against the army and police, and intimidation was employed against civilians. In 1823 a Protestant resident of Pallaskenry, County Limerick, received the following message, after his out-offices were burnt down:

> This is to show all hereticks the way that we will serve them, and to show them that they are not to put their trust in the Peelers or Army, for when they are asleep, we will be awake, and let all the bloody Orangemen of Pallas know that we are preparing for them against the first of July, and let them not boast of the forty thousand, for this is the death they may all expect.[30]

The proximity of the Second Coming provided intensity and purpose to such threats. Donnelly, whilst acknowledging the limits to our understanding of the millenarian revolt, suggests that cultural continuity existed between the millenarianism of the early 1820s and O'Connell's Catholic Association. 'King Dan' was believed by the Catholic peasantry to be the deliverer, who would fulfil the prophecy and destroy Protestantism. As evidence, he cites the well-known song, 'The Catholic Rent', sung to the air of St Patrick's Day, which has O'Connell scattering heretics, as foretold by Pastorini.[31]

Following this brief survey of popular religious culture in Ireland, during the first half of the nineteenth century, a few key points define the framework of religious inheritance that Irish migrants brought to Britain. Firstly, there was the diversity of religious practice in different parts of Ireland, not merely between Catholic, Anglican, and dissenting denominations, but also between English-speaking and Irish-speaking districts, urban and rural areas, and between large and small towns, in terms of recorded levels of attendance at a place of worship. Further diversity was evident within the Catholic population in the extent of modernisation as against the belief in folklore and Celtic magic.

Secondly, the process of modernisation, which began in the early part of the century, with the clergy attempting to clamp down on peasant superstition and unorthodox practice, had most effect among farmers and urban tradesmen and least among the labouring poor. Moreover, the influence of Cardinal Cullen's 'devotional revolution' must have come too late for the majority of the Irish migrating to Britain.

Thirdly, the wave of mass emigration that followed the end of the French Wars, in the period from 1815 to 1840, drew much of its strength from the decaying textile areas of Ulster and from rural Leinster and the midland counties. Consequently, a relatively high proportion of Irish Protestants found their way to the west of Scotland, to Liverpool, and to the textile towns of northern England. Before 1830, most of the London Irish migrated from Leinster, while, after the Famine, more emigrants came from Munster. The Irish in Britain were predominantly drawn from the central and eastern counties of Ireland.

Fourthly, religious conflict in the form of sectarian violence was a part of the popular culture. Yet it was not a uniform condition throughout Ireland, nor where sectarianism was most evident did it spring from the same causes or take the same forms. If head-on violence was most likely in communities where there was a roughly equal division between Catholics and Protestants, the experience of a reinvigorated Catholicism and a militant Orangeism in County Armagh was quite different from the millenarianism of the Catholic assault on 'heresy' in the midland, and southern counties.

Finally, and this is only now receiving serious attention, there was the problem of the non-practising Irish, who represented a very sizeable proportion of Irish migrants to Britain. Alongside the obvious economic forces that promoted migration, it is reasonable to assume that a serious motivation was the desire to escape from sectarian strife and the accompanying intimidation by neighbours, that people fled from religious oppression of whatever kind. Emigration to Britain was not merely in search of better economic opportunities, it offered the prospect of emancipation from a restricting, religious control. It is no coincidence that the most Anglicised and most commercially advanced parts of Ireland bred such individual attitudes among young people.

Britain

What impact did predominantly Catholic migrants have upon the English Catholic Church? Did Ireland, as Gerard Connolly asks, export a greater proportion of modern 'devout' Catholics from Leinster and Munster to sustain, as legend has it, a flagging native Catholicism in England?[32] Connolly finds no easy answer to the question, but at the present state of knowledge it can be asserted that the answer would depend on which city and in which decade the question was directed. Religious diversity in Ireland was compounded by the variety of the religious structures and provision that faced Irish migrants to Britain.

The English contrast with what happened to Ireland in the second half of the country could not have been more pronounced, and therefore provided a very different context for religious organisations pursuing their respective missions. In Ireland, the Catholic population was halved while the numbers of clergy increased, and a spectacular success was achieved in the very high levels of church attendances recorded by the end of the century. In England, the number of baptised Catholics increased eightfold, so demanding a huge increase in the provision of clergy, schools, chapels and religious houses. In the circumstances, what was accomplished at the end of the century by the English

Catholic Church may be judged as no less spectacular than the corresponding achievements in Ireland.[33]

A good deal of historical writing on the plight of Irish migrants in Britain has been presented as an epic struggle fought against overwhelming odds. It forms part of the nationalist story which depicts the Catholic Church as playing a vital role in establishing and sustaining Irish communities in Britain, maintaining a form of cultural continuity through a close identification between priest and people in the urban slums, and moulding the Catholic and Irish dimension into a single identity. The conventional script has the Catholic Church helping to preserve Irish traditions but at the same time advancing the moral condition of the Catholic poor in Victorian cities. Cast as central heroes were the missionary priests, who first ministered to poor Irish immigrants in sheds, upstairs rooms or disused shops. They faced hostility and even physical violence from local Protestants, who were deeply suspicious of Catholic ritual and the ambivalence of religious loyalty to Rome. Yet when the curtain comes down on the end of the century, the English Catholic Church has become reinvigorated and firmly established within the hierarchy of the religious establishment.[34]

If this sounds a rather hollow endorsement, it is not to question the heroic work of Catholic priests among Irish communities in Victorian Britain. Rather, it is to confront the issue of non-practising Irish Catholics who lived in the more concentrated Irish quarters and were found scattered throughout every district of Victorian cities. For some authorities[35], the influence of the Catholic Church extended beyond those who attended mass regularly to the bulk of non-practising 'Catholics' who retained the 'ancient faith of the Irish' and were, by reason of temperament and culture, regarded as 'instinctive Catholics'.[36] It is a vital point because if we are to accept that the Catholic Church was the chief agency for sustaining Irish cultural life in mainland Britain, it is only by ignoring *half* the Catholic Irish who rejected its ministry. Is it too narrow a definition that excludes people from religious allegiance merely on the measure of regular attendance? Or is it too sentimental to include the Irish who failed to observe their religion in any public fashion? It is not a problem confined to the Catholic or Protestant Irish. For contemporary Victorians, no less than for modern historians, it remains a lively subject of concern.[37]

Gerard Connolly has outlined a broad picture of the Catholic faithful in England and Wales, distinguishing, from among an estimated total of baptised Catholics, an average level of regular worship and the remainder of non-practising Irish. Taking the Irish population, by birth and descent, as 1.5 million in England and Wales, minus an estimated 300,000 Protestants, leaves 1.2 million as the total figure of the Catholic Irish. If an average attendance figure of 50 per cent is accepted, then the Catholic faithful emerge as approximately 600,000. However, this figure represents the peak of Catholic renewal and a very considerable improvement on the low levels of religious observance during the early decades of mass Irish migration to Britain.[38]

In London, various estimates put the level of Catholic attendance at between 25 and 30 per cent of the baptised population.[39] In Cardiff, despite the efforts of Catholic missions, only a quarter of Catholics performed their Easter duty in the period 1841 to 1861.[40] In Liverpool, barely a tenth of the 100,000 Catholic population practised their faith. The opening of St Patrick's in Irish Town, Manchester, the largest Irish community outside London or Liverpool, posed the familiar problem of filling it with the Catholic faithful.[41] W. J. Lowe found considerable variation in church attendance figures in seven Lancashire towns where there existed a relatively strong English Catholic presence. With most Irish emigrants to Lancashire forming part of the pre-famine generation of non-practising Catholics, Lowe argues that the strong commitment of the Catholic clergy assisted the migrant Irish to adjust to a more secular, urban way of life. Catholicism remained as an important source of continuity for those newly settled, whether from Gaelic or English-speaking parts of Ireland. Catholic schools acted as important agents of socialisation for the younger generation growing up in urban England. Yet Lowe's findings are striking not for showing the influences common to Irish Catholics in Lancashire, but for pointing out the different levels of attendance at mass in Liverpool, Manchester, Oldham, St Helen's, and Widnes. Liverpool recorded the lowest figures—48 per cent of Catholics attending mass regularly in 1855 and only 43 per cent in 1865. In Preston, where the Irish formed between a quarter and a third of all Catholics, attendance was as high as 63 per cent in 1855 and over 50 per cent in 1865, but was probably higher among the English rather than the Irish Catholics.[42] Why such differences occurred is difficult to explain.

The evidence of the figures appears to point to the specific influence of the size of the Irish presence in each town, which crucially affected the ability of the Catholic Church to provide priests, chapels and schools to match the need. The religious tradition or habit of casual piety that migrants brought with them must also have continued to shape their religious behaviour in England. Hugh Mcleod found that the previous rural patterns of English migrants to London, in the late Victorian period, showed up in varied patterns of urban attendance within the metropolis, the relatively high attendance of East Anglian migrants into north London contrasting with the lower attendance figures of migrants from counties to the south and west of London.[43] The other important influence lay with the particular character of each community affected by Irish settlement. A tradition of toleration and the presence of a wealthy, Catholic community could assist Irish Catholics to settle without the hostility that was met with in towns suffering severe economic dislocation.

It is also as well to recognise the natural inclination of religious historians to celebrate the progress of their particular faith. The perspective that develops from an absorption in ecclesiastical sources tends to reinforce instinctive loyalties. Given the story of the nineteenth-century struggle by Catholics and Protestant dissenters to remove restrictions on public life for those excluded from the Established Church, it is not surprising that a sentimental attachment runs deep. Inevitably, attention follows the outlook of the religious community, its hopes, fears and eventual triumphs against denominational rivals and an alarmingly sinful world. Quite understandably, the darker or unknown side of religious behaviour—the non-practising Catholics, for instance— has received comparatively little investigation, partly because its characteristics are more difficult to define or to discover in the available sources and, partly, because it does not fit the heroic mould of national and religious struggle.

Two broad trends may be identified in the religious experience of Irish Catholics in nineteenth-century Britain. An undue emphasis on one of them can give a misleading impression, whether of unqualified success or of abject failure.

The first, and best documented, is the improvement in the status and provision of the English Catholic Church. In many respects, it was able to rise to the challenge posed by the influx of Catholic Irish into British cities. From a very low base in the early decades of the century, the Church was able to accommodate and minister to practising Catholics, to instruct them into a Tridentine orthodox faith, and to provide a Catholic education for poor children and young adults in schools and confraternities. The very first provision for immigrant Irish Catholics was often extremely primitive, and only through the missionary zeal of Catholic ministers were the first humble steps taken:

> The very talented and zealous pastor of Merthyr Tydfil has under his care about 700 poor Irish, who are employed in the iron and coal works at Merthyr Tydfil and other places scattered at the distance of seven or eight miles around. He has no chapel, but says two Masses every Sunday; one at Merthyr, in a granary over a slaughter house, and the other at six miles distance (which he travels on foot) in a wash house. He has a school for about 50 poor children of both sexes, in a one-horse stable, about eight feet wide and sixteen feet long. His own dwelling is a workman's cottage, without a single article of decent furniture and often, it is feared, without a sufficiency of food . . .[44]

The classic story of the Catholic mission has been brilliantly reconstructed by Raphael Samuel. In a moving and, at times, sentimental study, Samuel describes the magnificent work of Catholic priests who devoted their lives to their ministry. Living among their parishioners, they gave advice on all matters, assisted with letters home to Ireland, found work and lodgings for newly arrived migrants, gave comfort to the sick and dying, and intervened in cases of violent disorder when the police were powerless to act. In short, priests acted as secular and religious leaders of their flock. Priests maintained a mystical authority in the community. Henry Mayhew, cited by Samuel, describes the priest on his rounds moving among the street Irish in London:

> Everywhere here the people ran out to meet him . . . women crowded to their door-steps, and came creeping up from the cellars through the trap-doors, merely to curtsey to him. One old crone, as he passed, cried, 'You're a good father, Heaven comfort you', and the boys playing about stood still to watch him. . . . At a conversation that took place between the priest and a woman who kept a dry fish-stall, the dame excused herself for not having been up to take tea

'with his rivrince's mother lately, for thrade had been so busy, and night was the fullest time.' Even as the priest walked along the street, boys running at full speed would pull up to touch their hair, and the stall women would rise from their baskets; while all the noise—even a quarrel— ceased until he had passed by. Still there was no look of fear in the people. He called them all by their names, and asked after their families, and once or twice the 'father' was taken aside and held by the button while some point that required his advice was whispered in his ear.[45]

The traditional belief in the magical powers of the clergy survived among the London Irish. Although the Church discouraged the belief in healing powers, traditional folk magic lingered on. Epidemics brought crowds to confession and priestly authority was sustained in transmitting Irish culture as well as Catholic doctrine.

Samuel's description of Fr Sheridan, the priest at St Patrick's, Soho Square, in the 1880s, provides a wonderfully evocative portrait of a 'miserable outcast community' presided over by a kindly man entertaining his flock through the reciting of Irish comic stories. It was his custom to read selected anecdotes and stories about Irish life, chosen 'to excite the risible qualities among the listeners'. The sacred portions of his evening meetings were often confined to the recitation of the Rosary which closed the proceeding:

> Monday 31.1.81—Medals and cards procured of Sisters. Feast of St. Bridget for February 1st to be observed. Read story of the pranks of Irish fairies Carleton's Poor Sch. and other tales com. p 214. Said Rosary; but did not speak on any religious topic. Present about 60.[46]

Other examples from his journal show Fr Sheridan more concerned to amuse than to instruct, and delighted if his 'performance' elicited hearty laughter. The story of Fin MacCoul and a giant from Carleton had his audience 'amused but [they] did not laugh to my satisfaction'. For the 'Curse of Roshogue', 'there was a great deal of laughing and would have been much more had I carefully prepared the reading of the piece'. 'Shemus O'Brien' and 'The Donnybrook Spree' 'seemed to excite the risible qualities wonderfully', and the 'Waiver of Duleck Gate' prompted 'a few good roaring laughs'.[47]

In introducing medals, banners, and processions, Fr Sheridan encouraged a sense of pride in the wearing of religious regalia. The text of the sermon by his fellow priest, Fr Roche, on gala day in April 1882, featured the brazen serpent put up as a sign, and this was interpreted as representing how the Irish, like the Jews of ancient time, were God's chosen people.[48] In this way, pride in an Irish identity became synonymous with Catholicism.

Throughout the century, the Catholic mission to the Irish poor was seen as a herculean task. Initially the English Catholic Church lacked the means to minister to the needs of poor immigrants, and great pressure was exerted on the wealthy Catholic gentry to finance the chapels and schools that were desperately needed. If, as Samuel argues, the Irish allegiance to faith and nationality was 'hallowed by persecution', it is as well to remember that this 'exalted sense of their own religion', however lowly their social status, appeared to work for only half of the Catholic Irish in Britain.[49] There is no doubting the loyalty of practising Catholics but there were as many who chose to avoid persecution by becoming less obviously Catholic and less possibly Irish.

Here it is a question of definition. Samuel includes Mayhew's London Irish among the Catholic faithful who dismissed the secularism they found among English costermongers: 'They talk like haythens. . . . They haven't the fear of God or the saints. They'd hang a praste—glory be to God! they would.'[50] Also included were the Irish who defended the Church under attack from militant Protestants. Samuel accepts that 'religious' disorder and riot represented a continuation of primitive rural violence into an instinctive defence of Irish urban communities. He champions 'the turbulent Irishwoman with her sleeves tucked up and her apron full of stones or, flourishing her rolling pin in battle . . . as distinguished a presence in the Irish mob as the labourer with his shillelagh'.[51] Such a defence of 'Catholicism', invariably against the advice of the Catholic clergy and often only ended by their intervention, owed more to a cultural and communal solidarity than to allegiance to the faith.

Were they, as Gerard Connolly asks, Catholics in any meaningful sense? And what are we to make of Mayhew's Irish lodging-house keeper who hung pictures of the bleeding heart of Christ, the Saviour bearing the Cross, and the adoration of the shepherds, alongside a portrait of Daniel O'Connell and a red-coated sailor smoking a pipe?[52] Are these evidence of the practice of the Catholic faith? More likely, they represent nostalgia for a lost Irish past, just as English rural migrants decorated their rooms with china dogs, aspidistra pots and landscape pictures. And do we share Mayhew's scepticism about the religious language of the decrepit and diseased Irishwoman, running a brothel in Bluegate Fields, already convicted for allowing three women to sleep in one bed?

> all which she told us with the most tedious circumstan-
> tiality, vowing, as 'shure as the Almighty God was sitting
> on his throne,' she did it out of charity, or she wished she
> might never speak no more. 'These gals,' she said, 'comes to
> me in the night and swears (as I knows to be true) they has
> no place where to put their heads, and foxes they has holes,
> likewise birds of the air, which it's a mortial shame as they
> is better provided for and against than them that's flesh and
> blood Christians. And one night I let one in, when having
> no bed you see empty I bundled them in together. Police
> they came and I was fined five pounds, which I borrowed
> from Mrs. Wilson what lives close to—five golden sovereigns,
> as I'm alive, and they took them all, which I've paid back
> two bob a week since, and I don't owe no one soul not a
> brass farthing, which it's all as thrue as Christ's holiness, let
> alone his blessed gospel.'[53]

The main issue of the non-practising Catholic Irish not only gave a great impetus to the Catholic mission to build more chapels and schools, but also boosted the status of the clergy. Irish immigrants in strange surroundings were inevitably more reliant upon the priesthood, who, of necessity, took on a central role in combating Protestant attempts to convert the Irish poor.[54]

Certainly, there was a pronounced fear of the migrant faithful being tempted away or becoming lapsed Catholics without adequate support:

> In all our great towns, there is a large body of people,
> beyond and above those of whom the local clergy have
> personal cognizance; who ought to be Catholics, and who
> might be brought within the Church were it possible to
> look after them.[55]

Lynn Lees is inclined to question contemporary fears of the 'lost faithful', on the grounds that clergymen exaggerated the numbers in appealing for money from the Catholic middle class. Whilst acknowledging that there were two Catholic populations, a minority of active attenders at a place of worship, Lees invites us to accept that through the influence of women and children at mass, 'far more families and individuals had contact with Catholic norms and rituals than the low attendance rate at mass indicates'.[56] Yet, with all the litany of forces ranged against the Church holding on to its people—the shortage of clergy, the lack of chapels and schools, the poverty of Irish parents—it is difficult to see how this was achieved when the religious habit was scarcely evident among Irish migrants when they arrived in Britain.

Despite the restrictions lifted on Catholic education after 1829, and a rapid expansion in the number of Catholic schools, educational provision was available for only 30 per cent of Catholic children in Britain on the eve of the Famine. By 1851, children aged 6 to 10, in Lees' sample of London Irish, had lower school attendance figures than English children: 28 and 25 per cent for Irish boys and girls compared with 25 and 33 per cent for English boys and girls in the same sample. The Catholic infant schools provided only 2–3 years schooling, and attendance was poor. In fact, it was only after 1880 that Catholic children started to receive a fuller education with the introduction of compulsory schooling up to the age of eleven years.[57]

The Catholic Church provided a cultural continuity with the old country, a spiritual comfort against a sometimes hostile host community, and practical help and advice in adjusting to a new way of life. At the same time, the Catholic clergy sanctified work, poverty and virginity. What Sheridan Gilley has called 'holy poverty' in describing the Catholic mission to the London Irish, was a message, less of hope than of endurance.[58] Even the hymns that were sung confirmed a code of sexual denial. Moreover, Catholic schools taught children to know their place and to accept the existing political order.

Perhaps this was a less than attractive package for many young Irish migrants, who had left Ireland to escape the restrictive religious pressures of life in small Irish communities, and were looking for wider economic opportunities in England. By definition, they would have been the more restless, the most eager for adventure and to explore new social horizons.

How many young Irish people were like Tom Barclay, who grew up in Leicester in the 1850s and 1860s, and turned away from Irish language and culture? He rejected 'the old bardic legends and laments' that his mother recited: 'But what had I to do with all that? I was becoming English. I did not hate things Irish, but I began to feel that they must be put away; they were inferior to things English. . . . Outside the house everything was English: my catechism, lessons, prayers, songs, tales, games. . . . Presently I began to feel ashamed of the jeers and mockery and criticism.'[59]

Faced with the threats from Protestant evangelists, the rival influences of Anglicisation and the secular culture of urban working-class communities, the Catholic Church had an uncertain hold over Irish Catholic migrants in Britain. Faith could not flourish in a vacuum and so attachment to the Church was fostered through a whole range of social agencies that brought practical benefits to those prepared to accept an accompanying code of respectability. Catholics were encouraged to join confraternities, temperance groups, choral societies, bands and drill teams. Where possible, the Church prompted charitable activities, encouraging moral virtue through prizes at boys' and girls' clubs and musical entertainments. Mothers' meetings encouraged low-budget homemaking. Relief organisations gave practical help to assist the poor and the unemployed during the winter months or with plans for emigration. Irish Provident Societies, burial clubs, and Temperance Benefit Societies all proclaimed the same self-help message as their Protestant counterparts.

A process of moral reformation formed a major part of the Catholic mission to the Irish poor throughout the century. As early as 1816, Dr William Poynter, Vicar Apostolic of the London district, saw the principal object of Catholic education as 'the preservation or correction of the morals of the lower orders'.[60]

The Catholic Church suffered an acute disadvantage in that most Irish weddings took place in Anglican churches where the scale of Protestant charity was more munificent. The much greater number of charity and missionary organisations that grew up under the influence and protection of the Protestant Churches was a further source of leakage from the Catholic faith. Even in the prisons and the workhouses, the established position of Anglican chaplains gave a powerful advantage for pressing home the blessings of a Protestant allegiance.

Within the Catholic churches, class differences posed painful difficulties over seating arrangements for the rich and the poor in the congregation. 'The wealthy Catholic', wrote Lucas, 'pushes his way to a comfortable two-shilling pew through files of Christ's poor, who are thrust down into places of dishonour, crammed together in the midst of dirt, noise, damp, cold and a pestilent congregation of vapours.'[61]

The fear of driving wealthy Catholics away by enforcing close proximity to the stench and fleas of the poor Irish, remained a delicate issue, especially with the need to tap the moneyed part of the congregation to finance missions to the poor. In the 1851 Religious Census, 40 per cent of the seats in London's Catholic churches were still appropriated for pew rents which, in effect, meant that many of the poor were compelled to stand.[62] As rich and poor Catholics lived within easy distance of each other in London, the problem of accommodating class differences in religious worship was more acute for the Catholic Church than it was in Protestant churches and chapels, which more closely mirrored the physical and social class segregation of Victorian cities.[63]

In addition to the two broad trends identified earlier, which encompassed the experience of practising and of non-practising Catholics, historians have been concerned to assess the importance of a third dimension, in the nature and extent of religious sectarianism in Britain.

Tom Gallagher has shown how the communal strife of nineteenth-century Belfast was exported, via the trading links of the industrial triangle, to Glasgow and to Liverpool.[64] As the main reception areas for Irish migrants, Glasgow and Liverpool acquired the biggest Irish communities, which grew too quickly for easy assimilation. The tensions between Irish migrants and the local population were compounded by the inclusion among the settlers of Ulster Protestants, who were traditionally hostile to Irish Catholics. Sectarian conflicts added a further dimension to potential unrest in Glasgow and Liverpool, unlike the experience of some other cities where the Irish community was overwhelmingly Catholic.[65] Nevertheless, important differences characterised the religious rivalries to be found in Glasgow and Liverpool, and both avoided the permanent division and open warfare that scarred the city of Belfast.

The differences relate to the pace of Irish immigration and reflect the economic structures of the two great western ports. A slower rate of Irish immigration to the west of Scotland is explained by Ulster suffering less than other parts of Ireland during the famine years. As the main source of Irish migrants to Scotland,

Ulster was also the most industrialised province. A close physical proximity, added to the rapidly expanding industrial economy of west-central Scotland, facilitated the absorption of large numbers of Irish over a period of several decades.

Mostly found in the ranks of the casual labour force, as navvies, dockers, or in domestic service, the Irish in Britain did not acquire a reputation for upward social mobility, as did the Irish in America.[66] Yet in the west of Scotland, Irish immigrants found employment in the mills and mines, from which they were largely excluded in the north of England. Gallagher suggests that the more enterprising immigrants changed their religion and 'shook the dust of the exile community from their feet, certainly in Glasgow'.[67] Irish immigrants posed little threat to local Scots in a city with a high proportion of skilled jobs, especially in the shipyards and engineering work, where craft unions and free-masonry provided severe restrictions on entry. Elsewhere in west Scotland, in Greenock and on Clydeside, unskilled labour predominated, and Irish Catholics and Protestants worked, uneasily, in the sugar refineries and on the dockside.

Economic rivalry over employment, in the first instance, produced conflicts with the host community, which became manifest in religious or cultural differences. Complaints about Irish immigrants were often illogically expressed in a coded language that tended to obscure real intentions. The Irish share of poor relief was a general target of criticism wherever there was a heavy Irish presence. At the same time, wherever there was a sizeable share of employment, designed to aid distressed Highlanders, it was a further cause of complaint when taken up by the Irish. Invariably, migrant Highlanders lost out to the migrant Irish in canal-building, sugar refineries and the Scottish coalfields.[68] Yet the implications of the complaints were that the Irish were both too lazy to work, being content to receive poor relief, and also worked too hard and for too little, in competition with local labour.

Criticism of the Irish as cheap labour was voiced by local workers and trade unionists, when the real targets should have been the activities of powerful employers. It has been suggested that some coal owners and iron-masters in west-central Scotland employed the Irish as strike-breakers and encouraged sectarian conflict by recruiting rival 'Orange' and 'Green' Irish workers as a divisive tactic to weaken the labour force.[69]

The Orange Order was probably imported from Belfast to Glasgow in the middle decades of the nineteenth century, and really took off with the return of Clydeside shipyard workers from Belfast in the late 1850s. Shipyard workers were the staunchest members of Belfast's Orange Order, and this loyalty was transplanted to Partick and Springburn by the 1870s. The Belfast connection was further strengthened when Harland and Wolff, the Belfast shipbuilders, established a new yard on the Clyde, at Govan in 1912. This occurred at the height of the Home Rule crisis, when the defence of Protestant Ulster excited strong political feelings. The arrival of Belfast workers in Glasgow, at such a time, added to the sectarian tensions manifest in the ferocious rivalry between the city's two football teams. Glasgow Rangers were an exclusively Protestant club, and Glasgow Celtic, which was founded by Irishmen from Donegal, had strong links with the Catholic community. The religious abuse heard from the terraces at the titanic meetings between Rangers and Celtic owe their origins to the movement of Protestant and Catholic Irish from the northern counties of Ireland.

A ritual form of rivalry also occurred in the annual Orange parades and St Patrick's Day demonstrations held in the city. However, large-scale disorder was rare, and when any damage was done, it was not unknown for apologies to be sent to the offended community. In contrast with Liverpool, Glasgow did not experience a residential segregation into Catholic Irish districts, nor was there the vicious street-fighting that became associated with Liverpool sectarianism.[70]

The Liverpool experience differed in scale and intensity, not only from Glasgow, but compared with any other town in Britain.[71] It was the major reception centre for Irish immigrants and as such bore the brunt of the acute problems facing the authorities. By the early 1800s, Liverpool had a sizeable Irish community, and, well before the famine period, the city experienced economic and political tensions that became expressed in sectarian conflict.

The Orange Order was established in Liverpool as early as 1819, and in the 1820s Orange processions became set-piece confrontations between Protestants and Catholics. The Irish held St Patrick's Day parades on a grand scale that made them safe from Protestant attacks. Sporadic riots took place, as in 1835, as evidence of deep-seated rivalry between the two communities. After the reform of municipal government in 1835, religious loyalties played a key role in the battle for political control of the borough council. In the first elections, held in December 1835 under the reformed system, the Liberals won an overwhelming victory, gaining 43 out of 48 seats, but by 1841 they had lost control and were not to regain it for a further forty years. Frank Neal explains how the Tories wrested control from their rivals by winning support for a virulent anti-Catholicism, directed at the Irish in Liverpool.[72]

The leader of militant Protestantism in Liverpool was an Irish Anglican priest, called Hugh McNeile, a brilliant, pugnacious orator who revelled in the theatrical rough-and-tumble of democratic politics. First he seized on the schools issue to rally support for the Tory cause. The Liberal Council, influenced by the Irish national education system established in 1832, wanted a non-denominational scheme, agreeable to Protestants and Catholics. McNeile, who genuinely believed that the Roman Catholic Church was the enemy of Christianity, argued that no concessions should be made to the Roman Catholic Church, which was engaged in a ruthless pursuit of power to crush all Protestant 'heresy'. McNeile's tone was apocalyptic, his defence of militant Protestantism unrelenting, and his rejection of Liberal toleration emphatic:

> They were asked why they would not keep quiet and allow Protestants and Catholics to live quietly together; his answer was that the Roman Catholic system was opposed to the perfect law of God and the gospel of his saviour. . . . The law of God taught the full and free forgiveness of sin by the blood of Jesus Christ, having therefore no place for purgatory of the soul, without which the whole system of Popery crumbles into the dust. That was a system with which they would not and ought not to live in peace.[73]

It was not merely the influence of an aggressive anti-Catholicism that won votes to the Tory side. McNeile and his clique of Irish supporters realised more quickly than the Liberals how elections were decided at the margins, and the crucial importance, in the new era of platform politics, of party organisation.

In practice, council seats were won on very narrow majorities with a limited franchise, and the winner-take-all nature of elections rewarded the majority party with an unassailable domination, quite disproportionate to its share of the vote. The great

Liberal triumph in 1835 was on the basis of 58 per cent of the votes cast, and this fell to 47 per cent in its disastrous defeat of 1841.[74]

The basis of the Tory victory was laid through enlisting the support of the newly enfranchised tradesmen and craftsmen through the Tradesmen Conservative Association and the Operatives Conservative Association, in a network built on opposition to Roman Catholicism. Anglicans and dissenters joined forces against the perceived threat of the Roman Catholic Church.

If the political rhetoric was violently anti-Catholic, the underlying tensions and anxieties were economic. While the Liberals supported the abolition of the slave trade, Catholic Emancipation, and the Repeal of the Union, the Tories played on the threats to employment arising from Whig policies. In Liverpool, as in Bristol, it was feared that abolition would reduce the volume of trade and shipping in the port.[75] This would directly affect the jobs of those dependent on the port—carpenters, shipwrights and ropemakers, who were already suffering from the breakdown of the apprentice system, resulting in apprentices being hired before completing their time at the expense of experienced carpenters. New shipping technology also posed a long-term threat to port workers brought up in the age of sail. The introduction of the iron-framed hull ushered in a new era of iron-clad ships and screw propellors. Steam-driven vessels introduced a new labour aristocracy of enginemakers and boilermakers. The classic ingredients of anxiety and resentment over economic change were found amongst the carpenters and shipwrights—and these trades formed the mainstay of the Orange lodges in Liverpool.

Most Irish Catholics in Liverpool were unskilled labourers, and therefore posed no direct threat to carpenters and shipwrights, but they were held to be guilty by association with the Whigs, whose policies, at national and local level, appeared to threaten a loss of jobs.

Neal suggests that the Irish, by their own violent behaviour, exacerbated the tensions in Liverpool. They initiated the riots in 1835 and were involved in fighting with the carpenters on the occasion of an Anti-Corn Law meeting in 1841. The election of the same year resulted in various fights between the carpenters and the Irish, following the provocative playing of 'The Boyne Water' by an Orange band. An attack on St Patrick's Catholic Church in South End was matched by a revenge assault on St James's Anglican Church. By 1842, the feelings of the street ruffians, enlisted to intimidate the Irish under the 'No Popery' banner, were roused to a pitch beyond the control of Orange officials, and individual Catholics were picked on indiscriminately.

The violence and disorder in Liverpool became so great that the control of the police took over from the schools as a central political issue. Catholics complained of a police force dominated by Orangemen and of discrimination against the Irish population. The Liberal Council had appointed a Catholic Irishman, Michael Whitty, as head constable in 1835, and he was later forced to resign. Disorder on the streets and the inflammatory style of McNeile's 'No Popery' campaign, dismayed many English Anglican priests in Liverpool. There was also the suggestion, as in the Fisher Street martyr affair in 1838, that McNeile was involved in falsifying evidence against Roman Catholics accused of intolerance.[76] Stories that were patently untrue were retold with theatrical effect to audiences of Protestant activists, in order to whip up antagonism against the Catholic Irish. A stream of speakers came from Ireland with fantastic tales of the Irish belief in Celtic magic and superstition.[77] However, moderate Protestants accused the zealots of whipping up feelings and causing disorder and a threat to property.

What was to compound an already tense situation in Liverpool was the mass emigration of the famine years. From the first few months of 1847, Liverpool became inundated with poor Irish, and was totally unable to cope with a situation of famine relief. Neal estimates that 296,231 people landed in Liverpool between 13 January and 13 December 1847. Within the total, some 116,000, or 39 per cent, could be described as starving Irish who applied for poor relief during the year, and over the next seven years the flow of immigrants into Liverpool was probably of the order of half a million. Out of almost 300,000 in 1847, 130,000 emigrated to the United States, and others moved on to the textile towns of Lancashire and Yorkshire—leaving a substantial residuum to be fed, housed and employed in Liverpool.[78]

The poor law system was completely overwhelmed. No attempt was made to apply the principle of less eligibility, enshrined in the 1834 Poor Law Amendment Act. As the Irish disembarked, they were directed to a shed in Fenwick Street and issued with bread and soup. The rapid increase in the numbers of Irish receiving outdoor relief, rising from 29,437 in the week ending 9 January to 143,872 in the last week of January, prompted bitter complaints of fraudulent claims being made on the system by the resident Irish poor.

The cost of supplying poor relief to the starving Irish in the famine years is difficult to estimate with any degree of certainty. Overall, the expenditure on the Irish poor rose from £2,916 to £25,926 between 1845–6 and 1847–8. More specifically raising sectarian tensions, the poor rate increased by 2s a week, which may have meant an additional rates payment of 30s to be found by the skilled artisan occupying a house rated at £15 per annum. This was at least the equivalent of a week's wages, on top of other financial burdens—all at a time of uncertainty over employment. For the employers, there was a real value in a ready supply of cheap Irish labour that more than compensated for an increase in rates. For poor English ratepayers, not only was there an extra financial burden, but there was the fear of wages being reduced by the Irish presence, or even of jobs being lost to the Irish.

Local and national newspapers exploited these fears: 'The present question', *The Times* proclaimed, 'is whether every English working man is always to carry an Irish family on his shoulders, as he does at the present moment. Do the working men of England choose to have it so?'[79]

A catalogue of 'social evils', found in an extreme form in Liverpool in the 1830s and 1840s, provided ammunition for sustained attacks on the moral condition of the Irish. Liverpool had some of the worst housing in the country and experienced the highest national mortality rates before the Irish famine migration to the city. The housing crisis was worsened as 27,000 Irish invaded empty cellar dwellings, condemned as unfit for habitation, halting council policy to close them down.

High death rates and epidemic disease were firmly associated with Irish districts by Duncan, the medical officer of health. In the absence of medical knowledge about the transmission of disease, the Irish proved a handy scapegoat for hard-pressed authorities, anxious to allay the fears of the middle classes. Specific charges were made that assumed a moral weakness in the Irish character. They arrived carrying 'Irish fever' or with dysentry. They lived in abject squalor, the result of disgusting habits. They would keep a contaminated corpse in the house in order to have the wake. It was only a small step from these accusations, legitimised by local officials and clergy, to full-blooded racial and religious condemnation:

Let a stranger to Liverpool be taken through the streets that branch off the Vauxhall Road, Marylebone, Whitechapel and the North End of the docks, and he will witness such a scene of filth and vice, as we defy any person to parallel in any part of the world. The numberless whiskey shops crowded with drunken half clad women, some with infants in their arms, from early dawn till midnight—thousands of children in rags, with their features scarcely to be distinguished in consequence of the cakes of dirt upon them, the stench of filth in every direction,—men and women fighting, the most horrible execrations and obscenity, with oaths and curses that make the heart shudder; all these things would lead the spectator to suppose he was in a land of savages where God was unknown and man was uncared for. And who are these wretches? Not English but Irish papists. It is remarkable . . . that the lower order of Irish papists are the filthiest beings in the habitable globe, they abound in dirt and vermin and have no care for anything but self-gratification that would degrade the brute condition. . . . Look at our police reports, three-fourths of the crime perpetrated in this large town is by Irish papists. They are the very dregs of society, steeped to the very lips in all manner of vice, from murder to pocket picking, and yet the citizens of Liverpool are taxed to maintain the band of ruffians and their families, in time of national distress.[80]

The diagnosis of social evils enumerated in sections of the Liverpool press is offensive to the modern reader, but the language used was standard comment on the condition of the urban poor in the early Victorian period.[81] The imagery employed was carefully selected to shock middle-class sensitivities, and the message was invariably stark—weakness of character explained social problems. The added dimension in Liverpool was the attack on Roman Catholicism which militant Protestants saw as encouraging moral failings.

It was also the Catholicity of crime figures that was seized upon and influenced the neutrals to acquiesce in the low opinion of the Irish as an inferior race. As early as 1836, one-third of those taken into custody in Liverpool were Irish and two-fifths of those before the magistrate's court were Irish. In fact, these figures do not mean an over-representation of the Irish in crime totals, as they are in line with the Irish proportion of Liverpool's working-class population, but the impression of Irish criminality was created by hysterical editorials in the press. The Irish were also singled out as beggars—a condition seen as part of the Irish character. The Irish habits of having their children beg, of beggars dressed in rags and deliberately living in squalid cellars, were seen as illicit activities designed to create sympathy from a gullible public. When in 1848, there was fear of a general uprising in Ireland and a potential alliance between the Repealers and the Chartists, the charge of ingratitude and disloyalty was made against the Irish. Middle-class fear of widespread destruction of property, in the event of a popular rising, were added to the economic grievance of an unjust burden of the rates.

The Liverpool experience represents one extreme, where sectarian violence was encouraged by militant Protestants for political ends. The legitimacy accorded to racial and religious bigotry by council officials, clergymen, and in newspaper editorials, served to endorse street violence and indiscriminate attacks on Irish Catholics. In playing on fears of unemployment, and in targeting the Irish presence as an explanation of social problems like housing and crime, the authorities relieved themselves of the responsibility to find practical solutions.

However, even in Liverpool, which suffered from acute urban problems, militant Protestantism had an uncertain hold over the electorate or even within the Conservative party. Most Anglicans were neither Evangelical nor Tractarian in outlook, but believed in a broad Church and a degree of religious toleration. McNeile's demagoguery was regarded as dangerous to social order and, ultimately, as a threat to property. His style and behaviour made him subject to bitter controversy. Humane voices were also raised in support of the plight of the Irish immigrants in Liverpool. The warring factions in Liverpool politics probably represented a minority of opinion, and the Tory majority was secured as much by good organisation as by an overwhelming hostility to the Catholic Irish.[82]

Outside Liverpool, the balance of argument between toleration and bigotry was more even-handed. In Wolverhampton, Roger Swift found echoes of the criticisms levelled at the Irish everywhere—associated as they were with disease, crime and disorder.[83] Attempts by militant Protestant preachers, Baron de Camin in 1859 and William Murphy in 1867, to deliver anti-

Catholic lectures, were accompanied by disturbances and rioting, as Irish Catholics protested against public attacks made on their faith. The correspondence columns of the local press featured a debate over the issue of free speech versus public order. Moderate Protestants in Wolverhampton condemned the emotive Catholic-baiting of the militants.

W. L. Arnstein makes a similar point in an account of the Murphy Riots in Birmingham.[84] The scurrilous methods employed to whip up anti-Catholic feeling served only to bring out the Catholic Irish in strength to demonstrate their disapproval of Murphy. In effect, the Murphy Riots were anti-Murphy riots. Moderate English opinion was appalled by the disorder that accompanied Murphy, wherever he went.

In Edinburgh, there were a few instances of sectarian conflicts in the 1850s and 1860s, but rather less than in other Scottish cities. Aspinwall and McCaffrey offer a structural explanation.[85] The social composition of Edinburgh, with its rentier and professional classes living and working in a metropolitan city, attracted a higher number of English than Irish. The city prided itself on an enlightened Whiggish tradition, which incorporated religious toleration. The Irish also posed no real threat to the employment of local labour as they were more likely to oust migrant High-landers in the labour market.

In the longer term, the Catholic Irish in Edinburgh achieved a social advance, assisted by better education and a process of self-help. The Catholic Church, whilst providing a cultural cohesion for the Irish community, also encouraged a form of lace-curtain respectability. The encouragement of thrift and self-improvement boosted the morale of the Irish and nullified the common complaints made elsewhere. Towards the end of the century, the Catholic religion was regarded as a lifeline for the immigrant Irish and recognised as an influence for social good. In fact, in Edinburgh, the Irish were on a level above the lowest Scots, who combined a fondness for drink with a disdain for religion. The Irish in Edinburgh were also fortunate in the presence of Bishop Gillis, the flamboyant leader of the Catholic Church, who was able to develop a form of social harmony across the religious and social divide in the local community. He used his social links with the local gentry to foster a concern for the Irish poor through the agencies of savings clubs, reading societies and boys' brigades. All these worthy activities recommended themselves to the Presbyterian Scots and eased the way for better relations between Protestants and Catholics.

A similarly tolerant atmosphere predominated in the district of Durham and Newcastle-upon-Tyne. R. J. Cooter found only one riot, which occurred in Sandgate in 1851, on the occasion of a visit by the appropriately-named Ranter Dick.[86] A general spirit of tolerance and generosity informed the activities of local landowners and municipal corporations. The view was taken that the Catholic clergy would help to civilise the poor Irish, and the social work undertaken by priests was much admired and even envied by other denominations. There was little evidence of support for Orangeism or of disturbances accompanying Boyne Day or St Patrick's day celebrations. The visit, in 1851, of a 'No Popery' lecturer, Dr Tadini, resulted in a humiliating charge of charlatanism, and he was driven out of the town.

In London, Lees found that Fr Mathew's crusade had broken the links between drinking and mass recreation in the 1830s and 1840s.[87] His work paved the way for Cardinal Manning to develop a moral reformation by borrowing the forms and tactics of the Salvation Army. The League of the Cross, temperance soldiers, and brass bands were employed among the London dockers to ameliorate their condition.

In Cardiff, which shared with Liverpool a hysterical response to Irish immigrants in the 1840s, the Irish were blamed for the outbreaks of typhus and cholera between 1846 and 1849. Yet, through a similar process of socialisation in the chapels and schools, through self-help organisations like the Ancient Order of Hibernians, and through assimilation via mixed marriages, a genuine advance in status was achieved. At the time of the typhus outbreak of 1893, an adverse reference to the Irish in the Medical Officer of Health's report was eliminated, by order of the Council.[88]

What Raphael Samuel has barely hinted at, a 'Victorian' transformation, took place gradually over a couple of generations. By the end of the century, the Catholic Church was no longer feared as a potentially subversive threat, rather it was recognised by its track record with poor Irish immigrants as an important force for doing good.

The next two chapters concentrate on the Irish involvement in popular politics. Chapter 5 examines the debate about the Irish contribution to Chartism. Chapter 6 assesses the growth of Irish nationalism.

5

Chartism

Two hundred thousand men—and what men! People who have nothing to lose, two-thirds of whom are clothed in rags, genuine proletarians and sansculottes, and moreover, Irishmen, wild, headstrong, fanatical Gaels. One who has never seen Irishmen cannot know them. Give me two hundred thousand Irishmen and I will overthrow the entire British monarchy.
(Friedrich Engels, 1843)

Chartism continues to exercise a fascination for modern historians, not merely as the first great working-class movement in Britain, but as part of wider debates about the structure of industrial society, the growth of class consciousness, the transition to a period of 'social harmony' in the 1850s and 1860s, and the incorporation of the organised working class into the body politic during the second half of the nineteenth century.[1] However, Professor John Saville reminds us that the subject of Chartism did not command such interest in the years that followed its defeat in 1848. This resulted from a deliberate attempt to play down the scale of Chartist activity in Britain, compared with the more tumultuous scenes enacted in European capital cities. 'The agitation which derived its impulse from the convulsions of the Continent prevailed only so far as to disturb for a moment the serenity of her political atmosphere. Awed by the overwhelming strength and imposing attitude of the friends of order, the mischief subsided almost as soon as it appeared, and the cause of rational freedom was materially strengthened by the futile efforts made to undermine it.'[2]

The verdict of the Annual Register for 1848 was endorsed in Charles Kingsley's novel, *Alton Locke*, which pointed to the futility of mass, Chartist action without a widespread adoption of the Christian faith. In rejecting physical force and working-class attempts at reform, Kingsley advocated that social amelioration could only be achieved by an enlightened aristocracy. In the meantime, the climate of opinion in the 1850s shifted away from mass politics. The Great Exhibition in 1851 celebrated economic prosperity in a spirit of national self-congratulation, and Samuel Smiles articulated the dominant contemporary ideology of self-help, in his best-selling book, published in 1859. When, in the 1850s, R.G. Gammage published the first history of the Chartist movement, he stressed the bitter divisions within the movement, and his partisan judgments on the 'physical force' Chartists, Harney, Jones and Feargus O'Connor, contrasted with his support for the moderate and sensible leaders, Lovett, Vincent, and Bronterre O'Brien. Those judgments have remained highly influential in the subsequent histories of Chartism. Yet the context of the 1850s, when they were established, has not been fully recognised. The mid-Victorian period was ushered in with a sigh of relief that troubled times appeared to be over and a new age of prosperity was to be enjoyed by all the people, whilst retaining the existing political and economic structures.

A hundred years later, the climate of the 1950s was quite different. Following the 'People's War', a Labour Government with a huge majority and the establishment of a Welfare State, historians were interested, as never before, in historic working-class movements like Chartism. With hindsight and the vantage point of post-war Britain, Chartism was due for a retrospective revival. With the publication in 1959 of Asa Briggs' *Chartist Studies*, a generation of scholars have been engaged in providing new insights into the nature of the Chartist movement.

Professor Briggs argued that Chartism was not merely a movement that meant different things in different regions of the country but also represented an attempt to create a sense of class unity among three disparate groups that made up the working class. If Chartism won support among superior craftsmen, the new-style craftsmen, like the machine-builders, were never prominent in the movement. Those whom William Lovett described as 'the intelligent and influential portion of the working classes in town and country' were often converted to reform before the Charter and remained faithful supporters, irrespective of the trade cycle. Nonconformity exercised a powerful influence on this group which facilitated any dealing with middle-class radicals, but hindered them in reaching an accommodation with the hard hands of the manual working class. Factory operatives formed a second group. They were concentrated in Lancashire and the West Riding of Yorkshire, but were also found in parts of Cumberland, Derbyshire, Wales and the West of England, and in the West of Scotland. In the period before and into the Chartist period, this group was often severely affected by a transformation of methods of production. The support of factory operatives was dependent upon the trade cycle, 'the crowds ebbed and flowed with the economic tides'.[3] Thirdly, domestic outworkers, whether nailmakers in the West Midlands or hand-loom weavers in Lancashire, Yorkshire, the West Country, Wales and Scotland, found themselves in a desperate plight against the advance of new machinery. To them, Chartism was essentially a knife and fork question. While they retained some hope of restoring their old position, they looked to Chartism to achieve it, but once their industry was destroyed, they abandoned all hope and political agitation. To Briggs, a diverse labour force produced a variety of responses to a working-class movement that ordered its priorities differently according to region.

A further diverse element in the unresolved debate was the nature and extent of involvement on the part of the Irish who were living in Britain during the period of Chartist activity between 1838 and 1848. From the outset it should be recognised that the nature of the available evidence poses a major difficulty in attempting to resolve conflicting views on the level of support for the Chartist cause among the resident Irish population. What may be attempted at this stage is to identify a framework in which the debate may continue to develop. Five areas of Irish influence suggest themselves which enable us to focus on separate strands before attempting an overall assessment. They are:

1 The role of Irish national and local leaders in the Chartist movement.
2 The participation of the ordinary Irish population, as 'faces in the crowd' in Chartist activity.
3 Irish influence on the ideology and organisation of English radical movements in the first half of the nineteenth century.
4 The involvement of Irishmen employed as 'bully-boys' by such organisations as the Anti-Corn Law League to break up Chartist meetings.
5 The importation of policing methods from Ireland to be used against popular movements in Britain and the subsequent

strengthening of the coercive powers of the state against popular agitation.

The leaders of the Chartist movement have not enjoyed a good press from Chartist historians. Following the pioneering work of Gammage, divisions within the leadership have commonly been identified as one of the principal weaknesses of a movement that was fatally split over 'physical' and 'moral' force. These factions within Chartism are most closely associated with the personalities of Feargus O'Connor and William Lovett. As O'Connor was the most influential, so he has been the most vilified of all the Chartist leaders. The strength of the condemnation of O'Connor poses interesting questions. Firstly, did O'Connor's Irishness represent something of an Achilles heel for English historians to attack? Secondly, was there an important Irish influence in the conduct of O'Connor as the self-styled leader of the English Chartists?

If, as most authorities agree, Chartism, without the firm support of middle-class radicals, was doomed to failure in the 1830s and 1840s, why does so much blame attach to O'Connor as the architect of defeat? G.D.H. Cole, who was highly critical of O'Connor, conceded that 'he was in the unhappy position of leading—for, much more than anyone else, he was the leader—a movement which could not possibly succeed either in getting the Charter or, what was more important, in enforcing the social changes of which the Charter was only the symbol to the main mass of its supporters'.[4] Yet Cole goes on to blame O'Connor for his incomprehension of the forces of industrialisation that he claims were to shape the future direction of social progress for the working class. He ridicules the notion of regenerating England through a form of spade-husbandry. Cole depicts O'Connor's back-to-the-land philosophy, exemplified in his infamous Land Scheme, formed against the worst excesses of industrial capitalism, as not only reactionary but tactically inept, in alienating support amongst potential allies committed to the development of the machine age.

Yet the most damaging criticisms were levelled at the character of the man. Cole depicts him as vain and boastful, as a dissembler and a demagogue who deceived himself with his own brand of empty rhetoric. In a damaging attack, Cole claims that Feargus's father, Roger O'Connor, was certainly 'more than a little mad'

and disparages the addiction of father and son to their descent
from the ancient Kings of Ireland. As confirmation of insanity in
the family, Cole describes how, following the defeat of Chartism,
Feargus O'Connor was removed by the Sergeant-at-Arms after
being involved in a scene in Parliament, to be committed as
insane into a private asylum in Chiswick, shortly before his death
in 1854. By such means, O'Connor's reputation has been discredited and the defeat of Chartism put down to vainglory and
weakness of character.[5]

More recently, Feargus O'Connor has been the subject of
rehabilitation in the history of working-class movements. James
Epstein's biography, *The Lion of Freedom*, reminds us that O'Connor
in his prime was an immensely popular figure, who combined
the roles of earlier radical leaders such as the 'Orator' Henry
Hunt and the journalist William Cobbett.[6] Similarly, Dorothy
Thompson argues that Feargus O'Connor could not have kept
himself at the head of the Chartist movement for a period of ten
years, if he was just another charismatic huckster. He did possess
political skills of a high order.[7] Moreover, O'Connor was engag-
ingly steadfast in his commitment to universal manhood suffrage
and the dignity of the common man. Against the overweening
dominance of the propertied classes, he preached the independence
of working men through their own organisations—trade societies,
schools and land colonies. Thompson refutes the charge that
O'Connor was a lightweight braggadocio figure, claiming that
his theatricality in organising massive demonstrations was a rare
political gift, making him a commanding national figure, adored
by the 'hard hands and men of fustian jackets' in the Chartist
ranks.

John Belchem, writing on O'Connor's part in the collapse of
the mass platform in 1848, exemplifies this view with regard to
his speech on Kennington Common. He argues that the rhetoric
of mutual flattery provided the right message in trying to
prevent a clash with the police in a very tense situation. Leader
and movement were thus joined together through the employment
of Henry Hunt's favourite device, the death motif:

> I have received at least 100 letters, telling me not to come
> here today, for that, if I did, my own life would be the
> sacrifice. My answer was this—'I would rather be stabbed
> to the heart than resign my proper place at the head of my

children' (Shouts of Bravo!) . . . 'Will you obey my counsel
and follow my advice? (Yes, yes) I will remain among you
as a hostage, for, so help me God, I will not desert your cause
until life deserts me. (Loud and prolonged cheering) . . .
How shall I feel if I thought that by any act of mine I had
jeopardized the lives of thousands, and thus paralysed our
cause? (Hear, hear) How, I ask, would you feel if you were
conscious that you had been parties to my death? What
would be our trouble and our sorrow, how great would be
our loss![8]

In this highly charged situation, O'Connor was able to prevent
disorder and bloodshed in calling off a meeting which merely by
taking place was a victory for the right of mass protest against
the government. The speech and the action demonstrate the
stature of the man in terms of political skill. They also reveal the
qualities that inspired his followers and dismayed his critics.
How does one explain the violent passions O'Connor aroused
among his own supporters and the abuse he has received from
detractors? The Irish dimension goes some way towards explaining
it, and also promotes a better understanding of O'Connor's
contribution to the Chartist movement.

Dorothy Thompson describes how 'he addressed the people
more in the style of a chieftain encouraging his gallant clansmen
than a commonplace agitator talking down to the level of an
unenlightened auditory'.[9] His appeal to the people was as a
gentleman prepared to make personal sacrifices on behalf of their
cause. The style of the man was recalled in a visit O'Connor
made to Barnsley, in the early years of the Chartist movement:

His figure was tall and well-proportioned, and his bearing
decidedly aristocratic. He wore a blue frock-coat and buff
waistcoat, and he had rings on his fingers of each hand. In a
graceful manner and in emphatic language, he told the
Radicals of Barnsley that he had sold off his horses and
dogs, greatly reduced his establishment, and come weal,
come woe he would henceforth devote his whole life to
promote the well-being of the working-classes.[10]

What may be regarded as clever artifice or as theatrical show,
may be admired or deplored according to personal taste, but
O'Connor's style belonged to an English tradition of gentleman

radicals and an Irish tradition of popular leadership. The notion of the Leader, the chieftain, winning the adulation of his followers, yet, at the same time uniting with them in a common self-sacrifice, created a bond of tribal proportions. It is reminiscent of the old Irish belief in an elected kingship in which all members of the tribe were equal in the sense that all might be elected as chief. O'Connor's popular style, which far outstripped the moderate, rational appeal of his fellow Chartist leaders, owed something to his Irish background and culture.

There is further evidence of this in O'Connor's conduct of the *Northern Star*, the leading Chartist newspaper, published in Leeds. The *Star* not only provided O'Connor, himself, with a high profile amongst Chartist leaders but also gave the movement a truly national focus. George Julian Harney, who took on the ideas of continental socialism, found himself in disagreement with O'Connor in his writings. Nevertheless he gave credit to O'Connor for the entertainment value that he provided to other *Star* writers in the form of Irish jokes and poetry in his commentaries. It was also O'Connor's policy to give prominence to Irish issues in the *Northern Star*, not merely as a reflection of his own interests but as a conscious appeal to the Irish living in Britain.[11]

A third example of Irish influence on O'Connor's contribution to Chartism is his Land Plan which was to preoccupy his energies after the failure of the second Chartist Petition in 1842. The ideal of the Land Plan was a system of peasant ownership of smallholdings. It drew on Irish conditions, O'Connor's own experience as a farmer in Fortrobert, County Cork, and on knowledge of the system he gained as a barrister in Ireland. An early pamphlet, 'A State of Ireland', followed by 'Letters to Irish Landlords', published in the *Northern Star* in 1841, expressed the ideas that came to full prominence in the Land Plan, adopted by the Chartists in 1845.[12] If, as his critics have it, this was inappropriate for industrial England, it clearly made more obvious sense in the context of rural Ireland. The centrality of the land problem in O'Connor's politics grew out of the condition of a demoralised and dependent peasantry, attempting to eke out a bare subsistence living, especially in the south and west of Ireland. If there was more than a hint of the charge of 'Old Corruption' about O'Connor's blasts against the Aristocracy and Privilege in the tradition of Hunt and Corbett a generation before, there is surely a passionate sense of outrage that only rings true in view of the scale of distress and poverty to be found in Ireland. O'Connor's writing in 1847 drew on the emotional tragedy of the Famine in Ireland to attack the evils of English capitalism:

> I tell you, that, sooner or later, thin gaunt men, dying of famine, pestilence and hunger, must have been the result of the usurpations of a bloated aristocracy—an overpaid staff of Ministerial menials—a well-fed standing army—a gorged church, over-paid officials, and pensioned paupers; of the absorption of the honey of the factory bee, by the drone who owns the key; of a useless police, only rendered necessary to reconcile men to their degradation, of overgrown bankers, merchants, and traders, speculating on the blood, the misfortunes, and the distresses of their country; and, above all, that such must be the result so long as the rich oppressor monopolises all power over the poor oppressed.[13]

Feargus O'Connor truly embodied the raw, emotional appeal to social justice that was rooted in rural communities. Arguably, G.D.H. Cole underestimated the past rural experiences that shaped the thinking of many Chartists in the 1830s and 1840s. In emphasising the influences of urban organisations—trades unions and cooperative societies—he was anticipating their influence that was to become more prominent in the second half of the century. It is an example of writing history backwards or over-emphasising those trends that appear to be coming your way. Yet, at the time, O'Connor's appeal to a rural past clearly struck a chord with many among the labouring poor who were themselves recent migrants from the countryside.

Bronterre O'Brien, dubbed by O'Connor as the schoolmaster of Chartism, was the other Irish leader of national stature. Although educated by the Edgeworth family, Trinity College, Dublin, and the Inns of Court in London, O'Brien was confirmed in a radical career by a passionate sense of Ireland's wrongs. The familiar catalogue of Irish grievances is rehearsed in his writing; the military-style occupation, the discrimination against Irish trade and industry, the rapacity of absentee landlords, and the wretched miseries of the Irish poor. He told his readers in *Bronterre's National Reformer* in 1837:

> I have seen thousands of Irish who have never had animal food or fish or wheaten bread twice a year since they were

born. I have seen them whole days together without even potatoes or salt . . . I have seen them living, or striving to live, on nettles and other weeds, till their blood actually lost the colour of blood and turned yellowish. I have seen them living, or striving to live, in sooty mudcabins, or rather sties, and in deep holes burrowed under bushes on the roadside, or under turf banks, where there was not even the iron pot which Cobbett speaks of . . . All this . . . have I seen in Ireland—not in solitary instances, but over whole districts . . . and often did my blood boil with rage to think that I could not strike the assassins dead who caused such misery. I have always loved the poor. I have always felt how unnecessary as well as unmerited was their treatment.[14]

Strongly influenced by French Revolutionary thinkers and by Robert Owen's utopian socialism, O'Brien argued that the aristocracy acted as a parasitic class upon working people, and that the root of social evils was the absolute ownership of land.[15] The analysis of expropriation of the industrious, by the idle, echoing the strictures against absentee landlords in Ireland, the acute sense of injustice, and the references to starvation and sordid subsistence, have obvious force in the context of Irish experience:

Look then at the monstrous injustice done to the wealth-producing, or labouring people. It may be thus stated in a simplified way; they are compelled by laws, in the framing of which they have no voice directly or indirectly, to raise property to the amount of £150,000,000 annually to be distributed, under innumerable names and pretences, among men who give them nothing valuable in exchange. . . . As regards the result to themselves it is precisely the same thing as if they were compelled to support twenty millions of people at £30 for each family; that is to say, in a style of living far superior to their own. . . . But let no one for a moment imagine that this is the whole amount of injustice done to the industrious classes . . . after being compelled to toil and raise countless luxuries for the knaves and fools and strumpets and villains, who first rob them, and sometimes hang them—after all this, the working people are absolutely disabled by the system from raising even the necessaries of life for themselves though possessing all the skill and strength and leisure and will to do so. How many hundreds and thousands of men and women, and grown boys and girls are there in England and Ireland, who with all the eagerness in the world to get employment and give their labour and time for the tenth part of what they are fairly worth, yet cannot succeed in procuring a sordid subsistence even on those terms?[16]

O'Brien's most influential period as a radical journalist and speaker was in the mid-1830s, the years leading up to the Chartist period. Sadly, he fell out with O'Connor over the issue of 'physical force' but found no support among his opponents in the 'moral force' wing of the movement. Constantly plagued by debt, he was also frustrated that his ambitious writing projects, including a life of Robespierre and a Real History of the French Revolution, never came to fruition. If O'Brien may be considered the leading intellectual figure of the Chartist movement and certainly the most respected journalist among its leaders, ultimately he was a tragic figure, disappointed that his political vision and personal talents did not combine to achieve radical change. By all accounts his speeches were given in the form of long lectures, three to five hours in length, which nevertheless sustained interest and enthusiasm among his listeners. Yet, what is striking about O'Brien's writing, exemplified by the piece on the state of the Irish poor, quoted earlier, is the emotional force and fierce sense of outrage against injustice—all resting on a fundamental belief in human dignity. His was not the condescending kind of humanitarianism, sometimes found among English middle-class radicals, but a genuine egalitarianism. If Bronterre O'Brien was a student of the French Revolution and mixed with members of the London Radical Reform Association, his form of radicalism was also shaped by his Irish background and the unhappy experiences of his native Ireland.

In the characters of Feargus O'Connor and Bronterre O'Brien, Irish 'virtues' and 'vices' were equally represented. Both possessed great facility with words and an ability to command the affection and support of popular audiences. Both men were guided by a natural affinity with the interests and feelings of the common people. Both men retained a passionate conviction of the inalienable right of working men to share in the political process. What may be listed on the debit side are those qualities that were, in English eyes at least, the enduring weaknesses of the Irish character. The very passionate language employed was perceived as merely vulgar display. The bold words unsustained by matching practical action was seen as cowardice. The habit of quarrelling and recourse to unbridled personal abuse of fellow leaders would be deemed ungentlemanly. The showmanship and theatricality all too often looked like exhibitionism and an unbridled show of vanity.

For good or ill, the Irish dimension was a contributory influence for two of the most important Chartist leaders. Equally, the least acceptable 'Irish qualities' are just the ones that have attracted the disdain of English contemporaries and historians, amongst whom can be counted those who positively disliked the Irish, such as Mark Hovell. To early historians of Chartism, Irish influence was regarded as unfortunate, appealing to the worst elements in English popular politics—violence, brutality and a sentimental obsession with an idealised rural past. Hovell despised O'Connor as an Irish interloper, who having failed in Irish politics and quarrelled with O'Connell, brought the worst qualities of the Irish into English politics. He described Irish immigrants as 'swarming' into England to provide the shock troops for 'physical force' Chartism for which he had no sympathy or understanding.[17] The hysterical descriptions of the Irish in Britain, written in the 1840s by Thomas Carlyle and Friedrich Engels, may also be understood as a form of scapegoating in the alarming atmosphere of political unrest that threatened to overthrow the existing social order.[18]

The Chartist movement achieved national status through the leadership of O'Connor, Lovett, O'Brien, Rayner Stephens and Henry Vincent. Chartism was also characterised by regional diversity and its followers were often involved with other radical and reform movements of the period. Indeed, John Belchem has argued that a divergence existed between national proclamation and local practice.[19] Reform movements were eclectic in membership and individuals saw no conflict in supporting more than one cause at a time. The Chartist movement, and Irish involvement in it, cannot be understood merely in the pronouncements of its leaders.

Among Chartist leaders at the regional level, historians have identified a number of Irishmen who played an important part in the movement. However, there is a danger in collecting Irish names from the local leadership of Chartism and in assuming, as regards other radical movements, that where there were Irish leaders, so would there be Irish followers, especially if there was a known Irish presence in a particular town or district. In practice, it is difficult to sustain this connection in any consistent way. Local Irish leaders seem, if anything, to be rather marginal figures, not always representative of the Chartist rank and file, sometimes moving in and out of the Chartist movement and, in two cases at least, compelled to move to other towns to find more congenial surroundings.

Thomas Murphy, a Catholic coal merchant in London, led St Pancras opposition to church rates and the new poor law in the 1830s. He was one of the group that included Feargus O'Connor in forming the Great Radical Association and the London Workingmen's Association in 1836. Murphy also presented the People's Charter at the large meetings held in Glasgow and Birmingham in 1838.[20]

Philip McGrath, a tailor, who lived in an Irish quarter of East London, was president of the NCA for many years. Long settled in England, he was thoroughly English apart from retaining an Irish brogue. Daniel and Charles McCarthy were members of the Chartist trade locality of the City Boot and Shoemakers in 1842. In the turbulent politics of the 1840s, they moved between Chartism and the Repeal Association, holding positions in both movements. Robert Crowe, who was one of the political prisoners in 1845, may well have represented the experience of others when, as a member of the Irish Confederation, he recalled that by 1843, 'my spare time was divided between . . . the temperance movement of Father Mathew, the repeal movement under Daniel O'Connell and the Chartist or English movement under Fergus [*sic*] O'Connor.'[21]

Arthur O'Neill, who was half Scots and half Irish, was a leading lay preacher in Glasgow, pioneering the idea of Chartist Churches as he toured the west of Scotland. When the Lanarkshire Universal Suffrage Association was formed in 1840, Arthur O'Neill became its first missionary. He established branches throughout the country and preached to Chartist congregations on Sundays. Although he addressed huge crowds in Glasgow, he found little support outside the larger towns and encountered opposition from the local ironmasters and millowners. O'Neill was an educator and promoted the virtues of self-help, temperance and cooperative societies. He followed the moral force line that universal suffrage could only be achieved through sobriety, respectability and intelligence. Eventually, O'Neill moved to Birmingham, where he became pastor of the Christian Chartist Church and a leading figure in the midlands.[22]

The woolcomber, George White, was an Irish Chartist leader in Leeds, who found himself out of tune with the respectable dissenting Chartists in the city. Leeds, like Glasgow and Birmingham, was a centre of moderate Chartism, despite the presence of O'Connor's *Northern Star*. Leeds Chartism was not a proletarian movement but was dominated by local traders whose municipal concerns were confined to opposition to 'jobbery', suspicion of the police, and a desire to keep expenditure and the rates as low as possible. White described himself as 'not so much a Radical as a Revolutionist' and moved to the city of Bradford where he won support among fellow woolcombers.[23]

It is interesting that O'Neill and White both found it convenient to move to other towns, yet they were men of quite different political outlook, and it is not clear, in either case, that the presence of Irish leaders meant that there was Irish support among rank and file Chartists. Bradford, with Barnsley and Ashton-under-Lyne, probably had the highest level of Chartist activity among northern towns. In all three places, Dorothy Thompson has argued that Irish leaders were present; the Rev. Patrick Ryan in Barnsley, Timothy Higgins in Ashton and John W. Smith in Bradford. Moreover, in Bradford the first radical groups were established in the districts where there was the highest Irish settlement. Democratic associations and later members of the National Charter Association were set up in Wapping and White Abbey districts.[24] Thompson makes a case for a continuous radical tradition, involving local Irish leaders, that fed through into northern Chartism. Thompson is certainly a leading authority on the subject but in the present state of knowledge, some caution is needed.

In identifying Irish leaders, Thompson has extended our knowledge of local Chartism, yet she has acknowledged that the population of the manufacturing districts was diverse in character and highly mobile. More mobile than most were Irish families in search of employment, who, it is recognised, had come over to Britain in successive waves of immigration. Newly arrived immigrants were clearly less able to become involved in popular movements than those who had settled a generation earlier.

There was also considerable diversity of experience amongst Irish harvesters, textile workers, dockers and labourers. Variations occurred between groups of Irish workers in the same industries but working in different towns. On reflection, these established differences make it inappropriate to generalise about Irish involvement in the Chartist movement, as if the Irish were a homogeneous group.

The shortage of reliable evidence on the participation of ordinary Irish men and women is recognised by the key figures in the debate, either through a conscious declaration of the difficulty or it may be discerned at an unconscious level as arguments attempt to cover the paucity of direct evidence. Dorothy Thompson openly admits the limitations of historical evidence in identifying Irish Chartists in Britain: 'Of the hundreds, indeed thousands, of Chartists whose names and occupations we know, the extra information about religion and birthplace is missing. Apart from the inadequate method of name-spotting, we have no way of telling what proportion even of these were Irish, whilst of the crowds we can tell even less.'[25] Later in the same piece, the point is repeated, followed by an adroit escape from the difficulty. 'We shall, of course, never be able to measure the participation of anonymous Irish in the Chartist crowds. We know that at least seventeen Irishmen were among the three hundred-odd awaiting trial for Chartist offences in the winter of 1839–40, and we do not know the nationalities of all those three hundred.[26] Thompson concedes that after the Newport Rising in 1839, the most violent of all Chartist incidents, no Irishmen were brought to trial. Yet Irish involvement is resurrected through a quotation from Lady Charlotte Guest's diary which describes the distress of wailing women in Tredegar, 'among whom were many Irish' seeing the return of defeated men from their ill-fated expedition. This is hardly convincing proof of participation by Irish Chartists in the Newport Rising.

Daniel O'Connell opposed the Chartist movement and took pride in his fellow-countrymen who also remained aloof from it. In a speech in 1839, he defended the actions of the Irish in Cardiff who were found on the side of law and order:

> In the manufacturing towns in England, the mass of the poor population—not more poor than active—every one of them subsisting on small means—in every one of these

towns there was a large garrison of Irishmen. Did they join the Chartists? Did they join the insurrection?

Oh, blessed be God, no. Not only the Irish in Ireland refused to gain any advantage by force, but the Irish in England joined not the Chartists but opposed them, for they only looked for justice by turning the hearts of those who opposed them (*cheering*). Take the town of Cardiff alone. In that town there were a considerable number of Irish, poor people, who went there to earn their wages in this world, and who endeavoured to procure the means of having a clergyman . . . What did they do in respect of the Chartist insurrection? Why! 100 of the Irish who had come into the town of Cardiff were sworn in special constables.[27]

In opposing the claim that there was a high level of participation in the Chartist movement, J.H. Treble describes it as 'an untested hypothesis, no matter how plausible, [which] does not begin to serve as a substitute for the rigorous process of historical investigation . . . the view described above presents an essentially misleading picture of immigrant alignments . . . despite the firm grip which individual Irishmen exercised over Chartism's destinies, the vast majority of their fellow-countrymen domiciled in Yorkshire, Cheshire and Lancashire had little contact with the movement until 1848 the "Year of Revolutions".'[28] Yet, Treble is not averse to making assumptions from the evidence to support his contrary case, and is rightly taken to task by Thompson for relying on the pronouncements of a few political and religious leaders as a substitute for the opinions of ordinary Irish working men and women.[29]

John Saville, in his book on 1848, has adjudicated on the debate. He accepts the qualifications Thompson makes to Treble's thesis, but argues that the extent of the involvement of Irish communities in Chartism remains problematic because of the difficulty of knowing precisely where Irish allegiance lay between Daniel O'Connell's peaceful movement for the repeal of the Union and Feargus O'Connor's 'physical force' Chartism. Where, he argues, Treble was right, was in his insistence that the year 1848 was different. Following O'Connell's death in 1847, the establishment of the Irish Democratic Federation in London to campaign for repeal, Fintan Lalor's influence on the policies of Young Ireland, and O'Connor's denunciation of the Crime and Outrages Bill in

Parliament had the effect of forging an alliance between the Confederates and the Chartists in the European, revolutionary climate of 1848.[30]

However, Saville also finds himself having to resort to inference and speculation in offering his own interpretation. 'What soon became clear in 1848 was that the main centres of Chartist unrest were precisely the towns and regions where the concentration of Irish communities was most evident: London, Bradford and West Yorkshire, Manchester and its surrounding towns, and Liverpool.'[31]

Saville then turns to discuss the question of the attitude of the mainland English towards the Irish in their daily lives, 'a somewhat grey area for which firm evidence is not always available,' and accepts that antagonism can be documented by correspondence in the press, by recorded physical assaults or the larger scale riots, 'but much remains concealed from the historian although the contemporary significance of racial hostility was often important'. Saville offers the historical parallel of the experience of the Jews in the East End of London in the 1930s. There, too, radical movements coexisted alongside anti-Jewish feeling, so demonstrating 'a wide gap in social consciousness between ordinary people and political radicals'. 'So it was with the Irish in the 1840s.' Saville concludes his assessment of Irish involvement in Chartism with a negative judgment:

> It may be assumed that among middle-class strata the close connection between Chartists and the Irish, given the iden-tification of violence and outrage with the Irish, was an additional influence in the support by middle-class England for the forces of order which is such a remarkable feature of the year. It is also difficult to believe that the varying degrees of anti-Irish feeling among the working people did not play some part in the formation of general political attitudes during the crisis period.[32]

Saville's assertion for 1848 may be subjected to a simple test for an earlier peak of Chartist activity in 1842. From the census data of 1851, Colin Pooley has drawn up a list of the 'top twenty towns' in terms of the number of Irish-born people recorded. These tell us where the main centres of Irish settlement were located. From the recorded membership of the National Charter Association in 1841–2, we know where the main strength of the movement was found. What is not known is the number or proportion of Irish NCA members. However, if the assertion holds that the strongholds of Chartism were centres of Irish settlement, one would expect a close correlation between the two sets of data. If the correlation is slight, we know that other factors were of much greater significance in determining Chartist activity than the mere presence of Irish people.

What happens when the two sets of data are matched up? The result of a simple statistical test on rank order shows a very low correlation between an Irish presence and Chartist membership, so low in fact that no explanation from the first can be offered for the second. A Spearman rank order correlation test produces a figure of 0.23. Beyond the negative result of the test, it is possible to pick out anomalies in the two sets of lists. Liverpool ranks second in column A and sixteenth in column B. Three of the top six cities in terms of an Irish presence are in Scotland but none of them feature in the top twenty cities for Chartist membership. Leicester ranks third in column B but does not feature in column A. The fact that certain towns appear to match fairly closely in rank order may be coincidence more than anything else. London, inevitably, came first in both columns; Manchester, fourth and second; Birmingham, seventh and eighth; Newcastle, tenth and eleventh; Bristol, thirteenth in both; and Sunderland, seventeenth and eighteenth. These are more than outweighed by a much more random distribution amongst the rest. The marked differences between the two lists are more significant than the coincidences which have prompted the false conclusion of an Irish presence being significant in Chartist activity, at least before 1848.

If some doubt is cast on the Irish playing a positive role in the rank and file support of Chartism, or indeed in other radical movements before the repeal movement in 1848, there is the alternative view that Irish involvement was, if anything, negative. On this side of the argument, one could cite the damaging split between Daniel O'Connell and Feargus O'Connor in 1836, followed by bitter mutual recrimination and threats of violence. This not only divided the reform movement, but with personal loyalty divided, it weakened the potential support of the Irish in Britain for Chartism. Verbal insults led to violent clashes between O'Connell's Irish Catholic Repealers, supporting the Anti-Corn Law League and English Chartists. In June 1841 in Manchester, an outdoor League meeting was attacked: 'the Chartists showed their preparation

Table 1: Numbers of Irish-born and membership of the NCA

Column A		Column B	
Towns in rank order	No. of Irish-born 1851 census	Towns in rank order	No. of NCA cards taken out Mar. 1841– Oct. 1842
1 London	108,548	1 London	8,000
2 Liverpool	83,813	2 Manchester*	3,300
3 Glasgow	59,801	3 Leicester	3,100
4 Manchester*	52,504	4 Sheffield	2,000
5 Dundee	14,889	5 Bradford	1,500–1,900
6 Edinburgh*	12,514	6 Nottingham	1,650
7 Birmingham	9,341	7 Leeds	1,320
8 Bradford	9,279	8 Birmingham	1,000–1,200
9 Leeds	8,466	9 Merthyr Tydvil	1,100
10 Newcastle	7,124	10 Hanley	1,100
11 Stockport	5,701	11 Newcastle	1,000
12 Preston	5,122	12 Bilston	1,000
13 Bristol	4,761	13 Bristol	920
14 Sheffield	4,477	14 Oldham	700–900
15 Bolton	4,453	15 Stockport	880
16 Paisley	4,036	16 Liverpool	800
17 Sunderland	3,601	17 Loughborough	800
18 Wolverhampton	3,491	18 Sunderland	750
19 Merthyr Tydvil	3,051	19 Bolton	700
20 Hull	2,983	20 Huddersfield	630

* Manchester and Salford
* Edinburgh and Leith
Spearman rank order correlation column N and B = 0.23

Adapted from Colin Pooley, table 2.1, 'Segregation or integration: The residential experience of the Irish in mid-Victorian Britain' in R. Swift and S. Gilley, *The Irish in Britain 1815–1939*, Pinter Press, 1989, p.66; and from James Epstein, *The Lion of Freedom: Feargus O'Connor and the Chartist Movement 1832–1842*, Croom Helm, 1982, table 6.1, pp. 231–2 for a row by drawing forth short staves, with which they began to lay about them.' This provoked a response from the League's Irish supporters: 'our Irish friends, made desperate at seeing this, and particularly by the brutal conduct of a fellow who nearly killed a poor man with a blow from an iron bar, rushed at the [Chartist] flags, tore them down, and laid about them to such good effect as to drive the Chartists out of the square.'[33] Similar incidents of violence, involving the Irish breaking up Chartist meetings, occurred in the Manchester area in 1841 and 1842.

The respectable cause of Reform, dominated by the skilled artisans, with its preference for moral improvement, constitutional and educational reform, has seen fit to depict the Irish as lacking the political experience and sophistication to combine with working-class reformers in England and Scotland.[34] The Irish contribution is thus confined to providing the muscle for 'physical force' Chartism, or perforce, lacking political discrimination, to being hired out by the Anti-Corn Law League to act as bouncers in wrecking Chartist meetings.

This latter role overlaps with the view personified by the enemies of reform during the Chartist period. Anti-reformers found the Irish a convenient scapegoat for riot and disorder. The image of the decent English and Scottish working class could be preserved, if unfortunate incidents could be explained by the presence of the 'scourings of society' as the Irish were commonly depicted in a hostile press.[35]

In terms of both ideology and organisation, Chartism grew out of a radical tradition in Britain and was also inextricably linked with other popular movements of the 1830s and 1840s. It is commonly understood as an expression of disillusionment with the terms of the 1832 Reform Bill and, specifically, resentment at the failure to extend the franchise to the working classes. Bitterness and a sense of middle-class betrayal over the terms of parliamentary reform were compounded by the class-based legislation enacted by the Whig government. A government composed overwhelmingly of landowners which granted £20 million compensation to the slave plantation owners in 1833; which introduced the poor law 'bastilles' in 1834, as punishment for the agricultural labourers' revolt in 1831, and deprived the poor of an entitlement to 'parish pay'; which curtailed traditional rights of assembly and protest through new coercive legislation from 1837 onwards, this government inflamed radical opinion against it.

If such issues formed the immediate political context of Chartism, what the Chartists stood for and the way the movement was conducted may be said to belong to an older tradition, extending back to the eighteenth century. The six points of the Charter may be traced back to radicals such as Wyvill and Cartwright in the 1770s; the emphasis on political rights to Tom Paine and the influence of the American and French Revolutions.[36] William Lovett, the leader of the 'moral force' Chartists, employed the language of Robert Owen in a philosophy that espoused human rights and utilitarianism.[37] Feargus O'Connor's mass platform, a kind of 'forcible intimidation' against the government to get it to concede Chartist demands, may be traced back to the tactics of Henry Hunt at Peterloo in 1819.[38] At the same time, it should be recognised that each movement was composed of several strands of opinion and strategy, and at best the continuity was fitful and uncertain. The ritual invoking of a radical tradition, whether by the wearing of Jacobin caps or the cry of Peterloo, was the means of rallying support, not evidence of its continuing existence.

The English radical tradition, as Stedman Jones has argued, was 'confined within a constitutional rhetoric'. This included a respect for certain conventions, even if it was critical of the politics of 'old corruption', of placemen and sinecures and had scant regard to the wishes of the common people. The monarchy, the hereditary principle, traditional rights of landowners and the rights of property in general, remained inviolable. Alongside this tradition, one can detect a less deferential form of protest that included the use of inflammatory language, physical force, and even planned insurrection. It was not exclusively Irish in origin, nor was it practised solely by Irishmen, but there is a perceptible line of continuity that draws on Irish traditions of rebellion. Several authorities, such as E. P. Thompson, Marianne Elliott, and Roger Wells, have discussed the link, between the United Irishmen of 1798, the naval mutinies at the Nore, and the members of the London Corresponding Society.[39] The traditions of Irish secret societies, like the Caravats and Shanavests, were brought over to England by Irish migrants and surfaced in the activities of men with blackened faces and in the robbery of arms by the Luddites. It has been argued that the Luddite practice of oath-taking drew on the example of Irish Ribbonmen. In particular Lancashire Luddism had a revolutionary tone that echoed the sentiments of the 1790s.

The argument is that the tradition of agrarian secret societies in Ireland in the eighteenth and nineteenth centuries, such as the Whiteboys, the Defenders, and the Peep-of-Day or Break-of-Day Boys, who were known for their 'driftless acts of outrage', developed into more deliberate organisations with an agenda of economic and social objectives which became known as Ribbon Societies. Between 1820 and 1840, Rachel O'Higgins claims that Ribbonism spread into every part of Ireland and became established in several British cities—Liverpool, Birmingham, Manchester, Glasgow and Edinburgh. 'There is, it is true, no evidence specifically connecting Ribbonmen as such with English working-class radicals. But wherever Ribbon Lodges were formed in England, an unusually high proportion of Irish labourers is found participating in local radical and labour movements. There need be no doubt, therefore, that Ribbonism helped to strengthen radical and Chartist organisations in northern England.'[40]

Radical protest movements create their own symbolism, and none served better than the blood of martyrs to the cause. If Peterloo became a radical symbol for the English working class, it had its counterparts in Irish history. The tragic farce of the Irish Rebellion in 1798 and the cruel death of Robert Emmet in 1803 became part of radical folk memory—re-enacted in theatrical form to keep the flame of rebellion alive. That these rituals formed part of the activity of English radicalism deserves further explanation. In a very important sense, English and Irish popular protest found a common cause—that of 'Justice for Ireland'. Radical sentiment was united against an aristocratic and exclusive system. There was, probably, broader support for a negative assault against privilege than for a specific programme.

Even after heavy immigration from Ireland after 1815, the old cry of 'No Popery' was replaced by a groundswell of support for democratic reform. Catholic Emancipation and reform in Ireland found widespread radical support in England in the early decades of the nineteenth century. Not only was there a remarkably persistent commitment to the concept of social justice, uniting the disinherited in Britain and Ireland, but the continuing plight of Ireland was seen as driving the Irish into flooding the British market with cheap labour. By removing Irish grievances, the need to migrate to Britain in search of work would also be removed. In supporting the Irish struggle for justice, radicals were also defending the living standards of the English working class. Political principle and economic interest were thus conjoined.

English support for the cause of 'Justice for Ireland' was not confined to the main areas of Irish settlement in Britain. J.A. Roebuck, the radical MP for Bath, in a speech in 1837, linked the cause of Ireland with Parliamentary Reform in England:

> I insist that no law has been passed in favour of Ireland, yet there will be no benefit to Ireland until the House of Commons be strengthened. The friends of Ireland must pursue a vigorous course, though that does not consist in putting down titles. No one can have a worse opinion of the Irish Church than I have; but while I see that this is the case, that churchmen of that church are clinging to it with all their fondest hopes and most desperate energies, when I anticipate all the dreadful consequences, how they are banded together and backed by the orange lodges, I must look for justice in some other measures. I will fight for justice for Ireland as well as for England. (*Loud cheers*)[41]

The force of sentiment and sense of common purpose against an exclusive, aristocratic system of government was most powerfully expressed in the writings of the great English radical journalist and editor of the *Political Register*, William Cobbett. His Irish writings are less well known than much of his work, but they confirm the vital link between English radicalism and the cause of Ireland. Cobbett visited Ireland in 1834 and, after addressing Irish audiences in many towns, he wrote of his experiences in the form of a warning to the labourers of England:

> Every county town in England has at this moment a supply of Irish flour, Irish meat, and Irish butter; and, curious enough, as it was only last spring I entered into possession of my present place, I had not time to make up my own bacon and pork, and my fellows are now eating Irish bacon. (*Hear, hear and loud cheers*) There they are with their red cheeks, their fat round faces, their clean shirts, their Sunday clothes; they live well, and have decent table-cloths laid before them every time they eat their victuals. While this is the mode of the husbandmen and artisans living in England, what, I say can be the cause that those who raise the food in this country, and who send it over to the English farmers to eat, have not a morsel of food to put into their mouths?

I saw the day before yesterday a mother with her four little children living upon some straw, with their bodies huddled close together to keep themselves warm. I have written over to one of my labourers . . . that if I find that George, the man who minds the cattle, should suffer them to have under them straw so broken and so dirty as that poor woman was lying upon, I would turn him out of the house as a lazy and a cruel fellow. (*Cheers*) . . . The cause of the misery was, that those who work, and those were the majority of the people in every country, those who laboured had not what they ought to have, a due share of what they laboured for. (*Hear hear*)[42]

The theme of starvation amidst plenty—one that was to be developed into powerful charge against England by the Young Ireland movement and later by John Mitchel—was contrasted with a rosy picture of the well-fed English labourer. The great injustice done to the labouring people of Ireland was graphically portrayed, not merely to elicit sympathy but as a dire warning of what could happen in England, under an oppressive Whig government:

MARSHALL, I dare say that my letters have made you stare; but staring is not all that they ought to make you do: they ought to make you think about how you would like to have a naked wife and children; how you would like to have no shoes or stockings, or shirt, and the mud spewing up between your toes when you come down the road to your work of a morning. they ought to make you think abut what you shall *do, all of you*, to prevent this state of starvation, nakedness and filth, from coming upon you . . . The same Ministers and same Parliament who keep this people in this state, after having got them into it, are the same Ministers and same Parliament who have got the power of making laws, and of employing soldiers and policemen in England . . .

And be assured, that this would be the lot of the English working people if the Scotch vagabonds could succeed in their projects for sweeping away our poor-laws. If that were done, the English farmers would be a set of beggarly slaves, the landlords would take so much from them, that they would be able to give the labourers not more than 6d a day, and you would all be living in hovels without chimneys, and be eating with the pigs, that you would be rearing and fatting for somebody else to eat! I would rather see you all perish, and perish along with you!

Cobbett argued that the only way Irish grievances could be removed was with the support of the people of England, just as the citizens of Newcastle, Leeds, Manchester, Birmingham, Nottingham and London had supported the Catholic Emancipation Bill and opposed the Coercion Bill:

> In the answer, which I gave to the kind and cordial address with which the citizens of Dublin were pleased to honour me, I took the liberty to observe to them that I believed that their grievances would never be redressed, *unless by the aid of their fellow-subjects in England*; and I am now, after personal examination into the state of the country and after attentive observation of men and things, fully confirmed in that opinion.

Prophetically, Cobbett anticipated tragedies and conflicts that were to hang over the condition of Ireland for the rest of the century—famine, agrarian strife, the demand for Home Rule—all are heralded in his warning of what was to come;

> Gentlemen, it is impossible that Ireland can be suffered to remain in its present state! What! vessels laden with provisions ready to sail for England, while those who have raised the provisions are starving on the spot where they raised them! What! Landlords living in England, having a 'RIGHT' to drive the King's subjects out of this island, on pain of starvation from hunger and from cold! What! call upon England for meal and money to be sent in charity to save the people of Ireland from starving, and make the relieved persons *pay rent the same year*! What! demand allegiance from a man whom you toss out upon the road, denying that he has any right to demand from any part of the community the means of sustaining life!... What! give to 349,000 of the English people as many representatives in Parliament as you give to the whole Irish nation, and bid the latter be content![43]

At the same time as Ireland became a *cause célèbre* for English radicals like Cobbett it was, undoubtedly, a source of considerable alarm to ministers of the crown and to members of the judiciary. Historians like Stanley H. Palmer and John Saville, who have closely examined the role of the state and the development of police forces in England and Ireland, see the Irish dimension as prominent in the minds of the authorities during the Chartist period.

Palmer, in identifying centres of Chartist disturbances, argues that the geographical spread was impressive and Chartist support was scattered amongst diverse occupational groups and in surprising places. Chartism was found in rural Wales as well as among the mining districts, among the artisans and journeymen of Suffolk, and in the cloth towns of Wiltshire and Somerset. It was most deeply entrenched in areas described as the 'leading edge of industrial change', the woollen towns of Yorkshire and the cotton towns of Lancashire.[44]

In seeking to curb disorder, the authorities relied on traditional means—troops, yeomanry and special constables. In most of the industrial towns, there were no regular police forces to call upon. In Bolton, which had a population of 51,000 in 1841, there were only 10 police and 13 constables from the old court leet and some 40–60 'perpetual' constables appointed under different local acts.[45] Compare this with the city of Bath, having a similar population, and 10 inspectors and 132 constables.[46] In Manchester, the newly incorporated borough council created a police force of 48 officers and 295 constables, but there was opposition to the levying of a police rate and the old police commissioners established a rival force of 240 men. Local politics prevented the establishment of an effective police force. Major-General Sir Charles Napier, Commander of the Northern District, warned the Home Office:

> The civil force here is quite inadequate—What are 500 Constables and Specials in a town which would turn out 50,000 people to see a dogfight! Manchester should, as you no doubt know better than I do, have a strong well-organised police of, at least, 1,000 Men.[47]

Birmingham, a leading centre of Chartist activity, was also lacking a properly constituted civil force. For a population of 180,000, Birmingham had only 30 day street keepers, 170 night watchmen and 2,300 special constables, for emergencies. With mass meetings, like the one addressed by Feargus O'Connor at Holloway Head in August 1838 which attracted 100,000, the authorities became anxious. By the spring of 1839, meetings were held in the Bull Ring in the centre of the city and the magistrates decided to ban all public meetings but to no avail, as the crowds continued to gather almost nightly. Against this backgound of impotence, the Mayor of Birmingham requested the assistance of the Metropolitan Police. The arrival of uniformed 'Bourbon' police from London prompted riots, disorder and public humiliation as troops were called in to aid the civil power. No one was killed in the 'Birmingham Riots' but the damage to scores of properties was an estimated £20,000. More seriously, the authorities were clearly alarmed by a situation that appeared to be dangerously out of control.

For the government, Sir Robert Peel proposed that Birmingham, Manchester and Bolton should have a police force based on the Metropolitan Police. Against impassioned cries that a continental-style police was being imposed by the government, Peel cited the precedent of the Dublin police which was universally acceptable under government control. This was enough to silence national and local opposition to the measure proposed. In fact, Peel's earlier experience as Irish Chief Secretary when, as Home Secretary, he established the Metropolitan Police in 1829, is thought to have been influential. Although this is commonly believed to be the first police force of its kind in the world, the model was the system of Irish county police founded in 1787.

The Irish connection with the formation of the Metropolitan Police in 1829, and with Peel's temporary measure of government police for the three towns in 1839, was to continue with the growth of county police forces in the peak period of Chartist disorder from 1839 to 1842. Palmer points to the chronology of the formation of county forces and shows that 'fully fifteen of the eighteen English counties that adopted the police on a country-wide basis over the period 1839–1856 did so in the first four years, 1839–1842'. Also thirteen of the fifteen acted at the height of the crisis which was between October 1839 and May 1840. Palmer concludes that 'the clear lesson is that the police were created for and largely implemented during the years of Chartist crisis, 1839–42; with the decline of Chartism after 1842, the stimulus to create police forces also disappeared.'

For the authorities, the nightmare posed by Chartist disorder was the fear of a parallel uprising in Ireland at the same time as troops were needed to suppress popular unrest in England.

Major-General Napier, commander of the army in the northern industrial districts, was an Anglo-Irish radical, with sympathy for the legitimate grievances of the 'moral force' Chartists. Earlier in his career, he had been a witness to the violence of 1798 and 1803 in Ireland. He was deeply disturbed by the prospect of civil disorder during the period of his command, 1838 to 1842. His recipe for preventing violence was to have such a strong military presence available, with troop reinforcements brought in from Ireland, that any foolhardy show of force by the Chartists would be deterred. Napier requested that not only troops be sent from Ireland, but that English regiments, containing the greatest number of Irishmen, should be selected for northern duty. In fact, in the period of nine months to August 1839, six regiments were brought from Ireland to the Northern District. A total of 3,600 men, almost half the total military strength in the north, were Irish troops. Not merely Irish troops but the memories of earlier Irish rebellions played a key role in the containing of English Chartism.

Napier feared that troops might not be the only import from Ireland and Irish-style assassinations and attacks on military barracks might be introduced in England. Indeed his troops might be exposed to the kind of brutal attack he recalled witnessing in Ireland: 'In 1798 I saw poor (Captain) Swayne and his 100 Soldiers surprised at Prosperous in the County of Kildare by a suddenly assembled force of peasants who burned him and his 100 men alive in their Barracks.' Talk of assassinations was freely circulating in the spring of 1839 in Lancashire, following the murder of Lord Norbury in Ireland, when bullets merited the grim description of Norbury pills.

In the event, the alarmist atmosphere that prompted troop movements and fearful expectations of a mass uprising proved to be misplaced. The Chartist crisis years of 1838 to 1842, in fact, witnessed very little in the way of violence or loss of life. If physical force Chartism was indeed an attempt to intimidate the government, it would, in practice, have been no match for trained and fully-armed soldiers. Napier, the old campaigner, could see through the rhetoric to the dismal reality of the overwhelming odds against the Chartists:

> Poor people! . . . They will suffer. They have set all England against them and their physical force: fools! fools! They talk

of their hundred thousands of men. Who is to move them when I am dancing round them with cavalry, and pelting them with cannon-shot? What would their 100,000 men do with my 100 rockets wriggling their fiery tails among them, roaring, scorching, tearing, smashing all that came near? And when in desperation and despair they broke to fly, how would they bear five regiments of cavalry careering through them? Poor men! How little they know of physical force!

The presence of real armed strength, reinforced by Irish troops, proved mightier than the rhetoric of physical force Chartism in 1839. While Ireland was experiencing a period of relative calm it was possible to move Irish regiments to the north of England.

In 1842–3, popular protest surfaced in Ireland and England at the same time, and curiously the national stereotypes were reversed. The Plug Plot disturbances produced widespread violence in northern England, whilst in Ireland, Daniel O'Connell demonstrated his hold over the people through a series of massive meetings all over the country, in his non-violent campaign for the Repeal of the Union. Most of the Plug Plot disorders were concentrated in a period of two months when the police lost control in Staffordshire, Yorkshire and Lancashire. A mob of 5,000 destroyed the police station at Newton, killing two constables, and in Preston another mob brushed aside the force of seventeen men and seized the town. In Manchester, troops were held back as 5,000 Lancashire mill hands invaded the city. In despair at the inaction of the local magistracy, the government issued a proclamation banning all public meetings, and put the Duke of Wellington in command of an army sent by train from London. The army set up headquarters in the Town Hall, mobilised 2,000 special constables and provided military support to thirteen police stations and to tollgate houses on roads leading from the city. Such actions were taken in anticipation of the kind of violent attacks experienced only in Ireland.

The extent of Chartist violence may be measured by comparison with other episodes of popular unrest. Palmer estimates that there were twelve deaths in July and August 1842; eight rioters, three soldiers and a policeman. The Chartist disorders of 1839–40 included twenty deaths—all in the Newport Rising. The Reform riots produced sixteen deaths (ten of them at Bristol) and the

Swing Riots occasioned only one death. Retrospectively, these low levels of fatality appear mild, certainly not the stuff of revolutions. The ease with which the authorities suppressed disorders, with the rebels losing twice the number compared with troop and police losses, was emphatic. However, at the time, the authorities were using the same means in dealing with violent disorder in England and Ireland. During the period 1839 to 1844 in Ireland, there were sixty-one recorded affrays between the peasantry and an armed constabulary. During the relatively quiet years, sixteen deaths occurred, fourteen peasants and two policemen. In the earlier period, 1827 to 1835, a total of 196 deaths had occurred in battles with the police in Ireland. Certainly, Ireland had a tradition of more lethal violence and, in countering this, the authorities operated a military-style police housed in barracks like an army of occupation.

The level and intensity of the violence in Ireland not only served as a dire example of what might follow in England, but the experience of military-style policing in Ireland was imported into a few of the newly-established county forces, especially in the north of England where Irish immigrants were concentrated. Only two of the 15 county forces set up in 1839–42 were led by veterans from the Irish Police, but Irish-born recruits in the Lancashire force increased from 5 to 18 per cent in about twenty years. In Staffordshire, Irish experience was seen as particularly useful in preventing a reoccurrence of the Plug Plot riots. Captain John Hatton, who served for seventeen years in the Irish constabulary, was appointed as Chief Constable on his record against the Ribbonmen in Louth and the tithe resisters in County Wicklow. His Deputy was another Irishman, Col. Gilbert Hogg, who subsequently became Chief Constable at Wolverhampton in 1848 and was to succeed Hatton in Staffordshire in 1857. Five of Hatton's original thirteen officers in the Staffordshire police were Irishmen. These officers drew on Irish experience and recruited Irishmen into the English county police.

It would have been more worrying for the government if the Irish and English radical movements had united, but personal and tactical differences separated Feargus O'Connor and Daniel O'Connell in the 1840s. The notorious pact between O'Connell and the Whig government in 1843 led to bitter charges of betrayal. It was only after O'Connell's death in 1847 that the spark of European revolutions in 1848 rekindled the spirit of rebellion in

Ireland and England. For a brief period in 1848 an alliance was forged between English Chartists and Irish Repealers.

The Irish dimension to the events of 1848 was probably more important than at any time during the Chartist period. It also illustrates how fear and alarm in England about the level of unrest in Ireland occasioned coercive measures that, in turn, tended to increase popular protest in both countries.

Saville has pointed to the Irish context in which the Crown and Security Act of April 1848, commonly known as the Treason-Felony Act, was introduced. Sir George Grey, in introducing the bill, made it clear that the rising tide of unrest in Ireland was the reason for the measure. The purpose of the bill was to introduce a new category of offence—that of 'open and advised speaking' in what might be deemed a treasonable fashion.

The growth of radical movements in parts of England and Ireland during the month of May formed the background to the Government's change of heart over making arrests of 'trouble-makers'. Requests for more troops in the disaffected districts, as the police came under continuous strain, combined with concern over a succession of popular demonstrations in the streets of London and northern cities, to put pressure on the government to act.[48]

The trial and conviction of John Mitchel, who was sentenced to fourteen years transportation, unleashed widespread protests among Irish communities in both countries. The perpetual fear of Irish violence was compounded by the news of famine in Ireland. English judges were alarmed that hordes of starving Irish would cross to England, intent on maiming and killing. Heightening the sense of crisis were the events in European capitals which appeared to herald the dawn of revolution.

To the propertied middle classes of England, the violent, destructive behaviour, associated with Irish popular protest, was threatening in itself but the infectious action of popular sovereignty that united Irish Repealers and English Chartists was seen as especially dangerous. The Attorney-General, Sir John Jervis, summing up in the Fussell trial, represented the mood of the propertied classes: 'Europe was in tumult: There was raging in a sister-country [Ireland] a system of circumstances where the ill-judging people thought the property of the people was the right of the people.'[49] Such naïvety was clearly dangerous in persuading people into violent actions, and the involvement of the Irish with

Chartism in 1848 seemed to confirm the essentially violent character of the Chartist movement.

The Irish dimension in Chartism has a historical significance for both English and Irish politics and contained both positive and negative influences on the progress of the movement. It was positive in the way Ireland shaped the outlook of two of its leaders, O'Connor and O'Brien, and Irish influences contributed to the style and organisation of Chartism. Some of the Irish in Britain gave positive support among the rank and file, but this was most pronounced in 1848 with the alliance with Irish Repealers. However, Irish influence was probably a negative factor in the leading Chartist centres, albeit with a few exceptions, and was wholly negative in the use of troops from Ireland and in the employment of Irishmen to break up Chartist meetings. Most negative of all was the use of coercive legislation to suppress Chartism, which was prompted by fears of an Irish uprising and Irish-type violence in England. The violence in Ireland was an ever-present shadow over the mental landscape of the English forces of law and order. Memories of past atrocities in Ireland, and fear of future outrages in England, haunted the military, the police and the judiciary. The long-term legacy of these anxieties were developments in policing and in the extension of the coercive powers of the state which were justified in the context of concern over Irish disorder and violence.

For all intents and purposes the year 1848 marks the end of an era of popular disorder and mass protest as a political strategy in England. Of course, it did not mark the end of demonstrations or of rioting, but thereafter, English popular demands for reform were mostly directed through organisations which increasingly operated within the body politic. Gradually, too, sections of the working classes were to become incorporated within the system. Extensions of the franchise, the legal recognition of trades unions, state education, and the improving influences of the cooperatives and temperance societies, E.P. Thompson's 'warrening process', reduced the sense of exclusion that was a legitimate grievance in the first half of the century. It took time to heal the bitter class divisions of the Chartist period and it would be a mistake to accept at face value the self-congratulation and apparent social harmony of the 1850s and 1860s.[50] The reality was that established police forces, a strong military presence, and new coercive legislation combined to defeat the forces of popular protest. Other ways forward had to be found, painstaking and pragmatic, rather than revolutionary, because the state had shown itself to be impervious to the pressure of the mass platform. Unwittingly, the Irish played a part in strengthening the powers of a coercive state.

This process assumed a wider significance in the second half of the century when the 'Irish question' appeared to threaten not merely the forces available to the state but the unity of the British Empire. The final chapter examines the influence of revolutionary and parliamentary pressure in the unfolding story of Irish nationalism.

6

Irish Nationalism

*We appealed in vain to the reason and sense of injustice
of the dominant powers. Our appeals to arms were always
unsuccessful . . . We accept the conditions of appeal, manfully
deeming it better to die in the struggle for freedom than to
continue an existence of utter serfdom. . . . All men are born
with equal rights.*
(Proclamation of the Irish Republic, 1867)

In considering the question of Irish nationalism, there are images
of conflict, equally as enduring as those of religious oppression
and sectarian bigotry, because of the Irish association with
political violence. There are not merely the well-known incidents
of Fenian outrages in Manchester and London, in the 1860s, or
the murder of British statesmen in Dublin, in 1882. A tradition
existed of attempted rebellion, agrarian violence, and mass protest,
that seemingly spilled over from the troubles in Ireland into the
politics of England.

What part Irish people played in political movements in Britain
has been considered in a rather fragmented fashion, and as a
marginal force in British politics. A great deal more has been
written about the growth of Irish nationalism in the nineteenth
century in Ireland, as a prelude to the establishment of the Irish
Free State in 1922. The fact of Irish independence, albeit within a
divided island, has undoubtedly given a retrospective credence
and legitimacy to pioneering nationalist movements that would
have astounded contemporaries. It is very tempting to write history
with the benefit of hindsight, but in doing so, there is a dangerous
distortion of what was understood and believed at the time.
Moreover, the process of retrospection confers a moral authority
with the certainty of the outcome providing its own justification.
Most famously, Macaulay applied a Whig interpretation of history
to the 'Glorious Revolution' of 1688 and the establishment of a
constitutional monarchy in England. More recently, the 'forward

march of labour' is a well-trodden path for labour historians, charting the rise of the English working class in nineteenth-century Britain. Arguably, a third example is the treatment of Irish nationalism, written in celebration of the inevitable triumph of Irish independence. All share the common assumptions of a benevolent 'spirit of progress' at work in the unfolding of events.

Since so much of Irish nationalism was bound up with English radicalism, it is legitimate to pursue what may be called the Irish dimension in British politics. In discussing the influence of the Fenians and Gladstone's Irish policies, the importance of historical continuity in the radical tradition is recognised, but also the power of fear on the part of the authorities in shaping government reactions. Rather than an inexorable progress towards historical inevitability, a tension existed between conflicting forces that moved events one way and then another, without at all conferring certainty on the participants or on the outcome.

A process that was apparent in official reaction to the Chartists was to continue with the activities of the Fenian movement in Britain. Paradoxically, the Fenians, whilst keeping the spirit of Irish nationalism alive, also had the effect of strengthening the apparatus of state surveillance to be deployed against any extra-parliamentary organisation. Officially constituted as the Irish Republican Brotherhood in 1858, the Fenians took their name and inspiration from the Fianna army in the old legend of Fionn MacCumhail. Despite fiasco and defeat, the movement became associated with outrageous feats of bravery or terrorism, dependent on where your sympathies lay, and it is often argued that the Fenians sustained a revolutionary tradition for over half a century. Indeed, T. W. Moody has linked the United Irishmen of 1798 and the Young Irelanders of 1848, via the Fenians, to the men of the Easter Rising in 1916. Moody suggests that the Fenian doctrine of nationality, transcending creed, class or ancestry, was that of Thomas Davis and the the Young Ireland movement.[1] These connections convey a neatness that is only apparent with hindsight.

It should also be recognised that the Fenians, like the Chartists, drew on many influences and represented a broad spectrum of interests in Ireland, the United States and in Britain. Initially, the IRB was a conspiratorial, secret society based in Ireland, the Fenian Brotherhood was a military support organisation in America, and the sister society, Clan na Gael, offered financial and ideological commitment after its establishment in 1877. The central driving force of Fenian ideology was a romantic nationalism constructed around an idealised past version of Irish history and culture. Inspiration was found among continental revolutionaries like the Italian, Mazzini, engaged in nationalist insurrection, and among French socialists in Paris. Emotional and financial support for Irish nationalism was found among exiled Irish Americans and also came from Fenian clubs in the centres of Irish settlement in British cities. Sustaining and uniting all the disparate elements was the hatred of the conqueror. England was depicted as a tyrannical oppressor and assumed 'satanic' powers of an evil empire in Fenian propaganda.[2]

For the Fenians, the lesson of past defeats, in 1798 and 1848, was that 'England would never yield to the force of argument, only to the argument of force'.[3] Secret organisation and the opportunity provided by the distraction for Britain of engagement in foreign war were to offset obvious military weakness. However, impatience for action and the need to maintain morale overcame a realistic assessment of any chance of practical success in peacetime. The military exploit of the attack on Chester Castle in 1867, where arms were to be seized and taken on a captured train via Holyhead for an invasion of Ireland, was led by John McCafferty, an officer trained in the American Civil War.[4] The British authorities, having infiltrated the movement with spies, were well prepared to counter the attempted raid. The Home Secretary, Spencer Walpole, sent a telegram to the mayor of Chester, approving the arming of Volunteers, and, just to be on the safe side, a whole batallion of Scots Fusilier Guards was despatched by train from London. Ironically, the train passed by the hapless McCafferty, who was stuck in a railway siding unable to move. The presence of the troops meant that the planned attack was hopeless. The police and troops were ready waiting for the 1,200 armed Irishmen from British cities arriving at Chester Station, as if on an excursion to a football match, only to find that the match was off. After such a fiasco, it was a remarkable achievement for the Fenian movement to survive as a 'physical force' threat in England through sporadic activity in the use of dynamite and other occasional acts of terrorism.

One explanation of the survival of Fenianism must lie in the minds of the authorities, where fear of a general uprising, assassination threats, and the potential destruction of public property, represented a very real challenge to security. Following the abortive Chester raid, a terrorist campaign of sabotage and incendiarism was set in motion during the summer of 1867. The targets were gas works, railway stations and other public facilities.

The alarm amongst local authorities, following the rescue of Fenian prisoners in Manchester in November 1867, was registered in the appeals made to the Home Office for money, arms and troop reinforcements.[5] Exeter demanded the arming of its police and the creation of a national guard. Cardiff requested firearms and ammunition. Derby wanted cutlasses. The Home Office made only a tentative response, fearful of an armed constabulary provoking more trouble than it was worth in the additional expenditure required. No expense was spared in deploying CID detectives to the most sensitive danger spots. Twelve of them were sent to Balmoral to guard the Queen against the supposed threat of assassination and instructions were sent by the new Home Secretary, Gathorne-Hardy, to the mayor of Tunbridge that Irish immigrants were to be watched by the police. Such actions seem to suggest that both the Home Office and the local authorities were panicked into a quite unreal appraisal of the potential threat from the Fenian movement.

After the Clerkenwell prison explosion, details of which were known to the police beforehand without their being able to prevent it, panic appeared to sweep the country, in fear of a general uprising. Characteristically, the Queen urged her ministers to take strong measures—in particular, the immediate suspension of Habeas Corpus. Rumours of Fenian plots abounded, there were to be raids on the arsenals at Colchester, Chelmsford and Canterbury, railway lines in Lancashire were to be blown up, the water works at Hull sabotaged and the railway station at Shrewsbury to be dynamited. Most alarming of all was the story that thirty men had set sail from New York with a plan to assassinate the Queen and the entire cabinet. Echoes of past Catholic plots came to mind, most notably Guy Fawkes and the Gunpowder Plot, in 1605.

Hardy took unprecedented steps to guard against the Fenian menace. In January and February 1868, he enrolled 113,674 special constables armed with staves, with Volunteers allowed to carry rifles. In London alone, 53,113 specials enlisted—700 surrounded the Bank of England, 800 guarded the Post Office. Engineers from the Board of Works examined all the sewers near public buildings and sentries watched over the outlets. Fearing the worst, the Foreign Office ordered wooden shutters for the first-floor windows, while around strategic sites in the capital, like Nelson's Column, emergency lighting was installed.

The authorities misjudged the scale of Fenian operations and also misinterpreted the mood of most Irish immigrants in Britain. The expected rising and extensive bombing campaign never happened, and many Irish communities publicly disavowed all connections with Fenianism.[6]

Historically, Fenianism was important as the first movement to convert ordinary Irishmen to the ideal of an independent Ireland, by harnessing nationalism to the old demand for the land being returned to the people. Fenian support in Ireland came from the poorer classes—small farmers and labourers, schoolmasters, clerks and urban workers.[7] Fenians gave encouragement to the Land League in the 1870s and to the Home Rule movement in the 1880s, both of which put pressure on the Imperial Parliament. Subsumed within the single aim of Irish independence, the Fenian movement cultivated nationalist sentiment by association with the removal of tenants' grievances and the aspiration for self-government. There was also a Fenian recognition of Gaelic revivalism and an infiltration of the Gaelic Athletic Association, founded in 1884. Ostensibly, the GAA was established to preserve and foster Irish games as a means of strengthening Irish identity. In practice, it furthered Fenian and nationalist influence.

A limit to the popular support the Fenian movement could command from Irish Catholics, who formed the great majority of Irish at home and abroad, was established by the stance of the Roman Catholic Church. Just as with the Chartists, the Church was hostile to Fenianism. It condemned the secret organisation, oath-taking and revolutionary methods employed by the Fenians. The Church preferred to advocate the constitutional path to the removal of Irish grievances, which grievances included the privileges of an alien religious establishment in the Protestant Church of Ireland. Members of the Fenian movement were subjected to the threat of excommunication by Archbishop Cullen, and this must have represented a potent threat to many practising Catholics. For their part, Fenians continued to draw a distinction between the religious and the secular spheres in advocating the separation of Church and State.

Given the powers ranged against it, the question of how the Fenian movement survived for over half a century, far longer than any previous political organisation, deserves some explanation.

It survived, partly, as already observed, through association with popular grievances and with a variety of related organisations that enabled the movement to advance nationalist identity and aspirations. It survived, partly, through the longevity of its leaders. John O'Leary, O'Donovan Rossa and John Devoy, all lived to a ripe old age, surviving imprisonment and exile and spanning fifty years of political activity.[8] Ironically, too, the Fenian movement was given a sustaining credibility by the fear and alarm about their activities on the part of the British government. The actions of successive British governments in first of all deviating from a lenient policy towards Fenian prisoners and creating martyrs to the nationalist cause and, secondly, in responding to Fenian violence by introducing the Irish question into the centre stage of British politics, inevitably lent credibility to the Fenian movement. Perhaps most important of all the influences that kept the Fenians in the public eye was the journalistic and propaganda talents of the leaders of the movement. If Fenian incidents frequently ended in disaster and a corresponding loss of credibility ensued, Fenian leaders shared with earlier radicals a talent for publicity and theatricality that created a Fenian reputation for daring and heroism. Fenian leaders skilfully exploited military defeat into moral victory, and in the process created a living legend.

The death of Terence McManus, the Young Irelander in San Francisco in 1861, provided James Stephens, the Fenian leader, with an opportunity for a publicity coup in arranging for the body to be returned to Ireland. Refused the use of Dublin Cathedral by Archbishop Cullen, Stephens acquired the services of a radical priest to officiate at the funeral. A crowd of 20–30,000 Dubliners turned up to watch the procession in the rain to Glasnevin cemetery and, not for the last time, did the funeral of an Irish patriot serve a symbolic purpose in fostering nationalist sentiment.

Even after the defeat and humiliation of the abortive raid on Chester Castle in 1867, opportunities were created to spread the Fenian message of defiance. A Provisional Government of the Irish Republic was accompanied by a proclamation sent to *The Times* in London. It contained the Fenian 'history' of expropriation, oppression and injustice, and claimed its moral authority from the sovereignty of the people and heroism in the struggle for freedom:

We have suffered centuries of outrage, enforced poverty and bitter misery. Our rights and liberties have been trampled on by an alien aristocracy, who, treating us as foes, usurped our lands and drew away from our unfortunate country all material riches. . . . But we never lost the memory and hope of a national existence. . . We appealed in vain to the reason and sense of justice of the dominant powers. . . Our appeals to arms were always unsuccessful. Today, having no honourable alternative left we again appeal to force as our last resource. We accept the conditions of appeal, manfully deeming it better to die in the struggle for freedom than to continue an existence of utter serfdom![9]

Historically, the most important incident involved the arrest of two Fenian leaders in Manchester in September 1867, and more dramatically, their rescue from an unescorted police van en route to Belle Vue Gaol. During the rescue, a police sergeant was killed, and from the subsequent police round-up, five Irishmen were tried on a charge of murder. It was immaterial in English law who had fired the fatal shot, as all those involved in the raid were liable to be found guilty. As it turned out, the trial received the full glare of national attention, and so provided the perfect platform for Fenian propaganda. William Allen, who was wrongly accused of shooting police sergeant Brett, was defiant to the last:

I want no mercy—I'll have no mercy. I'll die as many thousands have died, for the sake of their beloved land and in defence of it. I will die proudly and triumphantly in defence of republican principles and the liberty of an oppressed and enslaved people.[10]

Another of the five, Michael O'Brien, appealed to a higher form of justice than that found in the English courts:

Look at what is called the majesty of the law on one side, and the long, deep misery of a noble people on the other. Which are the young men of Ireland to respect: the law that murders or banishes their people, or the means to restrict relentless tyranny and ending their miseries forever under a home government. I need not answer that question here. I trust the Irish people will answer it to their satisfaction soon.[11]

The spirit of heroic defiance was met with a policy of ineptitude by the British government. One of the five men arrested, Maguire, was released on a free pardon; another, Condon, an American citizen, was reprieved. The other three, Allen, Larkin and O'Brien, were convicted and executed in public, in November 1867, and subsequently were remembered as the 'Manchester martyrs'. Legal doubts surrounded the trial and a sense of injustice took hold among Irish people that the men had been executed for political action as Irish rebels. The result was that the cause of Irish nationalism had achieved its first martyrs since the days of Robert Emmet and the reverberations continued for fifty years until the executions that followed the Easter Rising in 1916. T. D. Sullivan's verses, quoting Condon's remark in the dock,

> 'God save Ireland!' cried the heroes,
> 'God save Ireland!' say we all,

became universally popular when set to an American Civil War tune to become the unofficial national anthem for the Irish people. It was through the speeches of its leaders, through newspapers like the *Irish People*, distributed in England, through the symbolic adoption of nationalist emblems and banners, and the popularity of rebel songs that the Fenian movement kept the 'spiritual flame' of Irish nationalism alive over half a century.[12]

The episode of the 'Manchester Martyrs' was closely followed by an attempted rescue in December 1867 of the Fenian armaments organiser, Richard O'Sullivan Burke, who was on remand in Clerkenwell prison. The explosion in the outer wall of the prison, which was the chosen method of escape, failed to rescue Burke but succeeded in killing twelve people and a further thirty were badly injured. The political consequences of the Fenian outrages at Clerkenwell and Manchester, in the same year as the abortive raid on Chester Castle, were even more dramatic than the incidents themselves, and quite unexpected.

The cumulative effect of these events exerted a profound influence on English opinion. Irish grievances, in the form of agrarian outrages in Ireland, always appeared remote to the English public, even if these involved coercive measures imposed from Westminster. Irish outrages in English cities, involving loss of life and extensive damage to property, were quite another matter. Quite literally and painfully, the Fenians had converted the Irish problem into an English problem in posing a threat to the established government. In the open political arena, the Irish question became a central issue in British politics, whilst behind the scenes steps were taken to strengthen security and the secret investigation of Irish bombers.

It was American inspiration that was behind the dynamite war that began in January 1881 with an attack on Salford Barracks, Manchester. Further attacks took place in March at the Mansion House, London and in May at the Town Hall in Liverpool. The following year, a huge arms cache was found in Clerkenwell and a state of emergency was declared in Glasgow when the Tradeston Gas Works had one of its gasometers blown up, followed in quick succession by explosions in the coaling shed of the Caledonian Railway and the stone aqueduct on the Forth and Clyde canal.

Faced with a series of embarrassing explosions, planned from America and employing Irish bombers, the government appointed Col. Henry Brackenbury as spymaster in a secret intelligence unit in Dublin, and Howard Vincent, as Director of London's CID was made responsible for anti-Fenian activity in England. In 1883, a new bureau, the Special Irish Branch, was set up in Great Scotland Yard. Following the abortive attack on the Mansion House in London on 12 May 1882, the Home Secretary directed Vincent to beat up the Irish sections of London, 'the resorts of the lower classes of Irish are to be visited as far as possible tonight (13 May) by the most experienced officers'.[13] Since many of the planned attacks, including the one on the Mansion House, turned out to be total failures and the reaction of the authorities was misplaced, in needlessly antagonising innocent people, it was perhaps fitting that incompetence by the bombers was invariably matched by ineptitude on the part of the authorities.

In a parallel fashion to the threat posed by Chartism, the authorities reacted to the Fenian menace. At its peak in the late 1860s, Fenianism was more important for what it provoked than in terms of its direct achievements. Like the United Irishmen in 1798 and the Irish Repealers in the 1840s, the Fenians gained popular sympathy and aroused national sentiment. Yet they failed, just as surely as the earlier movements, in winning over a majority of Irish people to the notion of an independent Irish republic. With a membership, at its height, of around 50,000 and the ability to call on, perhaps, 6,000 firearms, the Fenians were never a serious force equipped for armed struggle. The idea of an independent Irish republic had more enthusiastic support in the

United States than it did in Ireland. R. V. Comerford's description of Fenianism 'as a voluntary social movement posing as a military organisation' accurately captures the theatrical quality of the movement.[14]

If the Fenians failed in winning sufficient support to exert pressure on the British government, they played a part, indirectly, in bringing the Irish question to the forefront of British politics. After the events of 1867, Gladstone sensed that the public were ready to accept reform measures designed to remove the long-held sense of injustice He acknowledged that Fenianism had conditioned the British population 'to embrace in a manner foreign to their habits in other times, the vast importance of the Irish controversy'.[15] Yet this may concede rather less than it seems to do, in the same way as Gladstone appeared to concede the principle of the franchise to the working class in 1864. What we know of modern public reaction to political outrages committed by the paramilitary organisations on both sides of the sectarian divide, appears to provoke an even more obdurate reaction, except for a committed minority amongst English opinion.

Perhaps the key to the Fenian breakthrough in Britain lay with the personality and politics of the 'people's' champion; William Ewart Gladstone. The knee-jerk reaction of successive British governments to Irish violence had invariably been to deploy even greater coercive measures and the suspension of civil liberties. It was only with Gladstone becoming leader of the Liberal party that the Irish question was brought into the mainstream of British politics. In fighting the general election of 1868, on the issue of the disestablishment of the Irish Church, Gladstone gave legitimacy to Irish national aspirations. In carrying out a legislative programme for Ireland, he recognised the right of Irish opinion to be heard.

Historical controversy surrounds Gladstone's Irish policy which, after the legislative reforms of his first two ministries, was to become an old man's obsession in the pursuit of Home Rule. All this contrasts with his earlier career in which Gladstone showed only a fleeting interest in Ireland. In 1845, the year in which he resigned over the Maynooth question, he wrote in prophetic vein to his wife:

> Ireland, Ireland! that cloud in the west, that coming storm, the minister of God's retribution upon cruel and inveterate and but half-atoned injustice! Ireland forces upon us those

great social and great religious questions—God grant that we may have courage to look them in the face, and to work through them.[16]

Yet, during his whole life, Gladstone only visited Ireland twice, in old age, for three weeks in 1877 and for a day in Dublin in 1880.[17]

The question arises why did Gladstone take up the Irish question in the 1860s? Even in the religious culture of the mid-Victorian period, Gladstone's exalted language and high moral stance, which was especially appealing to British nonconformists, also invited the charge from opponents of hypocrisy and opportunism. The Irish Church, Irish education and land reform were established issues in the 1860s and Lord Derby's Conservative government had been discussing the Irish university question. What was especially appealing about disestablishment to Gladstone, the Churchman, was the righting of a profound wrong as a means of preserving the Empire.[18] Gladstone believed that the removal of Irish grievances would reconcile the Irish people to the maintenance of British rule. The attraction of the disestablishment of the Irish Church to English dissenters was not so much based on moral principle, as on the expectation that the disestablishment of the English Church would follow.

In electoral terms, it was also sound political strategy to win the support of Irish Catholicism to the Liberal camp. R. V. Comerford has argued that Gladstone and his radical ally, John Bright, had targeted the Irish Catholic vote as early as 1864. Bright made the running in cultivating Catholic support with a popular visit to Ireland in 1866. He also won over nationalist sentiment by criticising the ill-treatment of Fenian prisoners and presenting a petition to the House of Commons on their behalf. Comerford argues that it was not the Fenians who put Ireland on Gladstone's agenda. Certainly, Catholic aspirations for 'justice' appealed to his moral conscience, but this appeal was never allowed to run ahead of practical politics. The overriding concern was to win Catholic support in Ireland for an electoral alliance with dissenting support in England and Wales. The fears arising from the events of 1867, especially the explosion at Clerkenwell, allowed Gladstone to create the impression that disestablishment would, in some mysterious way, defuse Fenian bombs. In the event, over half Gladstone's majority in the 1868 election came from the 66 seats he won in Ireland.[19]

However, it could easily have worked the other way. Disraeli informed the Queen that Gladstone had misjudged the mood of the country. He thought English hatred of 'Popery', and of the Irish, would probably prevent Gladstone from gaining power.[20] Disraeli, who resented Gladstone's assumption that the Almighty was always on his side, also underestimated the electoral appeal of Gladstone's high moral purpose. Gladstone wrote to his sister in January 1868 that he had taken up the Irish question in the name of 'the God of truth and justice'. His moral conscience was not on parade merely for the benefit of his family, or to be exercised in the privacy of his diary. He was able, as few politicians have ever done, to make it the basis of his appeal to the country. Gladstone, who was frequently distracted by issues of conscience outside politics, also needed to fire himself up with the conviction that he was called to lead a moral crusade. In a curiously modern style of electioneering, Gladstone set about his campaign with relentless energy and prodigious oratory.

During the 1868 election campaign, Gladstone made fifteen speeches in south-west Lancashire. On a famous occasion on 22 October at Wigan, he concluded a long-remembered speech by comparing the Protestant ascendancy in Ireland with:

> Some tall tree of noxious growth, lifting its head to Heaven and poisoning the atmosphere of the land so far as its shadow can extend. It is still there, gentlemen, but now at last the day has come when, as we hope, the axe has been laid to the root. (*Loud cheers*) It is deeply cut round and round. It nods and quivers from top to base. (*Cheers*) There lacks, gentlemen, but one stroke more—the stroke of these Elections. (*Loud cheers*) It will then, once for all, topple to its fall and on that day the heart of Ireland will leap for joy and the mind and conscience of England and Scotland will repose with thankful satisfaction upon the thought that something has been done towards the discharge of national duty, and towards deepening and widening the foundations of public strength, security and peace! (*Loud and prolonged applause*)

The famous sequel to the speech was Gladstone's reaction to the news, received at his country seat, Hawarden, on 1 December 1868, that the Queen's secretary would arrive from Windsor that evening. Gladstone was chopping down a tree in his park. 'Very significant,' was Gladstone's response to the telegram and he resumed his assault upon the tree. After a few minutes, he stopped and rested on the handle of his axe. He then exclaimed to his guest, Lord Shaftesbury's son, Evelyn Ashley, 'in a voice of deep earnestness and with an intense expression, "My mission is to pacify Ireland." He then turned once more to the tree and said not another word until it was down.'

It is a well-known story. Nevertheless, much of the essential Gladstone is encompassed by it—the high moral purpose, the sense of destiny, and the physical energy of the man are all present. Add to it, what Gladstone prized above all his other political talents, a sense of timing, knowing instinctively when to launch a moral crusade before the public, and there are the makings of a great political figure.

From 1868 to 1893, when Gladstone retired from politics, aged 86, he continued with his mission to 'pacify Ireland'. He was rarely the initiator of policy with regard to Ireland, conscious of the need to win public support, but once he had decided to adopt a measure, he took personal charge of it, immersed himself in the legislative detail of it and guided it through each reading of the House of Commons. More than any other politician, Gladstone remained steadfast to the idea of 'justice for Ireland'. This was often against very powerful and determined opposition, inside and outside the Liberal party, and from Queen Victoria and London society. Taken as a whole, Gladstone's Irish policy cannot be regarded as an election strategy. Over a generation, it brought him many reverses and much personal heartache.[21]

Gladstone's great electoral victory in 1868 was also achieved at some long-term political cost. As Gladstone's Irish policy became enacted in legislation, it aroused a deep anxiety on the part of the conservative establishment. To the Tory party, the disestablishment of the Irish Church in 1869 represented a fatal breach of the 1800 Act of Union, and thereby posed a threat to the unity of the British Empire. The first Land Act, which followed in 1870, was seen as a dangerous attack on the property rights of landlords. Among the propertied classes, it was regarded as an alarming precedent that might be followed in like measure in England. Such were the fears aroused by Gladstone's Irish policy that it created a countervailing force in the Conservative party, both to develop imperialism as a Conservative issue and to defend landownership against radical attack.

In fact, the Land Act, which was based on the Devon Commission (1845) recommendation to grant compensation for tenants' improvements, proved to be easily evaded by landlords. When there was a renewed agricultural depression in the late 1870s, the increase in evictions revealed how justified was the Irish demand for security of tenure. In response to severe agricultural depression in Ireland, and a wave of discontent represented by the Irish Land League, Gladstone introduced another Land Bill in his second ministry in 1881. This conceded to Irish tenants what was known as 'the three F's- fair rents, fixity of tenure, and free sale of holdings'. Judicial tribunals had the power to review rents and to prevent eviction of tenants who had paid a tribunal rent.

The first phase of Gladstone's Irish policy not only failed to solve the Irish question, but succeeded in creating a Tory backlash and the powerful party rallying cry of the defence of the Empire. At the same time, it did not appease the Irish sense of grievance but rather raised expectations among Irish nationalists, who remained opposed to piecemeal reform.

In 1870, under the leadership of a Tory, Protestant, Irishman, Isaac Butt, an organisation called the Home Government Association began a campaign for separate rule. Butt was a lawyer who had defended Meagher and Smith O'Brien after the 1848 rising, and the Fenian prisoners from 1865. Although conservative in outlook, he had become disillusioned with the failure of the Act of Union. His achievement was to unite three separate strands of Irish discontent, Tenant Right, the Amnesty movement for convicted Fenians, and his own Home Government Association, into a nationalist movement for Home Rule. Under Butt, the movement never commanded overwhelming support among Irish MPs. Only 51 out of 103 voted for a Home Rule motion on 30 June 1874.[22] Yet Butt had succeeded in bringing together disparate elements that could become a major political force in the hands of his successor, the formidable MP for Meath, Charles Stewart Parnell.

It was the renewal of severe economic difficulties in Ireland in the late 1870s, culminating in the land agitation during the period 1879 to 1882, that created the conditions for Parnell to become President of the Land League in 1879 and, in 1880, leader of the Irish Parliamentary party. After a generation of rising expectations in Irish agriculture, smallholders, larger tenant farmers and shopkeepers were all seriously affected by a drastic loss of production and removal of credit. The failure of the potato crop in the western counties brought the renewed onset of famine conditions; and land agitation, with Fenian support, began in County Mayo. Michael Davitt, who was a popular figure from his recent involvement in the Amnesty campaign for Fenian prisoners, waged a war of resistance against further evictions. When Parnell came to Westport, County Mayo, on 1 June 1879, he instructed tenants to pay only those rents that were 'according to the times' and to 'keep a firm grip on your homesteads and lands'.[23]

Not since the days of Daniel O'Connell had the Irish people such a charismatic champion. A Protestant landowner from County Wicklow, Parnell had inherited anti-British attitudes from the American side of his family and had learnt to resist English condescension at Cambridge University. Whilst he was attracted to the romance of Fenian nationalism, he was uniquely equipped to understand English customs and institutions. His great contribution was to harness the tradition of rebellion and nationalist sentiment within a parliamentary party capable of exercising real influence as a third force in the political battle between the two great parties at Westminster.

Parnell was both a skilful parliamentarian and a fine speaker combining the infuriating tactics of a mammoth filibuster in parliament with the rhetoric of extremism to capture eager audiences in America and in Ireland. He was able to use a form of moral intimidation, backed by the very real menace of agrarian violence in Ireland and the alarming threat of Fenian outrages in England. Roy Foster has described the sustained expression of such a political force, which embraced a wide diversity of interests, as a 'triumph of language'.[24]

As the land campaign spread throughout Ireland and a Fenian bomb campaign began in England, Gladstone was compelled to appease opinion in Britain by adopting coercive powers at the same time as the introduction of the Land Act in 1881. The Land League was declared illegal, and Parnell was arrested in October 1881. Following a spell in Kilmainham jail, which only added to his lustre in Ireland, Parnell was released in May 1882 to make an arrangement with the Liberal party. This involved the abandonment of violence in exchange for a parliamentary alliance. In the 1885 election, Parnell was able to deliver eighty-six Home Rule supporters among the Irish members to the Liberal camp. As it happened, this constituted the exact difference between the

Liberals (335) and the Conservatives (249). Parnell could not have given the Conservatives a majority, he could only sustain the Liberals in power.

Following the 1885 election, the pressure of Parnell and the Irish Parliamentary party appeared to move Gladstone towards the adoption of Home Rule as the price of continuing Irish support. The charge of opportunism was made against Gladstone in 1885 as it was in 1868. Yet the circumstances in 1885–6 were not so clear-cut, and the advantages by no means as certain. On a personal level, Gladstone had suffered in popular esteem over the death of General Gordon at Khartoum. He, himself, recognised that at that time any major Irish initiative of his own would not be favourably received by the British public. Whilst Gladstone had come round to the view that Home Rule was the surest way to retain Ireland within the United Kingdom, his critics in England and in Ulster exercised gloomy forebodings that, ultimately, it would lead not only to Irish separatism but to the spread of similar demands for independence throughout the Empire. Equally, Gladstone wished to present Home Rule as a logical extension of his 1868 mission to 'pacify Ireland', the continuation of an essentially conciliatory policy in the removal of just grievances in pursuit of 'justice for Ireland'. To his opponents, this looked like abject surrender in the face of violence and the fickle support of the Irish Parliamentary party.

Gladstone's first instinct was to create a consensus across both parties by winning over the Conservative leader, Lord Salisbury, to an acceptance of Home Rule as a constitutional issue. Lord Carnarvon, the Tory Lord-Lieutenant of Ireland, was known to favour Home Rule, but was overruled by the generally hostile sentiment among Tory leaders. Salisbury himself, could see dangers of a split in the Tory party and identified the maverick figure of Lord Randolph Churchill as the most likely to play the role adopted by Disraeli over Sir Robert Peel's policy on the repeal of the Corn Laws in 1846. The fatal split had kept the Conservative party unable to form a majority government until Disraeli's ministry in 1874. So, Salisbury, mindful in case history should repeat itself, rejected Gladstone's overtures.

Gladstone also faced powerful opposition within his own party such that, in the event, it was the Liberal party that became split over the question of Home Rule. The most serious defection was that of Joseph Chamberlain, a rising star on the radical wing of the party whose personal and policy ambitions were blocked by Gladstone's obsession with Ireland and its monopoly of parliamentary time. During the Home Rule debates, Chamberlain made effective criticisms of what was meant by Home Rule and certainly contributed to the level of dissent among the Liberal ranks. John Bright, another radical supporter in the past, was also fiercely critical of a policy which he described as 'surrender in Ireland, surrender in the Sudan, surrender in the Transvaal, surrender to terrorism'.[25] Other defectors included many leading Whigs who, as Liberal Unionists, moved over to the Conservatives in defence of the integrity of the Act of Union. If Gladstone had been persuaded to adopt Home Rule for party political reasons, he not only failed to understand the situation but succeeded in inflicting long-term damage to the prospects of the Liberal party. It is more likely that his own sense of moral duty and the stubborn conviction of old age propelled him on against all the forces ranged against him.

These included a curious alliance of intellectuals, the court and high society. Leading Victorian sages—Arnold, Froude, Spencer and Tennyson—all openly opposed Gladstone's Home Rule policy. A more sinister influence was exerted at court and in London society, where Gladstone was considered to be a lunatic or a traitor, and was largely ostracised in society. Queen Victoria was known to share the same sentiments. Personal relations between the monarch and her first minister had always been difficult, ever since Gladstone, during his first ministry, had encouraged the Queen to purchase a house in Ireland, and wanted the Prince of Wales appointed as viceroy there, as a way of instilling loyal affection among the Irish people. His efforts and manner were deeply resented as a gross interference into the personal lives of the royal family, and as an implied criticism of the Queen in neglecting her public duties. In the highly charged atmosphere surrounding the Home Rule issue, whispers in the Queen's ear by a few Conservative MPs, among whom Col. Tottenham was prominent, gave lurid details of Gladstone's nightwalking activities in rescuing prostitutes on the streets of London. On the advice of friends, Gladstone was forced to give up his rescue work because of the political damage that public disclosure would bring.

Little wonder that Gladstone, in his Home Rule address to the electors of Midlothian, on 1 May 1886, found himself beleaguered.

Ranged against him 'in profuse abundance, station, title, wealth, social influence, the professions, . . . in a word, the spirit and power of Classes and the dependents of Class!' Defiantly, Gladstone claimed that the classes had uniformly fought on the wrong side during the past sixty years and in the end were always beaten 'by a power very difficult to marshal—'the upright sense of the nation'.[26]

In presenting the Home Rule Bill in 1886, Gladstone prepared a carefully argued case in which he stressed not only the abominable way Ireland had been treated by England since the Union—'a broad and black blot' on the British record, but emphasised the economic interest Britain had in passing the administration of Ireland to Dublin. In moving away from the oblivion of the past, he declared, 'our interest is deeper than even hers'.[27] The blend of moral obligation and practical advantage was insufficient in argument to carry the day against the fears and emotions that surrounded the Home Rule issue. With ninety-one Liberals voting against the measure, the bill was lost by 343 votes to 313. In the subsequent election of 1886, which was fought over the issue of Home Rule, the Liberals suffered defeat as a divided party. With the Conservative party winning 216 seats, supported by seventy-eight Liberal Unionists, there was a combined majority of 118 over the 191 Gladstonian Liberals and eighty-five Irish Nationalists. The controversy among historians over whether Gladstone was guided by moral principles or by political motives may have posed a false dichotomy. A practical politician, intent on winning power, has to be mindful of electoral considerations. Yet Gladstone's assumption of the high moral ground formed part of his appeal to a substantial section of the electorate, who were prepared to trust to his lead on major issues. Gladstone's conversion to Home Rule encompassed both the profoundly moral case for the atonement of past misrule and the practical need to combat social disorder in Ireland.

A recent study by James Loughlin moves the debate forward by reassessing certain aspects of the Home Rule question.[28] Loughlin argues that it is too simple to accept Gladstone's Home Rule policy as wholly progressive and the Conservative and Unionist opposition to it as irredeemably reactionary. Gladstone relied on two or three close colleagues for information on the state of Ireland and was convinced, particularly by James Bryce's memorandum of 1885, that Ireland was on the verge of social dissolution. The land market had ceased to function. Only urgent action would rescue Ireland from a state of complete anarchy and the subsequent spread of violence in England.

Gladstone's historic model of Grattan's Parliament of the 1780s, as a precedent for a Dublin Parliament of the 1880s, incorporated assumptions of a restored gentry leadership in a stable and prosperous Ireland. Gladstone's diary reveals the influence of Edmund Burke on the formulation of Home Rule policy.[29] Burke's view of nationality, arising from an organic theory of society and the belief in the aristocracy as a governing class, was wholly acceptable to Gladstone. Yet, the reliance on historical precedent and on conservative philosophy, at once appealing to Gladstone's intellect, was far removed from the realities of Ireland in the 1880s. The faith in the Irish gentry to exercise political leadership and to sustain a stable social order was wholly misplaced since the landowning class was on the point of disintegration. The failure to recognise the role of agrarian struggle in the nationalist movement left him vulnerable to attack from political opponents concerned with the threats to property rights in both Ireland and in England.

In examining the arguments over the Home Rule issue, Loughlin attempts to penetrate beyond the expressed religious fears of the Unionist opposition to the practical objections to the proposed settlement. In particular, the issue of an estimated £4.5 million 'tribute' to be paid to the English treasury was seen as an obvious source of future resentment which would foster rather than defuse social disorder. John Bright spoke for a number of English Liberals and Radicals in opposing Home Rule: 'It would lead to friction, constant friction, between the two countries. The Irish Parliament would be constantly struggling to burst the bars of the statutory cage in which it sought to confine it.'[30]

Even more serious was the unresolved problem of Ulster. Certainly, the fears of Ulster Unionists were dismissed too lightly in the nationalist press and the threat of resistance to a Dublin Parliament and to 'Rome Rule' were discounted as empty bluster, reminiscent of the events of 1829 over Catholic Emancipation and 1869 over the Disestablishment of the Irish Church. Northern Protestants, at the time of the Belfast riots in 1886, might proclaim a loyalty to the British Empire and identify with an Anglo-Saxon sense of superiority over the Celtic Irish, but these sentiments provided only a token covering for religious and economic fears. Tales of Catholic atrocities and religious persecution formed an essential part of Unionist folklore. Ancient memory was called on to demonstrate how the Catholics could never be trusted. A leaflet entitled, 'Read What Was Done To The Protestants When The Rebels Had Home Rule' pointed to the involvement of Catholic priests in the atrocities of 1641. Deepseated fears were aroused by the prospect of a Dublin Parliament imposing the Roman Catholic Church throughout Ireland. Protestants feared that they would be driven from their farms and holdings through religious persecution. Protestant anxieties were the more painful because of a sense of betrayal made manifest by the consideration of Home Rule by the Westminster Parliament. Ulster loyalists believed in a contractual relationship with Britain—having come to Ireland to colonise the country, England, for its part, was surely bound not to hand them over to their Catholic enemies.[31] The presence of the Catholic majority, not only throughout the whole of Ireland, but in five of the nine Ulster counties, and the prospect of betrayal in England through Home Rule, created a beleaguered mentality, unwilling to trust or to compromise with friend or foe.

After the election of 1885, high hopes were expressed that the Irish vote in Britain would advance the cause of Home Rule. The Irish Nationalist party claimed that almost forty constituencies were lost by the Liberals as a result of the Irish vote responding to Parnell's call to the Irish to vote against them. John Denvir was confident that the spirit of national pride among the Irish in Britain could make a vital difference in electoral terms to the creation of national freedom.[32] The work of modern scholars, however, shows that such aspirations were guided more by wishful-thinking than by a realistic assessment. Alan O'Day, for instance, in reviewing the evidence for the Irish influence on parliamentary elections in London, has concluded that the Irish could command a numerical presence in certain constituencies, but that they were unable to change the outcome of elections even if they had voted en bloc.[33] This was simply because Irish voters formed part of the predominantly working-class community where they lived. If some had voted Conservative in 1885, thereafter they were 'overwhelmingly Liberal'. As part of the opposition to the Conservatives, Irish voters were unable to change things, either by abstaining or by bartering their votes. Also, unlike the situation in Liverpool, there was no significant anti-Irish 'backlash' discernible in the pattern of London voting, as the Irish were merely one among many different ethnic groups, and a multiplicity of factors determined how votes were cast. The electoral map of London showed that very few constituencies could change hands with a small shift in voting behaviour. Also the size of parliamentary constituencies after 1885 was simply too large for a group like the Irish to exercise sufficient leverage on the political parties.

A further attempt was made to push through Home Rule after Gladstone returned to power in 1890, despite the fall of Parnell over the O'Shea affair, followed by his death in 1891. Although an amended second Home Rule Bill passed the Commons in 1893, it was massively defeated in the House of Lords. Gladstone retired, beaten but unbowed, lamenting the failure of his great Irish mission. Parnell's death had left a divided Irish Parliamentary party but under the leadership of John Redmond in 1900, it was able once more to play a balancing act between the two great parties, and succeeded in re-introducing the Home Rule issue in the Edwardian period. Despite a growing consensus in both parties that Home Rule could not be indefinitely delayed it was ultimately defeated by a fiercely determined armed resistance by Ulster Protestants led by Edward Carson ('Ulster will fight and Ulster will be right'), and encouraged in illegal recourse to arms by leading members of the Conservative party. Hence the curious paradox of a threat of armed resistance to the forces of the crown by people who swore complete loyalty to the institutions and authority of the Union.

Home Rule represents one of the great 'if only's' of British history. If only Gladstone had succeeded in passing one of his Home Rule bills through parliament, or if the third Home Rule bill had been passed in 1912, it is conceivable that the whole of Ireland would still form part of the United Kingdom, albeit largely administered from Dublin, with its own parliament and separate facility to raise taxes. It follows that without subsequent partition and the Protestant exploitation of the Catholic minority in what became officially known as Northern Ireland, but remained the six counties to the nationalist community, there would have been no need for the civil rights marches in the 1960s and the onset of the modern 'troubles' that appear to resist all political or military solution.

Sadly, such a scenario is too selective in its focus. True, there was a large measure of acceptance for the policy of Home Rule in

Ireland, when it was offered, but that was because it was all that was on offer at the time. The Tory argument that, once the Act of Union was set aside and a measure of independence was granted, then there was no way of preventing further extensions until a completely separate state was established, rightly carried weight. It was as prophetic as the Tory defence of the pre–1832 parliament. Once the principle of reform was accepted, further extensions of the franchise were inevitable. Parnell, himself, chose not to put a limit on nationhood. His strength lay in his equivocation in choosing not to engage in definitions and specific proposals. The Home Rule movement, indeed, was an umbrella that concealed a diversity of aims and interests. Gladstone, in framing legislation, had to offer precise models of a system of self-government that could be made to work. In doing so, he suggested a new model of Britishness that incorporated a multi-national state of the four home countries.[34] Whereas the Welsh and the Scots had reconciled their symbols of nationality within a wider British identity and the Scots had their own legal and educational systems, the Irish had clearly suffered from the imposition of English law. Home Rule would have allowed diversity of legislation with a Dublin Parliament whilst preserving imperial unity and the ultimate supremacy of Westminster.

It is not entirely fanciful to imagine the appeal of a royal presence and the waving of the Union Jack throughout Ireland continuing beyond the First World War. The surprisingly high proportion of Catholic Irish (36,775 out of a total of 75,795) who had enlisted by December 1915 is one indication of a shared British identity.[35] The hostile reaction of the Dublin public to the captured rebels in 1916 has been interpreted as a betrayal of Irish boys fighting at the front, but it also reflects a wider sense of Britishness among the Irish people. When the Irish troops returned from the war in 1919, they were welcomed back with union flags.[36]

The Home Rule movement inherited the earlier radical commitment not only to 'Ireland for the Irish' but also to 'the land for the people'. Tenant right and freedom from eviction secured most of what was demanded but further threats to property rights were ultimately resisted by the rich graziers and 'strong' farmers who provided the mainstay of nationalist support. Although the Irish Parliamentary party employed anti-landlord rhetoric, the Land League and subsequent legislation strengthened class divisions within the farming community, protecting the wealthier farmers and resisting a challenge from the poor smallholders. A bottom third of Irish farmers remained discontented by the failure to safeguard their interests. The wave of Irish national sentiment unleashed with the execution of the 1916 rebels, Pearse and Connolly, overwhelmed sectional conflicts in a united hostility to the British government. As Paul Bew has argued, the conservative majority of substantial farmers, who had gained most from the land legislation of the British Parliament, imposed their own vision on the new nationalism after 1916 and on the new Irish Parliament in the 1920s.[37]

The ultimate settlement of the land question, although it achieved a remarkable transformation in the structure and owner- ship of Irish agriculture, virtually eliminating the landowning class, fell some way short of the dream of a peasant proprietorship for the whole of rural Ireland. Landowners were replaced by rich farmers and graziers, who formed a powerful élite, each occupying several hundred acres, whilst the poorest smallholders lost out in the inexorable march of capitalist agriculture.

All this was clearly understood by Ulster Protestants in dis- missing Irish nationalism as a sham and in describing the Home Rule movement as led by a 'collection of disreputable, violent and opportunistic politicians backed by Land Leaguers and Fenian dynamiters'.[38] Certainly there was fear of Catholic domination with the prospect of Home Rule or 'Rome Rule' administered from Dublin, and a loss of faith in a Westminster Parliament that could contemplate such a thing. The economic perspective was also different from that of Ulster, where prosperity in the industrial heartland of the Belfast region was strongly identified with the British imperial markets for linen textiles and shipbuilding. The Act of Union was seen as an act of providence contributing to Britain's powerful status in the world during the nineteenth century. Moreover, the contemporary examples of the unification of Germany and of Italy showed that breaking up the Union would seem to fly in the face of history and only undermine the basis of British power.

From the British perspective, economic, political and strategic interests, all pointed to the importance of preserving the Union. In British eyes, the execution of the Irish rebels in 1916 was nothing more than normal military practice in wartime, more justifiable in fact than the shooting of English or Irish deserters at the front. It can now be judged a monumental blunder which only prompted a tide of nationalist fervour on behalf of Irish patriots. The contrast between the hostile treatment Dubliners gave to the captured rebels and the wild jubilation that marked the release of their comrades who were not executed, a few weeks later, is the measure of the British mistake. This was compounded by the government's response to republican violence on the part of the Irish Volunteers, the IRA. The unlicensed destruction carried out by the 'Black and Tans' in Ireland was partly a result of the brutalising effect of the Great War. Battle-hardened veterans of the British army were in no mood to respect civilian rights and, disgracefully, were not discouraged or restrained from bully-boy methods in a search and destroy policy deployed against Irish rebels.

These actions represented a failure by the British government to accept the Irish people as 'fully-fledged citizens of the British state, let alone members of a British nation'.[39] Perversely, in seeking to bludgeon the Irish into submission and acceptance of Westminster rule, the crown forces had succeeded in driving the Irish into separatism. A profound sense of revulsion set in against conduct that belied the British sense of fairness and decency.

Whilst pursuing policies that were entirely counter-productive there was no British recognition of Irish nationality. The Prime Minister, Lloyd George, who had regard for Welsh as a living language, was contemptuous of the pretensions of the Irish language: 'they put up names at street corners to the confusion of every patriot'.[40] Exasperated in negotiation with Irish politicians, he thought up the idea of two nations in Ireland, with an entirely artificial separation drawn up between north and south. The Ulster Unionists were decreed to be a quite separate entity and an unhistoric Ulster created out of the six counties. The Government of Ireland Act in 1919 established a parliament at Stormont when it was not the wish of the Ulster Unionists, and the familiar British concept of dominion status was conferred on the Irish Free State in 1922. The Irish Republic was established in 1948.

Looking back to what was hoped for and forward to what came about in the period 1916 to 1922, there are three distinctive phases in the development of Irish popular movements in a British political context. All were to exercise influence over the eventual outcome—a period of conflict out of which emerged the Irish Free State in 1922. Inherent contradictions were built into the eventual settlement of a partitioned island.

The first phase, lasting from the Act of Union in 1800 until the Fenian outrages of 1867, was marked by mass protest, best exemplified by O'Connell's Catholic Association and Repeal movement, but was also linked up with the English Chartists in 1848. This was a form of moral intimidation supported by agrarian violence and the threat of physical force. Both Chartism and the Repeal movement appealed to an imaginary past and a sense of justice, with rather vague notions of the sovereignty of the people and the sovereign right of the people to possess their own land, acting as guiding principles.

The reaction of the British authorities was uniformly repressive to the demands of English radicals and to Irish nationalists. Coercive measures, additional use of police powers and the strengthening of military force, were invariably adopted, with the suspension of civil liberties. Such measures were brutally effective in removing dangerous leaders and in suppressing violent uprisings or sporadic disorder.

The second phase began with Gladstone's mission 'to pacify Ireland' in 1868 and ended with the final failure to achieve Home Rule in 1912. Gladstone accepted the principle of Britain's misrule of Ireland in the past and, through the legislative removal of just grievances, endeavoured to retain the loyalty of the Irish people within a United Kingdom framework. Although agrarian violence recurred, particularly during the Land War of 1879–1882, and Fenian and American bombings featured in the 1880s, the period was dominated by activity in the parliamentary arena. Parnell made a major contribution to the focus on Parliament in harnessing the support of extra-Parliamentary activists such as the Fenians and the Land League to lend credibility to the rhetoric of the Irish Home Rule party.

If Gladstone succeeded in legitimising Irish national aspirations through his piecemeal reforms, the attacks on landlords and property rights, and the threat to the integrity of the Act of Union aroused deep-seated conservative instincts on the question of the Empire. This was to prove electorally important in British politics in uniting the Conservatives, splitting the Liberals, and in reinvigorating the Ulster Protestants.

The third phase came into full prominence in the 1890s and so overlaps with the second. It took the form of a cultural nationalism that was quite separate from Parliamentary legislation or political manoeverings. Essentially, the argument for a separate Irish state was based on the notion of a separate Irish identity and culture. With enthusiasm for the revival of the Gaelic language and a renewed interest in the customs and ancient history of Ireland, it was a movement championed by leading writers like W. B. Yeats, J. M. Synge and Douglas Hyde who attempted to de-Anglicise Ireland in search of some kind of Irish spiritual purity. It was fanciful and romantic but also contained within it the strangely appealing notion of self-sacrifice as a test of nationhood that was heroically enacted in the Easter Rising in 1916.

If it was fanciful to dream of a republican Ireland, united under a uniformly accepted Catholic religion and with all its people subscribing to a common Gaelic language and culture, it was the pursuit of such a dream, against all the odds, that led to the ultimate creation of a separate Irish state, occupying most of the island of Ireland. If it was fanciful to expect the Irish people to remain content to be ruled by the Imperial Parliament, there existed in Ireland a sufficient sense of shared Britishness and common experience of language, customs and institutions, to limit the appeal of a separatist nationalism, at least in Protestant Ulster. What was achieved in 1922 was a crude compromise, unwanted by virtually all the participants. The unrelenting pressure for legislative reform and repeal of the union ultimately created a countervailing force that resisted the pressure for change.

An indomitable belief, held by a tiny minority of romantics, in a nationalist ideal, was pitted against an implacable refusal to yield to violent pressure, on the part of the British establishment, which was determined to defend the integrity of the Empire. The methods employed on both sides were not pretty, or easy to defend, with hindsight. Yet, ultimately, the historical outcome determined that the insensitive blundering of the British authorities did more to popularise nationalism in Ireland than either the 'heroic' deeds of the 'bold Fenian men' or the literary output and activity of the Gaelic revivalists.

Notes

Since these reference notes give complete bibliographical information about works cited and/or consulted by the author, no bibliography has been compiled.

Introduction, pp.1–9.

1   J.E. Handley, *The Irish in Scotland, 1789–1845*, Cork 1943, *The Irish in Modern Scotland*, Cork 1947, *The Navvy in Scotland*, Cork 1970; J.A. Jackson, *The Irish in Britain*, London 1963. K. O'Connor, *The Irish in Britain*, London 1972, concentrates mostly on the Irish experience in twentieth-century Britain. For a recent bibliography, see M. Hickman and M. Hartigan, *The History of the Irish in Britain: A Bibliography*, London 1986.

2   J. Epstein and D. Thompson, eds, *The Chartist Experience*, London 1982; D. Brooke, *The Railway Navvy*, Newton Abbot 1983.

3   Lynn Lees, *Exiles of Erin: Irish Migrants in Victorian London*, Manchester 1979; Frank Neal, *Sectarian Violence: The Liverpool Experience, 1819–1914*, Manchester 1987; Frances Finnegan, *Poverty and Prejudice: Irish Immigrants in York, 1840–1875*, Cork 1982: R. Swift and S. Gilley, eds, *The Irish in the Victorian City*, London 1985, id., *The Irish in Britain, 1815–1939*, London 1989.

4   Kerby Miller, *Emigrants and Exiles: Ireland and the Irish Exodus to North America*, Oxford 1985; Patrick O'Farrell, *The Irish in Australia*, Kensington, New South Wales 1987.

5   Colin Holmes, *John Bull's Island: Immigration and British Society, 1871–1971*, London 1988.

6   Swift and Gilley, *The Irish in the Victorian City*, op. cit., pp.1–12.

7   See chapter 1, Emigration.

8   See chapter 2, Little Irelands; Lynn Lees, op. cit.; D. Large, 'The Irish in Bristol in 1851', in Swift and Gilley, *The Irish in the Victorian City*, op. cit., pp. 37–58.

9   Census of Great Britain 1861, Appendix to Report, Table 126, p. 160.

10 J. Denvir, *The Irish in Britain*, London 1892; J. Hickey, *Urban Catholics*, London 1967.

11 Frank Neal, op. cit., pp. 37–121.

12 Swift and Gilley, *The Irish in the Victorian City*, op. cit., pp. 115, 207–24; Hickey, op. cit.

13   W.L. Arnstein, 'The Murphy Riots: A Victorian Dilemma', *Victorian Studies*, xix (1975), pp. 51–71.
14   R.J. Cooter, 'The Irish in County Durham and Newcastle c. 1840–1880', unpublished. M.A. thesis, University of Durham (1972), p. 57; Swift and Gilley, op. cit., pp. 37–58; H.J. Paine, *Report to the General Board of Health on the town of Cardiff*, London 1850; J.P. Kay, *The Moral and Physical Condition of the Working Classes employed in the Cotton Manufacture in Manchester*, Manchester 1832.
15   Bernard Aspinwall and John F. McCaffrey, 'A Comparative view of the Irish in Edinburgh in the Nineteenth Century', in Swift and Gilley, op. cit., pp. 130–57.
16   Jim Young, 'The Irish in Hull', *History Workshop Conference*, Leeds 1986.
17   See chapter 2, Little Irelands.
18   Alan O'Day, *The Irish in England in 1872*, London 1989.
19   Brenda Collins, 'Irish Emigration to Dundee and Paisley during the First Half of the Nineteenth Century', in J.M. Goldstrom and L.A. Clarkson, eds, *Irish Population, Economy and Society: Essays in Honour of the late K H Connell*, Oxford 1981, p. 195.
20   Denvir, op cit.
21   S. Gilley, 'English Attitudes to the Irish in England, 1798–1900', in C. Holmes, *Immigrants and Minorities in British Society*, London 1978, pp. 81–110.
22   See chapter 1, Emigration.
23   R. Dudley Edwards and T.D. Williams, eds, *The Great Famine: Studies in Irish History, 1845–52*, Dublin 1956.
24   Rachel O'Higgins, 'Irish influence in the Chartist Movement', *Past and Present*, vol. 20 (1961), pp. 83–96; J.H. Treble, 'O'Connor, O'Connell and the attitudes of Irish Immigrants towards Chartism in the north of England 1838–1848' in J. Butt and I.F. Clarke, eds, *The Victorians and Social Protest: a Symposium*, Newton Abbot 1973; D. Thompson, *The Chartists*, London 1984; Neville Kirk, *The Growth of Working-Class Reformism in Mid-Victorian England*, London 1985; J. Saville, *1848: The British State and the Chartist Movement*, Cambridge 1987; Stanley H. Palmer, *Police and Protest in England and Ireland, 1780–1850*, Cambridge 1988. See also chapter 5, Chartism.
25   K.R.M. Short, *The Dynamite War: Irish-American Bombers in Victorian Britain*, New Jersey 1979. See also chapter 6, Irish Nationalism.

Chapter 1, pp. 10–50.
1   R. Dudley Edwards and T. Desmond Willams, eds, *The Great Famine: Studies in Irish History 1845–52*, Dublin 1956; Cecil Woodham-Smith, *The Great Hunger*, London 1962.
2   P. Johnson, *Ireland: Land of Troubles*, London 1980, pp. 96–109; O. Macdonagh, 'The Irish Famine Emigration to the United States', *Perspectives in American History*, vol. X (1976), pp. 357–446.

3   On the eve of the Great Famine between the censuses of 1841 and 1951, the population of Ireland was probably in the region of 9 million.

4   O'Grada, 'A Note on Nineteenth-Century Irish Emigration Statistics', *Population Studies*, vol. 29 (1975), pp. 143–49.

5   Ibid, p. 148.

6   Joel Mokyr, 'Malthusian Models and Irish History', *Journal of Economic History* vol. XL, No. 1 (March 1980), pp. 159–66.

7   Joel Mokyr, *Why Ireland Starved: A Quantitative and Analytical History of the Irish Economy 1800–1850*, London 1983, chapter 3, pp. 30–80.

8   Kerby Miller, *Emigrants and Exiles: Ireland and the Irish Exodus to North America*, Oxford 1985, p. 193.

9   R. Crotty, *Irish Agricultural Production*, Cork 1966; J. Lee, 'Irish Agriculture: Review Article', *Agricultural History Review*, vol. 17 part 1 (1969) pp. 61–76; J. Donnelly, *The Land and the People of Nineteenth-Century Cork*, London 1975.

10   Thomas Gallagher, *Paddy's Lament: Ireland 1846–1847: Prelude to Hatred*, Dublin 1985, p. 148.

11   Eoin O'Malley, 'The Decline of Irish Industry in the Nineteenth Century', *Economic and Social Review*, vol. 13, No. 1, (1981), p. 33.

12   Brenda Collins, 'Proto-industrialisation and pre-Famine emigration', *Social History*, vol. 7 No. 2 (1982), pp. 127–46.

13   O'Malley, op. cit., pp. 21–42.

14   Ibid., p. 22.

15   The singular success of the Guinness Brewery, a further example of concentration, in this instance in Dublin, is referred to by O'Malley drawing on R. Crotty's unpublished work on the subject.

16   L.M. Cullen, *An Economic History of Ireland since 1660*, London 1972.

17   See also Crotty, op. cit.

18   Kerby Miller, op. cit., p. 198.

19   S.H. Cousens, 'The Regional Pattern of Emigration during the Great Irish Famine 1846–51', *Institute of British Geographers*, Transactions and Papers, No. 28 (1962), pp. 126–9.

20   S.H. Cousens, 'The Regional Variations in Population Changes in Ireland 1861–1881', *Economic History Review*, vol. 17 (1964), pp. 301–21.

21   Ibid., p. 310, fig. 4.

22   Ibid., p. 320.

23   C. O'Grada, 'Seasonal Migration and post-famine Adjustment in the West of Ireland', *Studia Hibernia*, vol. 13 (1973) pp. 48–76.

24   Ibid, p. 60.

25   Ibid, p. 60.

26   D. Fitzpatrick, 'Irish Emigration in the Late Nineteenth Century', *Irish Historical Studies*, vol. 22 (1980), pp. 126–43.

27   Ibid., p. 129.

28   M.A. G. Ó Tuathaigh, 'The Irish in Nineteenth-Century Britain: Problems of Integration', *Transactions of the Royal Historical Society*, 5th series, vol. 31 (1981), pp. 149–74.

29   Patrick O'Farrell, 'Whose Reality? The Irish Famine in History and Literature', *Historical Studies*, vol. 20 (1982), pp. 1–13.

30   Seamus MacCall, *Irish Mitchell: A Biography*, London 1938.

31   Sean Cronin, *Irish Nationalism: A History of its Roots and Ideology*, London 1983, p. 79.

32   J. Mitchel, *Jail Journal or Five Years in British Prisons*, author's edition, 1876, p. 16.

33   Ibid., p. 15.

34   Ibid.

35   Ibid.

36   J. Caird, *English Agriculture in 1851*, 1852.

37   J. Mitchel, *The Last Great Conquest of Ireland (Perhaps)*, 1876, p. 219.

38   Ibid., p. 105. The charge of genocide was not a new one. Dean Swift's infamously satirical *A Modest Proposal*, which recommended that eating of babies as a cure for overpopulation in Ireland, had been written more than a hundred years earlier.

39   O'Farrell, op. cit., p. 3.

40   See, for example, Liam O'Flaherty, *Famine*, Dublin 1937.

41   Later published in a trilogy, R. Kee, *The Green Flag*, vol: 1: *The Most Distressful Country*, Harmondsworth 1989.

42   *Cork Examiner*, 2 November 1846, quoted in Robert Kee, *Ireland: A Television History*, London 1981, p. 90.

43   Gallagher, op. cit.

44   *Cork Examiner*, 26 December 1846, in Gallagher, op. cit., p. 69.

45   Woodham-Smith, op. cit., p. 169. An example of the charitable activity of English workmen is found in a report of a meeting of English artisans at Ransome's Iron Foundary, Ipswich, where it was agreed among the 500 workmen that they would give 1d a week for the next six months, apprentices ½d, for the charitable relief of distress in Ireland, *Mayo Constitution*, 16 February 1847.

46   *The Times*, 26 March 1847, in Gallagher, op. cit., pp. 68–9.

47   Woodham-Smith, op. cit., p. 69, letter of Mr Nicholas Cummins, Cork Magistrate.

48   Ibid., p. 156.

49   Ibid., p. 162.

50   Ibid., pp. 163–4.

51   James S. Donnelly Jnr, *The Land and the People of Nineteenth-Century Cork*, London 1975, pp. 123–4.

52   Roger McHugh, 'The Famine in Irish Oral Tradition', in Dudley Edwards and Williams, op. cit., pp. 391–436.

53   Ibid., pp. 395–6.

54   O. MacDonagh, 'Irish Overseas Emigration during the Great Famine', in Dudley Edwards and Williams, op. cit., p. 325.

55   J. Lee, *The Modernisation of Irish Society*, 1848–1918, Dublin 1973, pp. 2–3.

56   Donnelly, op. cit., p. 74.

57   Ibid., p. 103.

58   Ibid., p. 98; see also Christine Kinealy, 'The Administration of the Poor Law in Mayo, 1838–98, *Cathair Na Mart, Journal of the Westport Historical Society*, vol. 6, No. 1 (1986), p. 105.
59   *Cork Constitution*, 24 April 1847, in Donnelly, op. cit., p. 87.
60   Paedar O'Flanagain, 'An Outline History of the Town of Westport, part IV, The Famine Years, Its Aftermath 1845–1855', *Cathair Na Mart, Journal of the Westport Historical Society*, vol. 4, No. 1 (1984), pp. 74–9.
61   Kinealy, op. cit.
62   Donnelly, op. cit., p. 90; see also *The Mayo Constitution*, 4 May, 18 May and 26 May 1847.
63   Ibid., p. 88.
64   O.MacDonagh, 'The Irish Famine Emigration to the United States', *Perspectives in American History*, vol. X (1976), p. 421.
65   S.H. Cousens, 'Regional death rates in Ireland from 1846 to 1851', *Population Studies*, vol. XIV (1960–1), pp. 55–74, especially p. 70.
66   Donnelly, op. cit., p. 87.
67   Ibid, p. 91.
68   Kerby Miller, op. cit.
69   Ibid, p. 125.
70   Ibid, p. 126.
71   For instance, an emigration scheme for Catholic families from the Tullamore district to settle in Queensland, Australia, in 1862, was planned to rival an earlier Protestant settlement there.
72   *Galway Packet*, 15 May 1852.
73   *Galway Packet*, 30 June 1852; see also *Mayo Constitution*, 6 April, 8 June, 1847.
74   Hugh Loudon to Thomas Hewat, Provincial Bank of Ireland, London, from Skibbereen, 8 February 1865, National Library, Dublin.
75   O. MacDonagh, 'The Irish Famine Emigration to the United States', *Perspectives in American History*, vol. X (1976), pp. 379–83.
76   H.S. Irvine, 'Some Aspects of Passenger Traffic between Britain and Ireland 1820–1850', *Journal of Transport History*, 1960, vol. IV, Part 4, pp. 224–41.
77   Kerby Miller, op. cit., p. 253.
78   Irvine, op. cit., p. 231.
79   *Cork Constitution*, 15 April 1851.
80   J.E. Handley, *The Irish in Scotland*, Cork 1943, pp. 34–5.
81   *North British Railway and Shipping Journal*, 23 December 1848, in Handley, op. cit., p. 35.
82   Irvine, op. cit., pp. 230–1.
83   Charlotte Erikson, 'Emigration from the British Isles to the U.S.A. in 1831', *Population Studies*, vol. XXXV, No. 2 (July 1981), pp. 175–97.
84   Patrick MacGill, *Children of the Dead End*, first pub. 1914, 1980 edition Ascot, pp. 69–72.
85   *Mayo Constitution*, 15 February 1853.

86   P.S. O'Hegarty, *John Mitchel: An Appreciation with some account of Young Ireland*, Dublin and London 1917, p. 77.

Chapter 2, pp. 51–82.

1   For the Irish in the poor districts of eighteenth-century London, see M. Dorothy George, *London Life in the Eighteenth Century*, London 1925, reprinted 1979, pp.120–31.

2   See M.A.G. O'Tuathaigh, 'The Irish in Nineteenth Century Britain: Problems of Integration', *Transactions of the Royal Historical Society*, 5th series, vol. 31 (1981), pp. 149–74; Roger Swift and Sheridan Gilley, eds, *The Irish in the Victorian City*, London 1985. Their conclusions echo those of J.M. Werly, 'The Irish in Manchester 1832–1849', *Irish Historical Studies*, vol.18 (1973), pp. 345–58; T. Dillon, 'The Irish in Leeds 1851–1861', *Thoresby Miscellany*, vol. xvi (1979), pp.1–28; E.D. Steele, 'The Irish Presence in the North of England 1850–1941', *Northern History*, vol. 12 (1976), pp. 220–41— writing in the 1970s Steele's work represented something of a reaction against the work of J.A. Jackson, *The Irish in Britain*, London 1963, and E.P. Thompson, *The Making of the English Working Class*, London 1963.

3   L.P. Curtis, *Apes and Angels: The Irishman in Victorian Caricature*, Newton Abbott 1971; S. Gilley, 'English Attitudes to the Irish in England, 1798–1900', in C. Holmes, ed., *Immigrants and Minorities in British Society*, London 1978, pp.81–110.

4   Jackson, op. cit., p.11.

5   O'Tuathaigh, op. cit., p. 152.

6   D. Fitzpatrick, 'Irish Emigration in the late Nineteenth Century', *Irish Historical Studies*, vol. 22 (1980), p. 134; for discussion of the myth of Irish ghettos and for Irish settlement abroad, see D. Fitzpatrick, *Irish Emigration 1801–1921*, Studies in Irish Economic and Social History 1, Dublin (1984), pp. 32–7.

7   C. O'Grada, 'A Note on Nineteenth-Century Irish Statistics' *Population Studies*, vol. 29 (1975), pp. 143–9. A revised estimate of Irish emigration to Britain suggests that it represented between one-fifth and one-quarter of the total Irish emigration between 1852 and 1910 of almost 5 million.

8   B.M. Kerr, 'Irish Seasonal Migration to Great Britain, 1800–1838', *Irish Historical Studies*, vol. 2 (1942–3), pp. 365–80; D.Brooke, The Railway Navvy, Newton Abbot 1983; J.H. Treble, 'Irish Navvies in the North of England, 1830–50', *Transport History*, vol. 6 (1973), pp. 227–47.

9   Census of Great Britain 1861, Appendix to Report, Table 126, p.160.

10   E.H.Hunt, *British Labour History 1851–1941*, London 1981, p.34.

11   The figures have been calculated from B.R. Mitchell and P. Deane, *Abstract of British Historical Statistics*, Cambridge 1962, reprinted 1971, *Population and Vital Statistics*, 8, pp. 24–6 and J. Papworth,

'The Irish in Liverpool, 1853–71: Family Structure and Residential Mobility', unpublished Ph.D thesis, University of Liverpool (1982), Table 1.1, p 14. For a retrospective overview of the Scots and Irish in England and Wales, see Census of England and Wales, 1881, vol. 4 pp. 52–5.

12 A. Armstrong, *Stability and Change in an English County Town—a Social Study of York*, 1801–1851, Cambridge 1974; M. Anderson, *Family Structure in Nineteenth Century Lancashire*, Cambridge 1971.

13 See for example, C. Richardson, 'Irish Settlement in mid-nineteenth century Bradford', *Yorkshire Bulletin of Economic and Social Research*, vol. xx (1971), pp. 40–57.

14 Werly, op.cit., p. 346.

15 Ibid., p. 347.

16 Ibid., p. 346 from *Report on the State of The Irish Poor in Great Britain*, Parliamentary Papers (1836) (40) XXX, , pp. 546–7.

17 O'Tuathaigh, op. cit., p. 154.

18 Ibid.

19 J. P Kay, *The Moral and Physical Condition of the Working Classes Employed in the Cotton Manufacture in Manchester*, first published Manchester, 1832, reprinted 1969.

20 The influence of Malthus, Ricardo and Bentham is strongly evident in the pamphlet.

21 Frances Trollope, *Michael Armstrong, the Factory Boy*, 1840; Benjamin Disraeli, *Coningsby*, 1844, id., *Sybil*, 1845; Mrs Gaskell, *Mary Barton*, 1848, id., *North and South, 1845*. For a discussion of early Victorian Manchester as a major focus of literature, see Gary S. Messinger, *Manchester in the Victorian Age: The Half-known City*, Manchester 1985, pp. 89–112.

22 Kay, op.cit., pp. 34–5.

23 Ibid., pp. 21–2.

24 Dr Lyon Playfair, Supplement to the *Report on the Sanatory Condition of Large Towns in Lancashire*, Parliamentary Papers (1845), Appendix to the *2nd Report of the Commission*.

25 Ibid., p. 384. It is likely that life expectancy among Irish migrants in Liverpool and Manchester declined around 1840, see Robert E. Kennedy Jr, *The Irish: Emigration, Marriage and Fertility*, Berkeley 1973, p. 45.

26 John Redman, visiting overseer of the township of Manchester, Report on the Irish Poor, (1836) p. 523.

27 Ibid., James Guest, cotton manufacturer, pp. 540–1 James Taylor. silk millowner, pp. 542–3.

28 Replies to Questions for Circulation in Populous Towns and Districts, Borough of Liverpool, No. 51, Appendix to *Second Report of Commissioners of Inquiry into the state of large towns and populous districts*, Parliamentary Papers (1845) p. 392.

29 The average household size for the St Bartholomew's district in 1841 was 8.3.

30   G.P. Davis, 'Image and Reality in a Victorian provincial city: a working class district of Bath 1830–1900, unpublished Ph.D. thesis, University of Bath (1981) p. 165.

31   For the Irish in Avon Street, Bath, see Davis thesis, pp. 188–94 and 352–6.

32   Lynn Lees, *Exiles of Erin: Irish Migrants in Victorian London*, Manchester 1979, p. 63.

33   The wide dispersal of Irish migrants in every district of a city has also been identified in Bristol and York; D. Large, 'The Irish in Bristol in 1851' in Swift and Gilley, op. cit., pp. 37–58; F. Finnegan, *Poverty and Prejudice: A Study of Irish immigrants in York, 1840–75*, Cork 1982.

34   Lees, op. cit., p. 62

35   Ibid., p. 37; Kerby Miller, *Emigrants and Exiles: Ireland and the Irish Exodus to North America*, Oxford (1985) p. 293.

36   Papworth, op. cit.

37   J. E. Handley, *The Irish in Scotland*, Cork 1945 p. 261

38   S. Gilley, 'Catholic Faith of the Irish Slums', in H.J. Dyos and M. Wolff, eds, *The Victorian City: Images and Realities*, vol. 2, London 1973, pp. 837–53.

39   Papworth, op. cit., (p. 355) refers to the low persistence rate among the Irish of 10 per cent between one census and the next.

40   Engels, op. cit., p. 125

41   *Bath Chronicle*, 27 January 1848, Lord Ashley speaking at the Assembly Rooms, Bath.

42   H.J, Paine Report to the General Board of Health on the town of Cardiff, London 1850, p.44 in V.J.Hickey, 'The Origin and Growth of the Irish Community in Cardiff', unpublished M.A. thesis, University of Wales (1959).

43   *Cardiff Advertiser and Merthyr Guardian*, March 1850, in Hickey, ibid., p. 45.

44   R.J. Cooter, 'The Irish in County Durham and Newcastle c.1840–1880', unpublished M.A.thesis, University of Durham (1972), p. 57.

45   Swift and Gilley, op, cit., p. 59.

46   Ibid., pp. 37–58.

47   Richardson, op. cit., pp. 294–316.

48   Dillon, op. cit., pp. 14–16.

49   Werly, op. cit., pp. 355–6 .

50   Roger Swift, 'Another Stafford Street Row: Law, Order and the Irish Presence in mid-Victorian Wolverhampton', *Immigrants and Minorities*, vol. 3 (March 1984), pp. 5–29.

51   Barbara Weinberger, 'The Police and the Public in Mid-Nineteenth Century Warwickshire' in Victor Bailey, ed., *Policing and Punishment in Nineteenth Century Britain*, London 1981, p. 75.

52   W.A.Walker, *Juteopolis: Dundee and its textile workers, 1885–1923*, Edinburgh 1979, pp. 113–47.

53   Handley, op. cit., p. 261.
54   Edward Gillet and Kenneth A. MacMahon, *A History of Hull*, Oxford 1980; I am also indebted to Jim Young of Hull WEA for his paper 'The Irish in Hull' at History Workshop Conference, Leeds 1986.
55   S.Thomas, *The Bristol Riots*, Bristol 1974.
56   P. Marshall, *Bristol and the Abolition of Slavery: the Politics of Emancipation*, Bristol 1975.
57   D.A. Reeder, *Urban Education in the Nineteenth Century*, London 1977.
58   Swift and Gilley, op.cit., pp. 41–2.
59   Roderick Walters, *The Establishment of the Bristol Police Force*, Bristol 1975.
60   R. B. Pugh, 'Chartism in Somerset and Wiltshire' in Asa Briggs ed., *Chartist Studies*, London 1959, reprinted 1972, pp.182–5.
61   P. Millward, 'The Stockport Riots of 1852: A Study of Anti-Catholic and Anti-Irish Sentiment' in Swift and Gilley, op. cit., p. 210.
62   *Bristol Times and Bath Advocate*, 25 March 1852. (Hereinafter *Bristol Times*).
63   *Bristol Times*, 11 November 1851.
64   *Bristol Times*, 8 July 1848.
65   A party of Irishmen took advantage of the landlord's hospitality when a new beer-house opened on St James back. Free drinks were on offer to attract custom and the evening ended in 'a real Irish scrimmage'. *Bristol Times*, 10 July 1851.
66   *Bristol Times*, 15 July 1848.
67   *Bristol Times*, 17 April 1852.
68   *Bristol Times*, 2 January 1847; 23 January 1847.
      Latimer, *Annals of Bristol*, Bristol 1887, p. 303.
69   *Bristol Times*, 6 February 1847.
70   *Bristol Times*, 17 April 1847.
71   Ibid.
72   *Bristol Times*, 15 May 1847.
73   Reprinted in the *Bristol Times*, 31 July 1847.
74   *Bristol Times*, 22 May 1847.
75   *Bristol Times*, 10 July 1847.
76   *Bristol Times*, 24 July 1847; individual Irish vagrants and smaller groups of 'principally Irish' were treated similarly in the same year.
77   Ibid.
78   Ten thousand or so were reported to have arrived in London from Cork, *Bristol Times*, 22 March 1851.
79   *Bristol Times*, 30 October 1852.
80   *Bristol Times*, 19 April 1851.
81   In an article on 'Irish Poor, Poor Laws and Poor Houses', *Bristol Times*, 19 July 1851.
82   Other Irish Poor-Law authorities were also involved in emigration schemes. In May 1853 the Cork Guardians decided that 'the interests

of the union would be benefited by adopting an extensive scheme of emigration'. *Galway Packet*, 29 May 1852.

83   *Bristol Times*, 19 July 1851.
84   Charged with defrauding 'a poor Irish girl' of £10, as reported in the *Liverpool Times* and reprinted in the *Mayo Constitution* of 15 February 1853.
85   *Bristol Times*, 10 July 1852.
86   *Bristol Times*, 24 April 1852.
87   *Bristol Times*, 3 February 1851.
88   Millward, in Swift and Gilley, op.cit.
89   *Bristol Times*, 3 July 1852.
90   *Bristol Times*, 10 July 1852.
91   Swift and Gilley, op.cit., p. 217.
92   *Cork Examiner*, 2 July 1852.
93   *Galway Packet*, 7 July 1852.
94   Reprinted in the *Cork Examiner*, 2 July 1852.
95   *Galway Packet*, 7 July 1852.
96   Miller, op. cit.
97   T.C. Heron Q.C., 'The Statistics of Ireland', *Irish Times*, 15 May 1862.
98   *Irish Times*, 27 June 1862.
99   *The Telegraph*, 25 June 1862.
100   Cecil Woodham Smith, *The Great Hunger, Ireland 1845–1849*, London 1962, p. 151.
101   William Makepeace Thackeray, *The Irish Sketchbook*, 1843, reprinted Belfast 1985, p. 84.
102   Ibid., p. 139.
103   S. Gilley, 'English Attitudes to the Irish in England, 1798–1900', in Holmes, op. cit., p. 85.
104   'Race in the Provincial Press, Birmingham', *The Guardian*, 12 July 1976.
105   E.P. Thompson, *The Making of the English Working Class*, London 1963, p. 439.
106   Werly, op. cit., pp. 345–6.
107   J.P. Kay, *The Moral and Physical Condition of the Working Classes . . .* 1832; M. Leon Faucher, *Manchester in 1844; its Present Condition and Future Prospects*, 1844; Friedrich Engels, *The Condition of the Working Class in England*, 1845; Elizabeth C. Gaskell, *Mary Barton*, 1848.
108   Thomas Gallagher, *Paddy's Lament: Ireland 1846–7; Prelude to Hatred*, Dublin 1985.

Chapter 3, pp. 83–123.
1   E.P. Thompson, *The Making of the English Working Class*, London 1963, p. 475.
2   *Report on the State of the Irish Poor in Great Britain*, Parliamentary Papers (1836) (40) XXX, iv, p. 432.
3   Ibid., p. 443.
4   Ibid., p. 443.
5   Ibid., p. 442.

6   Ibid., Appendix, p. 59, c.
7   Ibid., p. 459.
8   Ibid., Appendix, p. 59.
9   See the evidence of Mr R. Hyde Greg of Manchester and Mr Houldsworth, cotton manufacturer, of Glasgow, ibid., p. 461.
10   Ibid., p. 459.
11   Arthur Redford, *Labour Migration in England*, London 1926.
12   Ibid., pp. 159–60.
13   J.H. Clapham, *An Economic History of Modern Britain*, Cambridge 1930, vol. 1, pp. 57–66; Sydney Pollard, 'Labour in Great Britain', in P. Mathias and M.M. Postan, eds, *The Cambridge Economic History of Europe*, vol. VII, *The Industrial Economies: Capital, Labour and Enterprise*, Cambridge 1978, p. 103.
14   E.H. Hunt, *Regional Wage Variations in Britain 1815–1914*, Oxford 1973, p. 299.
15   J.A. Jackson, *The Irish in Britain*, London 1963; J.E. Handley, *The Irish in Scotland 1789–1845*, Cork 1943; E.P. Thompson, *The Making of the English Working Class*, London 1963.
16   E.H. Hunt, *British Labour History 1815–1914*, London 1981, p. 172.
17   Ibid., p. 173.
18   Ibid., p. 175.
19   Jeffrey Williamson, 'The impact of the Irish on British labour markets during the industrial revolution', *Journal of Economic History*, xivi, No. 3 (September 1986), pp. 693–721; *First Annual Report of the Poor Law Commission*, Parliamentary Papers (1835) vol. 35, p. 188.
20   *Report on the State of the Irish Poor*, Parliamentary Papers (1836), p. xxvi.
21   Op. cit., Williamson, p. 696.
22   David Fitzpatrick, 'A curious middle place', in R. Swift and S. Gilley, eds, *The Irish in Britain 1815–1939*, London 1989, p. 19.
23   Williamson, op. cit., p. 715.
24   Ibid., p. 720.
25   G.E. Mingay, *Rural Life in Victorian England*, London 1979, pp. 90–1.
26   Ibid., p. 111.
27   See chapter 2, Little Irelands.
28   R.D. Lobban, 'The Irish Community in Greenock in the Nineteenth Century', *Irish Geography*, vol. vi (1971) pp. 270–81; Alan Campbell, *The Lanarkshire Miners: A Social History of their Trade Unions 1775–1874*, Edinburgh 1979, pp. 178–204.
29   E.H. Hunt, *British Labour History, 1815–1914*, London 1981, pp. 164–76.
30   *Report on the Irish Poor*, Parliamentary Papers (1836), p. 469.
31   Ibid., see the evidence of Mr Samuel Perry, Agent to the City of Dublin Steam Packet Co., p. xliv.
32   *Bristol Times and Bath Advocate*, 24 July 1847.
33   *Report on the Irish Poor*, Parliamentary Papers (1836), p. 470.

34   The high mobility of Irish farm labour in Stafford is discussed in John Herson, 'Irish migration and settlement in Victorian Britain: a small-town perspective', in Swift and Gilley, op. cit., pp. 84–103.

35   *Report on the Irish Poor*, Parliamentary Papers (1836), Appendix p. 9, No. 176–80.

36   David Fitzpatrick, op. cit., in Swift and Gilley, op. cit., p. 19.

37   Sarah Barber, 'Irish Migrant Agricultural Labourers in Nineteenth Century Britain', *Saothar*, vol. 8 (1982), pp. 10–22.

38   Ibid., see the letter of Michael Sweeny, Appendix p. 21.

39   J.E. Handley, *The Irish in Scotland 1798–1845*, Cork 1943, p. 38.

40   Ibid., p. 39.

41   Fitzpatrick, op. cit., p. 18.

42   *Glasgow Examiner*, 28 September 1844, cited in Handley, op. cit., p. 35.

43   *Report on the Irish Poor*, Parliamentary Papers, (1836), p. 153, letter dated 29 March 1834.

44   *Jamaica Street and round about it in the year 1820*, by a Burgess of Glasgow, 1891, pp. 37–8, cited in Handley, op. cit., p. 54.

45   E.J.T. Collins, 'Migrant Labour in British Agriculture in the Nineteenth Century', *Economic History Review*, 2nd series, vol. XXIX, No. 1 (1976), p. 48.

46   *Report on the Irish Poor*, Parliamentary Papers (1836), pp. 97–116.

47   Collins, op. cit., p. 49.

48   Ibid., p. 50.

49   Ibid., p. 54.

50   Barber, op. cit., p. 14.

51   Handley, op. cit., p. 48.

52   *Report on the Irish Poor*, Parliamentary Papers (1836), p. 471.

53   Barber, op. cit., pp. 16–17.

54   Evidence of Chadwick, Appendix to the Report of the Poor Law Commission of Inquiry, in *Report on the Irish Poor*, Appendix, pp. 639–41.

55   Redford, op. cit., p. 152.

56   Lobban, op. cit., pp. 270–81.

57   C. Richardson, 'Irish Settlement in mid-Victorian Bradford', *Yorkshire Bulletin of Economic and Social Research*, vol. 20 (1968), pp. 40–57.

58   *Report on the Irish Poor*, Parliamentary Papers (1836), pp. 542–3.

59   Redford, op. cit.

60   Ibid., pp. 161–2.

61   *Report on the Irish Poor*, Parliamentary Papers (1836), p. 538.

62   Ibid., p. 539.

63   Ibid., p. 438.

64   Redford, op. cit., p. 153.

65   Duncan Bythell, *The Handloom Weavers*, Cambridge 1969.

66   B. Collins, 'Irish Emigration to Dundee and Paisley during the First Half of the Nineteenth Century', in J.M. Goldstrom and L.A.

Clarkson, eds, *Irish Population, Economy and Society: Essays in Honour of the late K.H. Connell*, Oxford 1981, p. 195.

67 Ibid., p. 202.
68 Ibid., p. 208.
69 Ibid., p. 209.
70 Ibid., p. 212.
71 W.A. Walker, *Juteopolis: Dundee and its textile workers 1885–1923*, Edinburgh 1979.
72 Ibid., p. 47.
73 J.E. Handley, *The Navvy in Scotland*, Cork 1970; T. Coleman, *The Railway Navvies*, London 1965.
74 D. Brooke, *Railway Navvy: 'That Despised Race of Men'*, Newton Abbot 1983, p. 108.
75 J.H. Treble, 'Irish Navvies in the North of England 1830–50', *Transport History*, vi (1973), pp. 228–9.
76 J.A. Patmore, 'A Navvy Gang in 1851', *Journal of Transport History*, vol. V (1962), pp. 187–8.
77 Brooke, op. cit., p. 374.
78 Treble, op. cit., p. 239.
79 Brooke, op. cit., p. 113.
80 Treble, op. cit.
81 Ibid., p. 246; letter of M.M. Guiness, *Freeman's Journal*, 4 December 1840.
82 Brooke, op. cit., pp. 113–14.
83 Brooke cites the example of navvies who became mixed up in a bread riot in Devon, ibid., p. 121.
84 Ibid., p. 122.
85 Patrick MacGill, *Children of the Dead End*, London 1914, pp. 226–7.
86 Alan O'Day, *The Irish in England in 1872*, London 1989; J. Denvir, *The Irish in Britain from the Earliest Times to the Fall and Death of Parnell*, London 1892.
87 O'Day, p. 34.
88 Ibid., p. 35.
89 Denvir, op. cit., p. 393.
90 Ibid., p. 398.
91 Ibid., p. 398.
92 See D. Fitzpatrick, op. cit., for a modern assessment of occupational distribution among the Irish in late Victorian Britain.
93 O'Day, op. cit., p. 66.
94 Ibid., p. 68.
95 Ibid., p. 69.
96 Denvir, op. cit., p. 437.
97 Ibid., p. 454.
98 Ibid., p. 437.
99 Ibid., p. 454.
100 O'Day, op. cit., p. 84–6.
101 Ibid., p. 86.

102   Denvir, op. cit., p. 442.
103   Ibid., p. 441.
104   O'Day, op. cit., p. 60.
105   Denvir, op. cit., pp. 446–7.
106   O'Day, op. cit., pp. 49, 52, 54, and 55.
107   Denvir, op. cit., p. 415.
108   Ibid, p. 418.
109   O'Day, op. cit., p. 47.
110   Denvir, op. cit.,p. 445.

Chapter 4, pp. 124–58.
1   'About 90 per cent of Catholics in cities and even higher percentages of Catholics in rural areas' are regular Sunday churchgoers. D.W. Miller, 'Irish Catholicism in the Great Famine', *Journal of Social History*, vol. IX (1975–6), p.83. There is evidence of a slight decline in attendance since the 1970s in Ireland, but it remains very high in comparison with other European countries.
2   Alexis de Tocqueville's *Journey in Ireland July-August 1835*, translated and edited by Emmet Larkin, Dublin, p. 21.
3   G. Best, 'Popular Protestantism in Victorian Britain', in R. Robson, ed., *Ideas and Institutions of Victorian Britain*, London 1967, pp. 115–42.
4   W. M. Thackeray, *The Irish Sketchbook*, 1843, reprinted Belfast 1985, p. 74.
5   D. W. Miller, op. cit., pp. 81–98.
6   Thackeray, op. cit., pp. 236–7.
7   Ibid.
8   D. W. Miller, op. cit., p. 90.
9   Lynn Lees, *Exiles of Erin: Irish Migrants in Victorian London*, Manchester 1979, p. 167.
10   Sean Connolly, *Religion and Society in Nineteenth-Century Ireland*, Dundalk 1985, p. 50.
11   Sir William Wilde, *Irish Popular Superstitions*, Dublin 1852, reprinted Totowa, New Jersey 1973, p. 14, cited in Elizabeth Malcolm, 'Popular Recreation in Nineteenth Century Ireland' in O. MacDonagh, W. F. Landle, and Pauric Travers eds, *Irish Culture and Nationalism. 1750–1950*, London 1983, p. 40.
12   E. Larkin, 'The Devotional Revolution in Ireland, 1850–75', *American Historical Review*, lxxvii (1972), pp. 625–52.
13   Ibid.
14   Lees, op.cit., pp. 169–72.
15   T. Crofton Croker, *Researches in the South of Ireland Illustrative of the Scenery, Architectural Remains, and the Manners and Superstitions of the Peasantry*, London 1824, p. 78.
16   Lees, op. cit.
17   Mary Carbery, *The Farm of Lough Gur*, Cork and Dublin 1973, p. 158.

18   Kerby Miller, *Emigrants and Exiles: Ireland and the Irish Exodus to North America*, Oxford 1985, p. 129, see chapter 1 Emigration.
19   Ibid., p.114; D. MacAmhlaigh, *Irish Navvy: Diary of an Exile*, London 1966 edn, pp. 39–42.
20   Gregory, *Visions and Beliefs in the West of Ireland*, New York 1970, pp. 182, 227.
21   Elizabeth Malcolm, op.cit., p. 46.
22   S. Gilley, 'The Roman Catholic Church and the Nineteenth-Century Irish Diaspora', *Journal of Ecclesiastical History*, vol. 35, No. 2 (April 1984), p. 197.
23   S. Connolly, op. cit., p. 18, citing H. Senior, *Orangeism in Ireland and Britain, 1795–1836*, London 1966.
24   D. W. Miller, 'The Armagh Troubles, 1784–95' in Samuel Clark and James S. Donnelly Jr, eds, *Irish Peasants: Violence and Political Unrest 1780–1914* Manchester 1983, pp. 155–91; Peter Gibbon, *The Origins of Ulster Unionism: The Formation of Popular Protestant Politics and Ideology in Nineteenth-Century Ireland*, Manchester 1975; L. M. Cullen, *The Emergence of Modern Ireland 1600–1900*, London 1981.
25   David Hempton, *Methodism and Politics in British Society 1750–1850*, London 1984, p. 122.
26   James S. Donnelly Jr, 'Pastorini and Captain Rock: Millenarianism and Secretarianism in the Rockite Movement of 1821–4', in Clark and Donnelly, op. cit., p. 126.
27   N. Cohn, *The Pursuit of the Millennium: revolutionary millenarians and mystical anarchists of the middle ages*, rev. edn., New York 1970; J. F. C. Harrison, *The Second Coming: popular millenarianism, 1780–1850*, London 1979.
28   Donnelly, op. cit., p. 123.
29   Ibid.
30   *Dublin Evening Post*, 24 June 1823, cited in Donnelly, ibid., p. 134.
31   Ibid., p. 136.
32   Gerard Connolly, 'Irish and Catholic: Myth or Reality? Another sort of Irish and the renewal of the clerical profession among Catholics in England 1791–1918' in R. Swift and S. Gilley, eds, *The Irish in the Victorian City*, London 1985, p. 226.
33   Ibid., p. 231.
34   Ibid., p. 235.
35   John Ó Riordain, *Irish Catholics: Tradition and Transition*, Dublin 1980; S. Gilley, 'The Catholic Faith of the Irish Slums: London 1840–70', in H.J. Dyos and M. Wolff, eds, *The Victorian City: Images and Reality*, 2 vols, London 1973, vol. 2, pp. 837–53.
36   G. Connolly, op. cit., pp. 233–5.
37   K. S. Inglis, *Churches and the Working Classes in Victorian England*, London 1963.
38   G. Connolly, op. cit., p. 232.
39   Lees, op. cit., pp. 180–2; J. A. Lesourd, *Sociologie du Catholicisme Anglais 1767–1851*, Nancy 1981, pp. 146–7; S. Gilley, 'The Catholic Faith of the Irish Slums: London 1840–70' op. cit.

40   J.K. Hickey, *Urban Catholics*, London 1967, pp. 90–4.
41   *Manchester Guardian*, 17 June 1846, cited in G. Connolly, op. cit., p. 230.
42   W. J. Lowe, 'The Lancashire Irish and the Catholic Church, 1846–71: the social dimension', *Irish Historical Studies*, vol. 20 (1976–7), pp. 144–7.
43   H. Mcleod, *Class and Religion in the late Victorian City*, London 1974, p. 28.
44   Hickey, op. cit., p. 71, note 2.
45   H. Mayhew, *London Labour and the London Poor*, London, 1861, vol. l, p. 114, cited in R. Samuel, 'The Roman Catholic Church and the Irish Poor', in Swift and Gilley, op. cit., pp. 275–6.
46   R. Samuel, ibid., p. 267.
47   Ibid., p. 268.
48   Ibid., p. 269.
49   Ibid., p. 279.
50   Ibid., p. 280.
51   Ibid., p. 280.
52   Mayhew, op. cit., vol. 2, p. 505, cited by Connolly, op. cit., p. 234.
53   Peter Quennell, ed., *London's Underworld: selections from H. Mayhew, London Labour and the London Poor*, vol. 4, London, pp. 68–9.
54   G. Connolly, op. cit., pp. 236–40.
55   Edward Lucas, 'The Conversion of England', *The Month*, 44, No. 1 (July 1885), pp. 310–11, cited in Lees, op. cit., p. 183.
56   Lees, ibid., p. 184.
57   Ibid., pp. 199–202.
58   S. Gilley, 'Heretic London, Holy Poverty and the Irish Poor, 1830–70', *Downside Review*, vol. 89 (1971) pp. 64–89.
59   T. Barclay, *Memoirs and Medleys: The Autobiography of a Bottlewasher*, Leicester 1934, cited in Lees, op cit., p. 190.
60   Lees, op. cit., p. 198.
61   Edward Lucas, *Tablet*, 6 January 1844, cited in S. Gilley, 'The Roman Catholic Mission to the Irish in London 1840–60', *Recusant History*, vol. 10 (1969–70), p. 132.
62   S. Gilley, ibid.
63   Ibid., p. 126.
64   Tom Gallagher, 'A Tale of two cities: Communal strife in Glasgow and Liverpool before 1914', in Swift and Gilley, op. cit., pp. 106–29.
65   Ibid., p. 106.
66   Ibid., p. 109; Kerby Miller, op. cit., p. 493.
67   Ibid., p. 109.
68   E.H. Hunt, *British Labour History, 1815–1914*, London p. 162.
69   S. and O. Checkland, *Industry and Ethos, Scotland 1832–1914*, London 1984, pp. 88, 94.
70   Gallagher, op. cit., p. 115.

71 F. Neal, *Sectarian Violence: The Liverpool Experience, 1819–1914*, Manchester 1988.

72 Ibid., chapter II, No Popery politics 1800–44, pp. 37–79.

73 Ibid., p. 46.

74 Ibid., p. 46.

75 P. Marshall, *Bristol and the Abolition of Slavery: The Politics of Emancipation*, Bristol 1975.

76 Neal, op. cit., pp. 49–50.

77 An example of the stories that formed the stuff of Protestant propaganda was that in the islands off the west coast of Ireland, the Virgin Mary was worshipped as a fish.

78 Neal, op. cit., p. 81.

79 *The Times*, 6 May 1847, cited in Neal, ibid., p. 109.

80 *Liverpool Herald*, 17 November 1855, cited in Neal, pp. 114–15.

81 See the language of the Rev. Whitwell Elwin, chaplain to the Bath Union, in Graham Davis, 'Beyond the Georgian facade: The Avon Street district of Bath' in Martin Gaskell, ed., *Slums*, Leicester, London and New York 1990, p. 166.

82 Neal, op. cit., pp. 63–4.

83 Roger Swift, 'Another Stafford Street Row: Law, Order and Irish presence in Mid-Victorian Wolverhampton', in Swift and Gilley, op. cit., pp. 189–94.

84 W. L. Arnstein, 'The Murphy Riots: a Victorian Dilemma', *Victorian Studies*, vol. xix (1975), pp. 51–71.

85 Bernard Aspinwall and John F.McCaffrey, 'A Comparative View of the Irish in Edinburgh in the Nineteenth Century', in Swift and Gilley, op.cit., pp. 130–57.

86 R. J. Cooter, The Irish in County Durham and Newcastle, 1840–1880, M.A. thesis, University of Durham (1973), pp. 114, 124, 153.

87 Lees, op. cit., p. 207.

88 Hickey, op. cit., pp. 102–3.

Chapter 5, pp. 159–90.

1 J. Foster, *Class Struggle and the Industrial Revolution: Early industrial capitalism in three English towns*, London 1974; Harold Perkin, *The origins of Modern English Society 1780–1880*, London 1969; T. R. Tholfsen, *Working Class Radicalism in mid-Victorian England*, London 1976; Neville Kirk, *The Growth of Working Class Reformism in Mid-Victorian England*, London 1985; G. Crossick, *An Artisan Elite in Victorian Society: Kentish London 1840–1880*, London 1977; R. Q. Gray, *The Labour Aristocracy in Victorian Edinburgh*, Oxford 1976; F. M. L. Thompson, *The Rise of Respectable Society*, Glasgow 1988.

2 J. Saville, *1848: The British State and the Chartist Movement*, Cambridge 1987, p. 200.

3 Asa Briggs, ed., *Chartist Studies*, London, 1959, p. 7.

4 G. D. H. Cole, *Chartist Portraits*, London 1965, p. 305.

5 Ibid., p. 335.

6   James Epstein, *The Lion of Freedom: Feargus O'Connor and the Chartist Movement 1832–1842*, London 1982.

7   D. Thompson, *The Chartists*, London 1984, pp. 96–101.

8   John Belchem, '1848: Feargus O'Connor and the collapse of the Mass Platform' in James Epstein and Dorothy Thompson, eds, *The Chartist Experience: Studies in Working-Class Radicalism and Culture 1830–1860*, London 1982, p. 282.

9   Thompson, op. cit., p. 99, quoting W. J. O'Neill Daunt, *85 Years of Irish History*, p. 244.

10   Thomas Frost, 'The Life and Times of John Vallance', *Barnsley Times*, May 1882, in Thompson, op. cit., p. 99.

11   Ibid., p. 98; John F. McCaffrey, 'Irish Immigrants and Radical Movements in the West of Scotland in the Early Nineteenth Century' *The Innes Review*, vol. XXXIX, No. 1 (Spring 1988), p. 54.

12   Rachel O'Higgins, 'Irish influence in the Chartist Movement, *Past and Present*, vol. 20 (1961), p. 94.

13   *Northern Star*, 23 January 1847.

14   *Bronterre's National Reformer*, 7, 28 January and 4 February, 1837, in A. Plummer, *Bronterre: A Political Biography of Bronterre O'Brien 1804–1864*, London 1971, pp. 24–5.

15   Rachel O'Higgins, op. cit., p. 93.

16   *A Penny Paper for the People by the Poor Man's Guardian*, 15 April 1831, in Plummer op. cit., pp. 6–8.

17   See Dorothy Thompson, 'Ireland and the Irish in English Radicalism before 1850' in Epstein and Thompson, op. cit., pp. 120–1.

18   Thomas Carlyle, *Chartism*, London 1839; Friedrich Engels, *The Condition of the English Working Class*, 1845, with introduction by Eric Hobsbaum, St Albans 1969.

19   John Belchem, 'English Working Class Radicalism and the Irish 1815–50' in R. Swift and S. Gilley, eds, *The Irish in the Victorian City*, London 1985, p. 85.

20   I. Prothero, 'Chartism in London', *Past and Present*, No. 44 (August 1969), p. 93.

21   Dave Goodway, *London Chartism 1838–1848*, Cambridge 1982, p. 64.

22   Alex Wilson, 'Chartism in Glasgow', in Asa Briggs op. cit., pp. 274–5.

23   J.F. C. Harrison, 'Chartism in Leeds' in Asa Briggs, op. cit., p. 76.

24   D. Thompson, 'Ireland and the Irish' in Epstein and Thompson, op. cit., p. 124.

25   Ibid., p. 123.

26   Ibid., p. 140.

27   *The Merlin*, 14 December 1839, in J. Hickey, *Urban Catholics: Urban Catholicism in England and Wales from 1829 to the present day*, London 1967, pp. 142–3.

28   J. H. Treble, 'O'Connor, O'Connell and the attitudes of Irish Immigrants towards Chartism in the north of England 1838–48', in J. Butt and I. F. Clarke, eds, *The Victorians and Social Protest: a Symposium*, Newton Abbot 1973.

29 Thompson, op. cit., p. 121.
30 Saville, op. cit., pp. 73–4.
31 Ibid., p. 74.
32 Ibid., p. 74; see also Neville Kirk, *The Growth of Working Class Reformism in Mid-Victorian England*, London 1985, pp. 311–48.
33 Treble, op. cit., p. 54.
34 McCaffrey, op. cit., pp. 46–7.
35 *Glasgow Herald*, 10 March 1848.
36 Tom Paine, *Common Sense*, 1776, *The Rights of Man*, 1790–2, *Age of Reason*, 1794.
37 Gareth Stedman Jones, *Languages of Class: Studies in English Working Class history 1832–1982*, Cambridge 1983, p. 126.
38 John Belchem, 'Feargus O'Connor and the Collapse of the Mass Platform', in Epstein and Thompson, op. cit., p. 271.
39 E. P. Thompson, *The Making of the English Working Class*, Harmondsworth 1963; M. Elliott, 'Irish Republicanism in England; the first phase 1797–9' in T. Bartlett and D. W. Hayton, eds, *Penal Era and Golden Age*, Belfast 1979; Roger Wells, *Insurrection: The British Experience 1795–1803*, Gloucester 1986.
40 Rachel O'Higgins, 'The Irish influence in the Chartist Movement', *Past and Present*, vol. 20 (1961), p. 85.
41 *Bath and Devizes Guardian*, 7 January 1837; see also support for 'Justice for Ireland' in the city of Leicester, in Asa Briggs, op. cit., p. 130.
42 Denis Knight, ed., *Cobbett in Ireland: A warning to England*, London 1984, pp. 69, 73.
43 Ibid., pp. 210–11.
44 Stanley H. Palmer, *Police and Protest in England and Ireland 1780–1850*, Cambridge 1988, p. 414.
45 Ibid., p. 415.
46 G. P. Davis, 'Image and Reality in a Victorian Provincial City: A working-class area of Bath', unpublished Ph.D Thesis, University of Bath (1981), p. 336.
47 Palmer, op. cit., p. 416. The following section is based on Palmer pp. 435–57.
48 Saville, op. cit., p. 170.
49 Ibid., p. 183.
50 Trygve Tholfsen, *Working Class Radicalism in Mid-Victorian England*, London 1976.

Chapter 6, pp. 191–216.
1 T. W. Moody, *The Fenian Movement*, Cork and Dublin 1968, reprinted 1985, p. 102.
2 R. F. Foster, *Modern Ireland 1600–1972*, Harmondsworth 1988, p. 341.
3 Moody, op. cit., p. 103.
4 For a narrative account of the Chester Raid, see R. Kee, *The Green Flag: Bold Fenian Men*, London 1972.

5   Donald C. Richter, *Riotous Victorians,* Ohio 1981, pp. 25–32.

6   For instance the Irish in Swansea came out publicly against the Fenians: 'We hereby express our abhorrence of all armed violence, and all resistance to the civil power, being convinced that such measures are evils . . . We cannot but disapprove of all secret societies and especially of what is called "The Fenian Brotherhood", quoted in Richter, op. cit., p. 29.

7   Moody, op. cit., p. 106.

8   John O'Leary (1830–1907), co-editor of *The Irish People,* author of *Recollections of Fenians and Fenianism,* 1896, mentor of W. B. Yeats, and prominent in the literary revival; Jeremiah O'Donovan (Rossa) (1831–1915), edited the *United Irishman,* published *Prison Life,* 1874, *Recollections,* 1898; John Devoy (1842–1928), founded the *Irish Nation,* 1882, and edited the *Gaelic American,* 1903, author of *Recollections of an Irish Rebel,* published 1929.

9   *The Times,* 8 March 1867, in Kee, op. cit., p. 38.

10   Ibid., p. 46.

11   Ibid., pp. 46–7.

12   Moody, op. cit., p. 111. The ballad, 'The Smashing of the Van', sung by Brendan Behan, celebrated the episode of the 'Manchester Martyrs'; Tim Pat Coogan, *The I.R.A.,* Glasgow 1988 edn, p. 30.

13   K. R. M. Short, *The Dynamite War: Irish-American Bombers in Victorian Britain,* New Jersey 1979, p. 91.

14   R. V. Comerford, 'Gladstone's First Irish Enterprise 1864–70, in W. E. Vaughan, A New History of Ireland, vol. V, *Ireland under the Union 1801–70,* Oxford, 1989, p. 436.

15   Kee, op. cit., p. 51.

16   John Morley, *The Life of Gladstone,* 2 vols, 1905, London vol. 1, p. 383.

17   Peter Stansky, *Gladstone: A Progress in Politics,* London 1979, p. 153.

18   Foster, op. cit., p. 395.

19   Comerford, op. cit., pp. 440–3.

20   P. Magnus, *Gladstone,* London 1954, 1963 edn, p. 193. The following section is based on Magnus's account, pp. 192–3.

21   Apart from the fateful split in the Liberal Party in 1885 over the Home Rule issue and the heroic defeats of his Home Rule bills that took a great personal toll of Gladstone, he was personally affected by the murder of his favourite nephew, Lord Frederick Cavendish, in the Phoenix Park murders in 1882.

22   Kee, op. cit., p. 62.

23   Foster, op. cit., p. 404.

24   Ibid., 'The Politics of Parnellism', pp. 400–28.

25   Magnus, op. cit., p. 356.

26   Ibid., p. 349.

27   Ibid., p. 357.

28   James Loughlin, *Gladstone, Home Rule and the Ulster Question 1882–93,* Dublin 1986.

29 'December 18, 1885—Read Burke: what a magazine of wisdom on Ireland and America. January 9, 1886—made many extracts from Burke—sometimes almost divine.' Gladstone's diary, quoted in J. Morley, *The Life of William Ewart Gladstone*, London 1903, vol. iii, p. 211.

30 Loughlin, op. cit., p. 121.

31 D. W. Miller, *Queen's Rebels: Ulster Loyalism in Historical Perspective*, Dublin 1978.

32 J. Denvir, *The Irish in Britain from the Earliest Times to the Fall and Death of Parnell*, London 1892.

33 Alan O'Day, 'Irish influence on Parliamentary Elections in London, 1885–1914: A Simple Test' in Swift and Gilley, op. cit., pp. 98–105.

34 D. G. Boyce, 'The Marginal Britons: The Irish', in Robert Colls and Philip Dodd, eds, *Englishness: Political and Culture 1880–1920*, London 1986, p. 235.

35 Paul Bew, Ellen Hazelborn, Henry Patterson, *The Dynamics of Irish Politics*, London 1989, p. 15.

36 Boyce, op. cit., p. 247.

37 Bew, op. cit., p. 21.

38 Ibid., p. 18.

39 Boyce, op. cit., p. 244.

40 Ibid., p. 245.

Index